KU-480-085

THE KASHMIR SHAWL

and its Indo-French Influence

Frank Ames

Antique Collectors' Club

© Frank Ames 1986
World copyright reserved
First published 1986

All rights reserved. No part of this publication may be reproduced, stored in a retrieval system or transmitted in any form or by any means electronic, mechanical, photocopying, recording or otherwise, without the prior permission of the publisher.

British Library CIP Data
Ames, Frank
    The Kashmir shawl: and its Indo-French
influence.
    1. Shawls
I. Title
746.9'2   NK8976

    ISBN 0-907462-62-6

Published for the Antique Collectors' Club
by the Antique Collectors' Club Ltd.

HERTFORDSHIRE
LIBRARY SERVICE

746. 9'2

Printed in England by the Antique Collectors' Club Ltd., Woodbridge, Suffolk.

Colour Plate 1 (Frontispiece). Shawl (fragment). Dogra, 19th century, late Mughal style. 51cm x 140cm.
The delicate branches forming the circular trellis pattern recall the spiralling ornaments often associated with early Ottoman art, such as Iznik ceramics, embroidered or silk brocaded panels, etc. This is especially apparent by the artist's effort to space the large, vibrantly colourful blossoms freely. Indeed, perhaps this piece was destined at one time for the Turkish market. Note the thin lunar crescent at the base of the blossom's stem of superbly drawn, serrated leaves.

TO MY PARENTS

Antique Collectors' Club

The Antique Collectors' Club was formed in 1966 and now has a five figure membership spread throughout the world. It publishes the only independently run monthly antiques magazine *Antique Collecting* which caters for those collectors who are interested in widening their knowledge of antiques, both by greater awareness of quality and by discussion of the factors which influence the price that is likely to be asked. The Antique Collectors' Club pioneered the provision of information on prices for collectors and the magazine still leads in the provision of detailed articles on a variety of subjects.

It was in response to the enormous demand for information on "what to pay" that the price guide series was introduced in 1968 with the first edition of *The Price Guide to Antique Furniture* (completely revised, 1978), a book which broke new ground by illustrating the more common types of antique furniture, the sort that collectors could buy in shops and at auctions rather than the rare museum pieces which had previously been used (and still to a large extent are used) to make up the limited amount of illustrations in books published by commercial publishers. Many other price guides have followed, all copiously illustrated, and greatly appreciated by collectors for the valuable information they contain, quite apart from prices. The Antique Collectors' Club also publishes other books on antiques, including horology and art reference works, and a full book list is available.

Club membership, which is open to all collectors, costs £12.95 per annum. Members receive free of charge *Antique Collecting,* the Club's magazine (published every month except August), which contains well-illustrated articles dealing with the practical aspects of collecting not normally dealt with by magazines. Prices, features of value, investment potential, fakes and forgeries are all given prominence in the magazine.

Among other facilities available to members are private buying and selling facilities, the longest list of "For Sales" of any antiques magazine, an annual ceramics conference and the opportunity to meet other collectors at their local antique collectors' clubs. There are nearly eighty in Britain and so far a dozen overseas. Members may also buy the Club's publications at special pre-publication prices.

As its motto implies, the Club is an amateur organisation designed to help collectors get the most out of their hobby: it is informal and friendly and gives enormous enjoyment to all concerned.

For Collectors — By Collectors — About Collecting

The Antique Collectors' Club, 5 Church Street, Woodbridge, Suffolk

Acknowledgements

I am very grateful to the many persons who shared generously of their time, knowledge and enthusiasm in the production of this book, and, I am deeply indebted to those private and public institutions who generously permitted the illustration of their shawls.

In France, great thanks are due to my friend Dr. Jim Williams whose unstinting help and expert advice on the initial organisation of the book was of invaluable assistance to me. Without Jim's vast knowledge of carpets and of things Oriental this project might never have seen the light of day; to Madame Krishna Riboud, president and founder of Association pour l'Etude et la Documentation des Textiles d'Asie (AEDTA), I am particularly thankful for the liberal access to her museum's rich holdings. AEDTA, under the efficient administration of Frédérique Delbecq, offered me a unique atmosphere for the study of Asian textiles in Paris; Madame Jacqueline Jacqué, Musée de l'Impression sur Etoffes, Mulhouse; Madame Madeleine Despierre, Musée de la Mode et du Costume, Paris; La Bibliothèque Nationale, Paris, and their excellent staff of librarians; Pierre Arizzoli Clementel and Evelyne Goudry, Musée Historique des Tissus, Lyon; Les Archives Nationales, Paris.

In London, Betty Tyers, Victoria and Albert Museum; M.J. Pollack Indian Office Library; Meg Andrews, Sotheby's Belgravia; Anne Marie Benson, Philips.

In the United States, Milton Sonday, Cooper Hewitt Museum; Richard Lanier, of the Asian Cultural Council, who introduced me to India's Museums; the Metropolitan Museum of Art; Lotus Stack Minneapolis Institute of Arts; Yale University Art Gallery; Fine Arts Museum of San Francisco; Boston Museum of Fine Arts; Textile Museum, Washington, D.C.

In India, O.P. Tandon and Devaki Ahivasi, Bharat Kala Bhavan, Benaras, and Dr. Anand Krishna for having read the manuscript and his inspiring letter of send-off; Krishna Lal of the National Museum Delhi, who surmounted incredible difficulties of access to the museum's collection; Martin Singh, Calico Museum of Textiles, Ahmedabad; Dr. M.L. Nigam, Salor Jung Museum, Hyderabad; the Jagdish and Kamla Mittal Museum of Indian Art, Hyderabad; Sushil Kumar and his staff at the Indian Textile Company, Bombay; Dr. Karin Singh and Madame Shobha Nehru who graciously permitted me to view the 'toshakhana' of the Maharaja of Kashmir; Dr. Asok Kumar Das and Chandrmani Singh of the Maharaja Sawai Man Singh II Museum, Jaipur; Sadashiv Gorakshkar, Prince of Wales Museum, Bombay; Vishnu Lall and Family, Agra; Dr. Bashir Ahmad Dar, Srinagar, for translation.

Warm regards and much appreciation to Lucien Arcache, Guillermo Arizcorreta (for the line drawings of shawl construction), Valery Beranstain, Anne Christine, Steven Cohen, Roseline Degrain, Jacqueline Daniel, Henry and Jacqueline Dumas, Francesca Galloway, Roland Gilles, Christian Grandin, Renate and Arthur Halpern, Tessa Hughes, Jack Ismidlian, Joan Lecoutour (for having read the manuscript), Monique Lévis-Strauss, Louis Lomüller, George Michel, Michel Spink, Jeff Spurr, Marie-Noëlle Sudre, Roben Tala and Gabriel Vial; to Joyce Ames and Eddie Fazio for their continued encouragement to see this project through; and to all my friends in Kashmir who brought me into intimate contact with their families, work and culture.

Lastly, a very special thanks to Evelyne Chevallier for typing much of the manuscript and for accompanying me on several study trips to India. Her devoted help in assisting me during many of the photo sessions went far beyond the call of duty.

Photographic Acknowledgements

The author is deeply grateful to the following people, museums and institutions who have so generously contributed photos and other documentation:

Meg Andrews, Hertfordshire: Plate 43
Bharany, New Delhi: Plates 20, 39, 187, 212
Evelyne Chevallier, Paris: Colour Plate 15
Marti and Maurice Clare, London: Plate 61
Rosaline Degrain, New York: Colour Plate 13
Tessa Hughes, London: Colour Plates 18, 45
Dr. Anand Krishna, Benaras: Plate 129
Sushil Kumar, Bombay: Colour Plates 3, 4, 5
Ganeshi Lall and Son, Agra: Plates 126, 180, 184, 194
Philips, London: Plate 59
Mr. and Mrs. A.J. Puri, Bombay: Plate 195
Sotheby's, London: Plates 97, 171, 192
Marie Noelle Sudre, Paris: Colour Plate 60
Dr. Jim Williams and Roland Gilles, Apamé, Paris: Colour Plates 61, 64

Museums & Institutions

Association pour l'Etude et la Documentation des Textiles d'Asie (A.E.D.T.A.), Krishna Riboud, President, Paris: Colour Plates 20, 21, 39; Plates 4, 23, 66, 85, 147, 209
Bharat Kala Bhavan (Benaras Hindu University): Colour Plates 22, 23, 31; Plates 87, 94, 95, 100, 101, 103, 104, 105, 107, 109, 111, 115, 116, 119, 120, 121, 123, 128, 132, 134, 135, 136, 138, 146, 148, 149, 150 151, 160, 166, 170, 172, 177, 189, 204, 205, 211, 214
Bibliothèque Nationale, Paris: Plates 44, 45, 46, 48, 49, 50, 57, 72, 75, 76, 77, 78, 79, 80, 81
Boston Museum of Fine Arts: Plates 74, 90, 92, 125, 131, 139, 140, 141, 152, 155, 157, 163, 164, 167, 169, 179, 181, 183, 185, 193, 196, 198, 199, 206, 213
Calico Museum, Ahmedabad: Plates 91, 96, 98, 142, 145, 188, 197
Conservatoire National des Arts et Métiers, Paris: Colour Plate 44; Plates 47, 64, 65, 69, 70
Fine Arts Museum of San Francisco: Plate 216
Indian Office Library, London: Plate 32
Jagdish and Kamla Mittal Museum of Indian Art, Hyderabad: Plates 88, 117, 144
Louvre, Paris: Plate 28
Metropolitan Museum of Art, New York: Plates 35, 36, 37, 38, 68, 219, 221
Musée de l'Impression sur Etoffes, Mulhouse: Plate 62 (Studio Basset)
Musée des Arts Décoratifs, Paris: Colour Plate 10; Plates 54, 55, 56, 60
Musée Historique des Tissus, Lyon: Plates 18, 63, 161a
Musées de Nice; Plate 29
National Museum, Delhi: Plates 102, 106, 108, 114, 127, 130, 133, 153, 154, 156, 158, 159, 162, 165, 174, 175, 177, 182, 186, 190
The Textile Museum, Washington, D.C.: Plates 83, 93, 99, 137, 161b, 220
The Victoria and Albert Museum, London: Plates 58, 73, 84, 86, 89, 97, 110, 112, 113, 118, 122, 124, 168, 176, 178, 191, 202, 203, 207, 208, 210, 217, 218
Yale University Art Gallery, Connecticut: Plates 82, 143, 201, 215, 222

Author's Collection, Paris: Colour Plates 1, 2, 6, 7, 8, 9, 11, 12, 14, 16, 17, 19, 24, 25, 26, 27, 28, 29, 30, 32, 33, 34, 35, 36, 37, 38, 40, 41, 42, 43, 46, 47, 48, 49, 50, 51, 52, 53, 54, 55, 57, 58, 62, 63, 65, 66; Plates 1, 2, 3, 5, 6, 8, 9, 10, 11, 12, 13, 16, 19, 21, 22, 24, 25, 26, 27, 30, 31, 33, 34, 40, 41, 42, 51, 52, 53, 67, 71, 173, 200

Colour Photography: Studios James Lignier and Jean Claude Valette, Paris

Contents

Colour Plates

Preface

The idea of putting together a comprehensive book on the Kashmir shawl was first suggested to me by a good friend while I was vacationing on New York's Fire Island during the warm summer of 1979. It had been almost ten years since I first left the States and had taken up residence in Europe. Paris had become my 'plaque tournante' for what was soon to become an endless number of voyages to India.

But before setting foot in the Orient, I had already become keenly intrigued by the European 'Kashmir' shawl. Seeing them lying around in the auction rooms of Paris, London or New York, thrown into a heap in some obscure corner of the sale room, I was continually struck by the richness of their colours and changing patterns, the ingenious combinations of which sometimes imitated the real Kashmir shawls so closely that it was impossible not to do a double take.

I have found the auction sale room a great place for learning about art and antiques. There even the most casual viewer can enter into intimate contact with the rarest of objects, be they paintings, jewellery, rugs or sculpture, in a way impossible in a museum. Once sold they will probably sit in the coveted world of private collections, glassed enclosed museums or securely locked vaults. But before the hammer falls, there is an opportunity to hold in your own hands the precious piece which, except possibly through a published photo, has for so long eluded the public's eye; a rare experience indeed. And even if one is not a connoisseur, there is always a powerful delight in being able to inspect the object briefly with a feigned and savoury expertise while others are forced to wait at the sidelines with bated breath wondering whether you've secretly condemned it as a fake or acclaimed it as a treasure.

Most fascinating of all is the chance of viewing an entire collection built up by one individual, a meaningful and homogeneous collection, reflecting the particular empathy and stamp of a single collector. Museums, dependent on the state for finance, find their budgets restricted and monies frequently inaccessible when the need arises thus preventing them from buying entire collections. Some institutions are more fortunate and make acquisitions through wealthy people who seek tax benefits. But in general an enormous amount of bureaucratic red-tape must be cut before an object becomes a new acquisition; the museums' collections suffer accordingly. In this respect a private citizen has much greater versatility. As new pieces come onto the art market which represent a more expressive aspect of the field in which he is interested, they can be used to replace earlier acquired pieces whose brilliance has waned, whereas rarely can a museum resell or exchange an object once it has been formally acquired.

After that warm summer, I found myself compulsively pursuing this project, tracing the boteh's slow, painstaking pictographic evolution. The world stood still while I forged the missing links in its chain of development.

As the 'canvas' of an expressive art medium, I began to discover that the Kashmir shawl, viewed in its earliest manifestations, harboured stylistic doors the keys to which remain frustratingly elusive. At the root of each Mughal flower lay a tiny trap door concealing another world; and crossing the threshold was as precarious as Alice's dreamworld pursuit after a pocket-watch rabbit. I suppose it is just this elusiveness which urges one continually to dig below the surface; to find the doors which will liberate from those great Oriental vaults of man's immortalized genius the missing links of spiritual antiquity, the lost horizons of an extinct art.

In India, outside the major collections of Benaras, Delhi and Calico, few shawls of importance exist. At the museum in Srinagar a few early nineteenth century pieces are on display, but the pitiful conditions in which they are kept will not assure them of a very long life. The Bharat Kala Bawan is endowed with by far the richest collection, the greater portion of which have come down directly from the family of the Maharaja of Jaipur. It is said that, just after India's independence, the Maharani decided to do some palatial spring cleaning. Bundles of seventeenth and eighteenth century shawls were thrown out into the courtyard and sold on a first-come-first-served basis for a handful of rupees.

Things have changed a lot since then. During one of my recent trips to India I had found myself in a rundown section of Old Delhi where a dealer and I were haggling over what he considered to be a very rare object and needless to say his price was 'top quality' too. Without batting an eyelid, he snatches off his dusty shelf one of the latest western catalogues on the subject replete with glossy colour plates and points out a vaguely similar object that had just been exhibited at a well-known Western museum. This is what shopping is all about in India today.

If one wants to view the 'kani' techniques in operation one must go to Kanihama (12 miles from Srinagar) where the government is making a vain attempt to revive the art. However, anybody who really appreciates the complexity of these tapestry weaves risks a terrible let-down. On the other hand the visitor will walk away rewarded by the even deeper understanding of the herculean effort and patience that was invested in them years ago, and the fine-tuned system of a highly sophisticated division of labour where the skill of the weaver, dyer or spinner was as much hailed and sought after as gold. In craftsmanship the Kashmiri still possesses one of the greatest abilities in the world, but for Kashmir once again to flex its true artistic muscles the stimuli will have to come through private enterprise.

F. Ames, March 1986
Sainte Apolline, Paris

Introduction

After many centuries, the Kashmir shawl still fires our imagination as an exotic souvenir of the Orient, representing a bygone and opulent era. The shawl's sudden migration in 1800 from Kashmir to Europe spawned important new developments in European design ideas, centering around one of the most ubiquitous motifs ever to come from the East: the 'buta' or 'boteh' as it is known in the West, a cone-like form that is commonly found on printed goods, on rugs, embroideries and many other textiles.

The present work attempts to define and classify the Kashmir shawl, analyses the wealth of images and symbolism found in its finely ornamented weave, and places its development within the context of the four major periods of Kashmir's history.

Unlike many near eastern textiles which have a continous and uninterrupted history, the Kashmir shawl remains unique as a weave which has not been produced in over a century; as a result, certain technical facets concerning its construction have almost completely disappeared, a fact which tends to intensify our perception of its mysterious beauty and illuminating colours.

Kashmir shawls, as a general rule, did not represent a folk art as did nomadic carpets, kilims, and Indian embroideries. They were made, rather, for an expanding commercial market ignorant of and so far removed from the hardships experienced by the poor shawl weaver striving to support his family. The shawl may represent an expression of the weaver's art, but economic necessity was his probable motivation.

The Kashmiris were not part of a nomadic group and remained far removed from contact with the outside world. To this day their origins are still in dispute. Indeed some claim they are one of the lost tribes of Israel. Perhaps the natural beauty and tranquillity of the Kashmir valley, despite its many invaders, enabled the weavers to devote so much painstaking effort to one of the most difficult weaves in the history of textiles.

Kashmir, bordered by Chinese, Indian and Muslim territories, resisted for a long time before acquiescing to the teachings of the Sufi dervishes who brought the Islamic religion into the Kashmir valley in the eleventh century, and from this time Islam became a continual inspiration in the creation of designs. By the fourteenth century it was firmly implanted and declared a state religion. Medieval Kashmir witnessed numerous lootings by Turkish invaders until the Sultan dynasty was founded by Sultan Sham-ud-Din (1339-1342). A century later, Kashmir's art and culture flourished under Zain-ul-Abidin (1440-1470). Under his rule Persian replaced Sanskrit as the official language of government.

The English word 'shawl' is derived from the Persian 'shal'. In Oriental tradition, shal describes not only one particular article of clothing, but a whole range of fine woollen fabrics.

This book is only concerned with the woven, decorated shawl for which Kashmir has been famous. The appellation 'kani' shawl, as it is popularly known in Kashmir, originally meant simply a woven shawl, but during the course of time the term kani has taken on a more special significance and is defined as a type of weave in which the design is formed by the manipulation of small wooden sticks called 'tojis' which interlock their respective coloured threads as they complete each weft of the shawl. Traditionally the most valued shawls were composed of threads of delicate wool from the underbelly of the wild Tibetan mountain goat, the pattern being worked by the technique known to Western textile historians as 'twill tapestry'. These are the 'woven jewels' of Kashmir.

Plate 1. Srinagar, capital of Kashmir, on the Jhelum River from the Zain-a-Kadal.

The prefix 'amli' means embroidered, which is, of course, the art of ornamenting cloth by needlework applied completely independently of the ground cloth. In the woven or kani technique, the colour thread forming the motif is part of the ground cloth itself and a hole will be made if a coloured thread is removed.

These two methods were sometimes employed together but were rarely equally important. A kani shawl, for example, might be embellished by the addition of specially embroidered colours or even small separate and independent motifs, but never in an exaggerated way. A shawl classified as an amli shawl would never contain kani work as this particular type of shawl was usually made as a speedy imitation of the former.

These appellations are extremely important not only for classifying the type of weave but also for placing the shawl in its proper historical context. These terms become especially important when studying the nineteenth century European imitations of the Kashmir shawls. European manufacturers used two other significant kinds of shawl-weaving methods: the draw-loom and the Jacquard loom. Although these techniques are in fact very different from the kani and amli weaves, the inexperienced eye is easily deceived by the remarkable similarities of colour and design which were achieved. The problem is further complicated, as we shall see later, by the French development of a 'counterfeit' Kashmir-shawl industry at the beginning of the nineteenth century. Here the same kani weave was employed in Europe with such success that these imitations were easily traded as genuine Kashmir shawls, both in the West and the Orient.

In order to clarify our understanding of these different techniques, we examine in this book the early development of French shawl design and production. It thus becomes clear that France, long neglected by textile historians was actually a leader in this revolutionary and highly industrial aspect of textile art. Around 1800, other European countries, of course, hopped on the fashion band-wagon, but France was the unchallenged frontrunner, both in artistic creation and manufacturing techniques.

By studying France's active role in this field, our knowledge of these elegant textiles is enormously enhanced. The Kashmir shawl and its French imitation will thus be seen to represent two inseparable and major art forms of the nineteenth century.

Chapter One
Classification of the Kashmir Shawl

The most striking fact about the history of Kashmir is that its people rose to great heights of art, culture and economic prosperity primarily when the impulses came from outside rather than from within. The Kashmir shawl developed over three hundred years, through four different periods of foreign political rule, during which Kashmir was ruled successively by the Mughals, the Afghans, the Sikhs, and the Dogras and the shawls illustrated in this book have been classified according to these four main periods.

It is impossible to speak of one 'great period' in the development of the Kashmir shawl; each culture brought its own unique contribution. The development of the Kashmir shawl is influenced directly by changing historical circumstances; it reflects times of peace and of war, of famine and prosperity, as well as changes in royal patronage.

In order to set the stage for the ornamentation of the Kashmir shawl this chapter provides a brief historical background of the four main periods. Detailed discussion of the evolution of the boteh is discussed in Chapter 4 again under the period headings. In this way the reader may gain a better insight from a narrative focused directly on elements of style rather than on one which attempts to combine historical facts with theories of artistic sensitivites. Nevertheless, and so that the basis of this system of classification may come into sharper focus, a few stylistic points are briefly discussed here to clarify the attribution of the shawls illustrated in this book.

It appears that the early Mughal period represents an important and prosperous moment for the kani shawl. At the time the Renaissance was flourishing in the West and the Orient too was experiencing great artistic achievements. However, there are no dated shawls of the Mughal period, and extant pieces attributable to the seventeenth century do not seem to date much earlier than the reign of Jehangir (1605-1627). His reign is important for our study because this is when the 'flowering plant' first appeared, a design of delicate beauty which had a great influence on future generations of shawl designs. But a word of caution is due here. Other contemporary patterns surely existed and probably enjoyed an equal popularity which should not be overlooked. Unfortunately, the dearth of early shawls inhibits any positive statements concerning concurrent schools of design. The situation becomes clearer in the eighteenth century, but it is not until the early nineteenth century that a firm overall picture of the multitudinous shawl patterns emerges. This is due, of course, not only to the numerous extant pieces available to us for examination from this period but also to pictorial references by Western painters.

The Kashmiri people suffered under their Afghan overlords and this is manifested in the more restrained expressiveness of many of the extant patterns. What was lost in the sensuous lines of the 'flowering plant' was gained in the regal stature of the more rigorous and hardy plant of the eighteenth century. Later on it was the outline shape of the boteh that reigned supreme which the artist filled with a floral mosaic. As the curtain fell on the eighteenth century, Sikh power began to proliferate slowly throughout the Punjab and two decades later it engulfed Kashmir. A prelude to what would constitute distinct stylistic elements of the Sikh period becomes progressively apparent during this time. Because the effect of political change can be seen in the shawl's design, an attempt has been made here to classify the shawl according to whoever held power over Kashmir at the time of its manufacture.

No system of classification is foolproof and obviously certain imperfections are bound to arise. For example, one of the biggest problems was how to classify a shawl piece exhibiting design characteristics from one period (such as the spacing of the botehs) while it was probably woven during the course of another. In such cases the shawl is classified under the period in which it is thought to have been woven, with a sub-classification attributing style to a different period.

Of course in the long run where certain examples proved difficult, an educated guess had to be made based on experienced gained over many years in the study and handling of literally thousands of both rare and common specimens in public and private collections. This collation is the result of extensive field work spanning three continents, the pieces have been chosen not only for their fine quality but also for the ways in which they document particular periods of styles.

Origin of the Kashmir Shawl

The shoulder mantle or shawl had been in existence, in a variety of forms, from the most ancient times, serving as a staple and protective garment not only for the rich and noble but also and above all for the common people. In ancient Buddhist literature the shawl can be found among recorded inventories of woollen textiles, and its manufacture appears to have been a cottage industry in Kashmir as early as the eleventh century.

Doubt still persists, however, as to the actual beginnings of the kani shawl industry. At present there is no extant kani piece which may be said with certainty to predate the seventeenth century, in spite of the nineteenth century legend recorded by the Baron Von Hugel who cites Zain-ul-Abidin's (1420-1470) enthusiastic encouragement of the arts of Kashmir. However, the high degree of sophistication of the early seventeenth century fragments suggests that the shawl industry may have been in existence at least as early as the late sixteenth century.

A recently-found document[1] provides new evidence suggesting that indeed it may have been during either the fifteenth or sixteenth century that the industry first began. This document was written by the well-known shawl merchant of nineteenth century Kashmir, Hajji Mukhtar Shah. Mukhtar Shah, whose ancestors began working in the shawl trade in the seventeenth century, was painfully struck by its sudden demise during the 1870s, and, at the request of the eminent linquist G.W. Leitner, wrote a history tracing the early development of the industry which, he said, had given 'a lease on life to five lakh[2] souls'.

Mukhtar's treatise, like any Oriental document, should be interpreted with care, since it reflects a vision of time and history often different from that of Western thought. It provides a remarkable picture of the development of the weaving industry. Furthermore conversations with present-day descendents of old weaving families bear out its arguments.

Mukhtar records that Kashmir came under the de facto domination of Mirza Haider Dughlat in 1540. Haider was born in 1500 in Tashghar at the Eastern end of Turkestan and was a first cousin to the great Mughal, Babur. At fifteen he left his cousin's protection to join the forces of Abu Said in Kashgar, whom he served for nineteen years. In those days the governments of Tibet, Ladakh and Kashmir were closely interrelated.

Mirza Haider Dughlat encouraged many of the industries originally introduced by Zain-ul-Abidin a hundred years earlier, and among the annual presents offered to him in tribute were a few rolls of very fine but crudely woven Ladakhi wool, called 'putto'. Woven from goat's wool, the cloth was softer and warmer than any

---

1. Shah.
2. Five hundred thousand.

yet manufactured in Kashmir, apparently because shawls, until then, were made only from sheep's wool. Mirza Haider felt that if this wool, called 'pashm', could be spun and woven by the expert craftsmen of Kashmir, perhaps an even better material could be produced.

According to Mukhtar, it was under the guidance of Haider's faithful adherent and cook, Naghz Beg, that a new industry was generated which induced the local people to develop the kani shawl technique. Beg, to whom Kashmir owes the kani shawl, instituted a thin instrument called a 'seekh', or spike, at each end of which different coloured yarns were placed. He also introduced a new feature of red and green spots in regular rows.[3] Following his death, shawl weavers continued developing the spike-shuttling method, using the double-colour scheme in various ways; generally white putto for men and red for women. Later, saffron yellow and indigo blue were also added.

The industry continued to flower, but, as Mukhtar points out, it was not until the Mughals' conquest of Kashmir in 1586 that the Kashmir shawl industry realised its full potential.

Mughal Period (1586-1753)

The Mughals (also known as Moguls or Mongols), inhabitants of the vast steppe land of Central Asia, were a race of warlike nomads who conquered Northern India in the early part of the sixteenth century. Under Mughal rule Kashmir abandoned its antediluvian isolation, and its natural beauty attracted people from all over Asia. The Mughals instituted great building projects and a sound system of administration, and Kashmir enjoyed a brisk trade as part of the great highway of Central Asia.

Akbar, grandson of the great founder of the Mughal dynasty, Babur, ruled Kashmir for nineteen years. He abolished many of the religious persecutions and iniquities suffered by the people under the rule of the Turkish Sultans. He also took a personal interest in the manufacture of Kashmir's artefacts and paid special attention to the shawl industry, which he admired greatly.

His interest in religion and his tendency toward free thought and mysticism were known and admired throughout the world. Akbar's genius lay in the shrewd reconciliation of the often opposing forces of Hindu and Muslim philosophies. He successfully achieved this by establishing a cult of monarchy, presenting himself as a semi-devine ruler, whom it was a religious duty to obey and sacrilege to oppose. His son Jehangir, impressed by the nimbus or halo he observed in Western religious painting, sustained this idea of divine rule by featuring himself in paintings glorified by shimmering gold nimbuses of exaggerated dimensions. The powerful military force and 'divine' monarchal aura which reigned during this great period of regal opulence should be borne in mind when studying the remaining Mughal textiles handed down to us.

No other Mughal textiles used the kani technique. It was used, however, in textiles of the Central Asian region and certain areas of Persia, especially in kilims, saddle bags and Soumak weaves. For example, the Bakhtiari tribes of Southern Persia produce a single faced weave just like the shawl, although without a twill and with the reverse side displaying a relief of ridges where the various colour areas join. Textiles of the kani technique were also woven by people of early Turkish origin, although weavings of this type are extremely rare, probably because they were not exported and served simply the utilitarian purposes of the nomadic tribes who wove them. Because of the scarcity of adept Kashmiri craftsmen, it is known that Akbar

---

3. Sufi, pp.563-564.

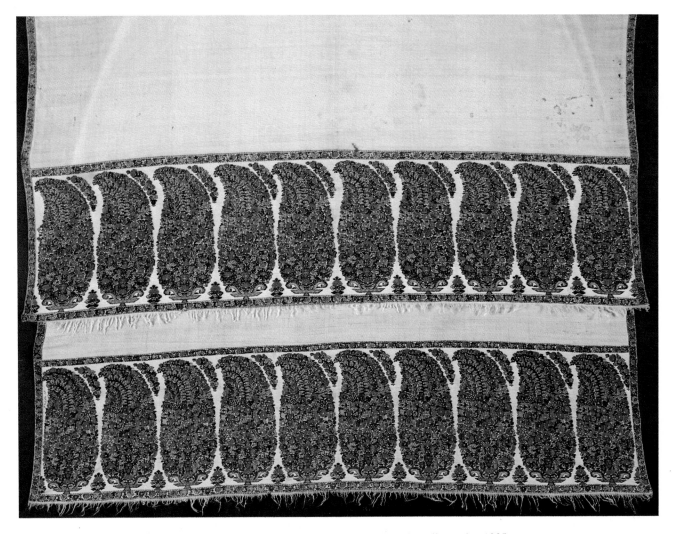

Colour Plate 2. Afghan period, Empire shawl. Dochalla showing both palla ends, 1805. See details in Plate 10.

brought many weavers from the city of Andizhan, Eastern Turkestan (about 750km (470 miles) north of Kashmir), down to Kashmir, and one inevitably speculates on whether the kani weave originated in these areas or in the Kashmir.

Akbar's keen interest in textiles is illustrated by the meticulous efforts undertaken to have them carefully arranged and preserved in the toshikana or imperial wardrobe. Textiles which had been offered to him as tribute, and various court commissioned pieces, shawls amongst them, were all labelled as to their date of entry, price, colour and weight.

Abul Fazl, his court chronicler, wrote that Akbar improved the shawl department by making a 'visual' improvement to the tus shawls. Tus was an extremely fine goat's wool which came from the wild ibex whose natural colour was brown or white or various shades in-between. The tus shawl was unrivalled for its lightness, warmth and softness; and it was generally dyed without altering its natural colour (see Wool, Chapter 3). Akbar experimented with various techniques in shawl dyeing and

Plate 3. Shoulder mantle (detail). Mughal, late 17th or early 18th century

Plate 2. Darbar hanging (detail) of silver embroidered velvet, 17th century.

discovered that tus wool was impervious to the colour red. He also reports that Akbar increased the size of the Kashmir shawl so that it could be made into a complete suit.

The way the shawl was worn captured Akbar's imagination. 'Previously the Kashmir shawl was worn folded in four', wrote Fazl, 'but now they were generally worn without folds and look well just thrown over the shoulder.' But the major change in style came when Akbar began wearing them in pairs, hence the name 'dochalla' or twin-shawl. An identical pair of shawls were sewn back to back to hide the rough ridges of the tapestry weave, giving the appearance of a single, reversible shawl.

George Forster, who visited Kashmir in 1783, was informed that during the Mughal period 40,000 looms were in operation (see Figure 1, page 30); of course not all of these were involved in the manufacture of kani shawls. Fazl cites one thousand workshops in Lahore alone, where mostly 'chirahs' (turbans) and 'fautahs' (loinbands) were made. These fabrics were known as 'mayan' and were made of silk and wool.

Following Akbar's death his son, Jehangir, succeeded to the throne. Jehangir had fallen in love with the natural beauty of Kashmir the day he paid his first visit to the Valley with his father in 1589. He described the incredible flora of the valley in his memoirs, *Tuzk-i-Jehangir:* 'The red rose, the violet, and the narcissus grow of themselves; in the fields there are all kinds of flowers and all sorts of sweet, scented herbs, more than can be calculated. In the soul-enchanting spring the hills and plains are filled with blossoms, the gates, the walls, the courts, the roofs are lighted up by the torches of banquet-adorning tulips.'

Kashmir became his favourite abode and he declared that he would rather be deprived of every other province of his mighty empire than lose Kashmir. In this connection Forster wrote: 'the interests of this province were so strongly favoured

Plates 4a and 4b. Silk brocade. Safavid, 17th century. Plate 4b (right) is from a waistband. These two silk fragments exemplify the high standards of Persian textile art from which 17th century India drew much inspiration.

at the Mughal court that every complaint against its governors was attentively listened to, and any attempt to molest the people was restrained or punished.' Under Jehangir's rule, Kashmir enjoyed one of its most prosperous periods.

Jehangir also writes about the shawls of Kashmir in his memoirs: 'The shawls of Kashmir to which my father gave the name of 'param-naram' are very famous; there is no need to praise them. Another kind is 'narharma'; it is thicker than a shawl and soft. Another is 'darm': it is like a 'jul-i-khirsak' and is put on a carpet. With the exception of shawls they make other woollen material better in Tibet. Though they bring the wool for the shawls from Tibet they do not make them there. The wool for the shawls comes from a goat which is peculiar to Tibet. In Kashmir they weave the 'pattu' shawl from wool, and sewing two shawls together they smooth them into a kind of 'saqarlat' (broad-cloth) which is not bad for a raincoat.'[4]

The Hindi name for shawls, 'param-naram', coined by Akbar continued, and it seems to have been given to an article regularly presented to the nobles. 'Narharma' means 'like a river', for the shawl had waves (maujdar) as a decorative feature (see Plate 108). Jehangir noted in his memoirs that he once presented to Mirza Raja

4. Jehangir, vol.2, pp.147-148.

Bhao Singh a special Kashmir shawl called a 'phup', derived from the sanskrit word 'pushpa', flower. We thus learn that the shawl, at that time, was ornamented with flowers.

Sir Thomas Roe, James I's ambassador to the Mughal court, was offered a gold shawl by the Governor of Surat in 1616. Decorative shawls such as these were apparently used as enticing bribes and this is mentioned in the early records of the English East India Trading Company. Roe, however, rejected the governor's offer, writing in his memoirs: 'and pressing me to take a gold "shal", I answered we were but newly friends; when I saw any constancy in his carriage and the money paid I would be more free with him yet I would receive no obligation.'[5]

Jehangir was succeeded in turn by his son, Shah Jehan, who ruled from 1627 to 1658. He took an even greater interest in the welfare of Kashmir than had his father. Among the Mughal rulers, Shah Jehan is remembered as a builder. His monumental constructions, like the Taj Mahal in Agra and the Red Forts in Agra and Delhi, testify to his unusually fine architectural taste, which synthesised several impulses: Hindu, Buddhist, and Persian.

The most coveted shawls during the Mughal period were often ornamented with precious metals. Manrique, a Spanish monk travelling in India in 1630, described fine shawls as having 'borders ornamented with fringes of gold, silver and silk thread. The princes and nobles wear them like cloaks, either muffling themselves up in them or else carrying them under their arms. These choice cloths are of white colour when they leave the loom but are *afterwards* dyed any hue desired and are ornamented with various coloured flowers and other kinds of decoration which make them very gay and showy.'

The remarks by this early traveller imply that embroidery was at that time used in shawl decoration. Had Manrique been speaking of the kani method, he would not have described it as having been removed from the loom. Curiously, no mention of 'tojis' (the wooden needles used in the kani weaving) nor any description of the intricacies and lengthy time required to weave the kani shawl is found in the writings left from the Mughal period. The descriptions focus on the uniqueness of the high quality wool (not necessarily Kashmiri wool), rather than on the techniques by which it was manufactured.

Aurangzeb came to the throne of his father, Shah Jehan, in the year 1658. With him the mighty Mughal empire founded by Babur and consolidated by Akbar and his two successors began to decline. Aurangzeb was a strict, orthodox Muslim, and his views and sentiments towards his Hindu subjects directly opposed those held by his predecessors. The great artistic tradition of Mughal India began to decline under Aurangzeb's regime.

François Bernier, the celebrated doctor, philosopher and traveller, spent twelve years in India as physician to Aurangzeb. He had the privilege of visiting Kashmir while accompanying Aurangzeb and of thus being the first Westerner ever to set foot in the 'enchanted land'. He contradicted Manrique's description regarding shawl decoration, saying that they were made with a 'sort of embroidery made on the loom'. These differences of observation are typical of Western travellers whose knowledge of loom techniques was poor. Since Bernier actually visited Kashmir, where one could hardly escape the sight of weaving being performed, his observation is probably the more believable.

Bernier also described the shawl industry in some detail. 'Large quantities of shawls were manufactured which gave employment even to children,' he wrote. 'These shawls measured five by two and a half feet, were ornamented at both ends with a sort of embroidery made in the loom, a foot in height. The Mughals and

---

5. Irwin, 1973, p.10.

22

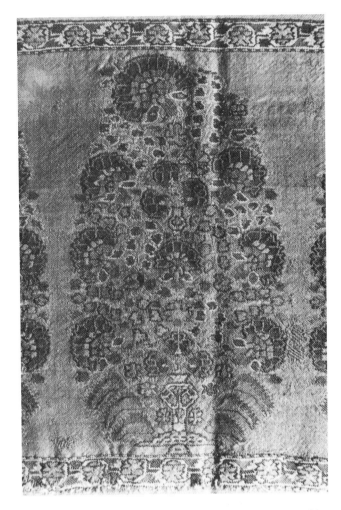 

Plate 5 (left). Shoulder mantle (detail of Colour Plate 36, p.236). Mughal, mid-18th century.

Plate 6 (right). Patka or waistband (detail of Colour Plate 24, p.199). Mughal, mid-18th century.

Indian men and women wore them in winter around their heads, passing them over the shoulders as a mantle. One sort was manufactured with the wool of the country and the other with the wool of the shawl goat of Tibet. The price of the tus shawl ranged from 50 to 150 rupees. Great pains were taken to manufacture similar shawls at Patna, Agra and Lahore but they lacked the delicate texture of Kashmir shawls.'[6]

Bernier also explained the ranks within the social and military hierarchy[7] in a letter to one Monseigneur Colbert and it appears highly possible that shawls reflected military rank, both through the variations in the 'boteh' patterns (see

---

6. Bernier, pp.402-403.
7. At the top of the military ladder of command were the 'Omrahs' or 'seigneurs'; often foreign adventurers who advanced through the ranks and were rewarded with attractive salaries and titles. The titles signified the number of horses under their command, such as 'hazari', one thousand, 'do-hazari', two thousand, up to the maximum 'Duazdeh-hazari', or twelve thousand. Such honourable titles represented exalted positions and were created expressly to attract public attention. Under the Omrahs came the 'mansadbars' or cavaliers. Although they lacked the Omrah's pomp and high status, they were nevertheless often able to ascend the ranks to eventually become Omrahs.

Plates 99 and 100), and through the actual colour of the shawl itself. The small number of extant Mughal pieces known does not offer enough evidence at present to comment definitively on the question of rank, with the exception of the pure white tus, or tooch shawls reserved for the king alone and used by him as gifts for foreign dignitaries.

Part of the shawl trade with India during the Mughal and Afghan periods was carried out through the agency of the government. Most of the shawls, for instance, were taken by officials and sent to Delhi and Agra where some were presented to the Emperor and the rest sold to courtiers and the nobility. The Mughal emperors, during their many visits, were frequently followed by a horde of traders from Hindustan who purchased shawls and other artistic wares and sold them at a profit in the chief cities of India.

A new shawl design which caught the eye of an Emperor often found immediate popularity among his followers and the nobles of the court. Accordingly, when the Mughal ruler, Muhammud Shah (1720-1742), was presented with a shawl of a fascinating floral design, he ordered that 40,000 rupees-worth be supplied to him annually. No real description of the design remains but, nevertheless, the shawl came to be called, after the name of the emperor, 'Buta Muhammud Shahi'.[8]

As the Mughal kingdoms began to collapse and Kashmir came under Afghan rule, the shawl trade began to focus increasingly on the West, while the Indian market fell into decline. In spite of this change, the government of Hyderabad in the Deccan, under the rule of Nizzam'ul Mulk, continued to be a rich outlet for the Kashmir shawl where it remained the conventional dress of the nobles at court.

Afghan Period (1753-1819)

The Afghan invasion in 1753 by Ahmad Shah Abdali put an end to the Mughal rule of Kashmir. Under the rule of the Afghans, the country was reduced to the lowest depths of penury and degradation, a slavery lasting for sixty-seven years. The Afghans' cruelty also threatened the life and property of all foreigners who had been residing in Kashmir. About ninety firms established by Hindu businessmen were closed down as their owners returned to their homeland, while nearly half the population of Kashmir left the terror-stricken land permanently. Nevertheless, shawl weaving continued during these difficult times and accounted for a significant portion of Kashmir's revenue. The shawl's popularity abroad resulted in a brisk trade.

Afghan's control of Kashmir represented just another provincial addition to an already vast empire carved out by Ahmad Shah Abdali. Ahmed Shah was chosen by the Afghan chiefs at Qandahar to be their leader. He thus inherited the incalculable treasures amassed by his predecessor Nadir Shah (assassinated 1747), including the famous Koh-i-nor diamond and the peacock throne taken as booty by the latter when he sacked Delhi in 1739. He assumed power over the eastern part of Nadir's empire, and Afghanistan took its place among the Kingdoms of the world. His empire at one time extended from Herat, Meshed, Khurasan and Nishapur in the West to Multan, the Punjab and finally Delhi in the East.

Towards the end of the eighteenth century and during the time of Abdali's rule, the Qajar dynasty arose in Southern Persia bringing with it an increasingly strong patronage of the arts. This was something absent from the life-style of the warring Afghans. The oil paintings produced during the reign of Fath 'Ali Shah (1798-1834) and those just preceding his monarchy do not necessarily represent new sources of Kashmir design inspiration but they do provide images of bejewelled royalty, rich in sumptuous brocades, embroideries and Kashmir shawls. The importance of these

8. Koul, p.37.

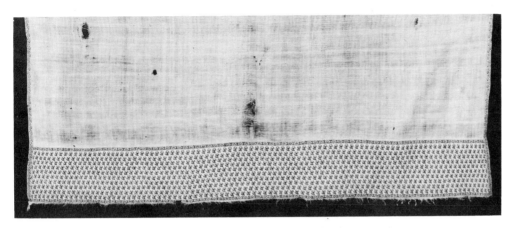

Plate 7. Shoulder mantle. Early Afghan period. This popular pattern of 'winged leaf' butis is framed by a conventional delicately drawn hashia pattern.

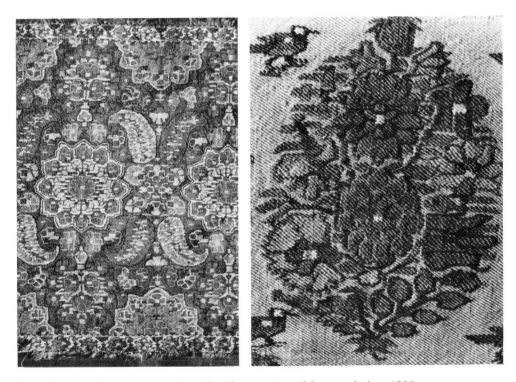

Plate 8 (left). Shoulder mantle palla (fragment). Afghan period, c.1800.

Plate 9 (right). Detail of Colour Plate 34, p.233. Afghan period, late 18th century.

Qajar paintings lies in their iconography and they represent some of the earliest known illustrations of Kashmir shawls and shawl designs. (For style development of the Kashmir shawl the reader is referred to the Chapter 4, 'Symbolism and the Boteh'.)

The darkest period in Kashmir's history occurred during the regime of the Afghan governor Haji Dad Khan (1776-1783). He imposed a heavy tax on the shawl-weaving trade, and began the system of 'dagshawl' or excise-tax on shawls which later became such a burden for the poor shawl weavers that they even preferred death to the weaver's profession. Bamzai explains that the dagshawl system first developed out of the need by the state to seek more taxes than that which it already received through the usurious sale of saffron and grain.[9] In lieu of taxes from such produce, Haji Dad Khan taxed the weavers directly, who then numbered 12,000, with a small tax called 'Qasur-i-shali'. Subsequently, this too was abolished and a new *ad valorem* tax was imposed on every shawl manufactured. By 1813, when Azim Khan was the governor of Kashmir, the number of looms rose to 24,000. Azim brought back the forcible sale of grain to the weavers but kept the *ad valorem* tax. Thus the poor weaver was squeezed into debt. Invariably he had to borrow against future shawl sales in order to purchase his grain. In order to eat he had to weave.

Although Forster does not mention the dagshawl system per se, the high taxes accumulated by a shawl caused him to remark with a slight note of astonishment:

> 'The price at the loom of an ordinary shawl is eight rupees, thence in proportional quality, it produces from fifteen to twenty; and I have seen a very fine piece sold at forty rupees the first cost. But the value of this commodity may be largely enhanced by the introduction of flowered work; and when you are informed that the sum of one hundred rupees is occasionally given for a shawl to the weaver, the half amount may be fairly ascribed to the ornaments.'[10]

Statistics on the number of shawl looms in Kashmir at that time are not always reliable. Usually they were estimates received through word of mouth and they probably took into consideration all types of looms which were set up for shawl weaving. Our attention here is basically focused on the kani shawl and not on the plain or simple, undecorated shawl which served as the staple product (and still does) for both Kashmir's inhabitants and foreign markets. The kani shawl was made

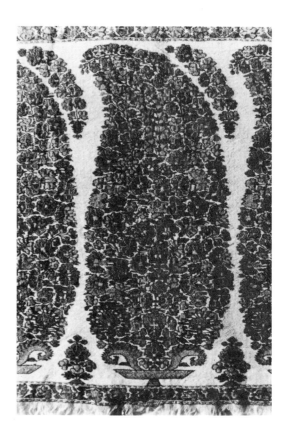

Plate 10. Long shawl (detail of Colour Plate 2, p.19) with 'Empire' boteh. Afghan period, c.1805.

---

9. Bamzai, p.489.
10. ibid., p.489, 490.

26

Plates 11a, b and c. Plaid patterns (detail). Afghan period, c.1800. These patterns proliferated around 1800, probably due to the newly formed Afghan court at Kabul and also the emerging Qajar dynasty of Persia. Many of these wonderful patterns owe much to 17th century Ottoman art and a look at silk embroidered panels of that period will reveal startling similarities.

almost exclusively for the foreign market. This market is non-existent today although the Indian government is trying to revive the industry and there may be a maximum of fifty kani looms in operation now. Unfortunately, the product of today cannot compare with the level of art which was achieved over a hundred years ago — even among the most inferior kani shawls made then.

Although 23,000 looms were mentioned as being in operation in 1823, Richard Strachey provides a conflicting statistic in his 1812 report to the Bengal Civil Service. He estimates, in what appears to be a more precise manner, that 16,000 looms were operating in Srinagar and its surrounding area, and calculates that 80,000 kani shawls were made in the course of a year (see Figure 1, page 30).

Sikh Period (1819-1846)

Kashmir became a vital frontier region in the nineteenth century. With the advance of the British Empire to the north, Tzarist Russia into Asia towards the North-West, and the extension of the Chinese borders to Sinkian, Kashmir occupied an important strategic area as the meeting place of three great Empires. It was to become a centre of activity of various foreign agents engaged in collecting information on its geography, administrative set-up and defence.

The Sikhs were originally a religious sect, founded by Guru Nanak in the late sixteenth century. Among the peoples of India, they are marked by a distinctive religion and by intense devotion to their homeland, the Punjab. The Sikhs repudiated mosques and Hindu temples and taught the worship of God as Truth. They proclaimed the town of Amritsar as the centre of Sikhism and as a place of pilgrimage. Perhaps because of their conflict with the Mughals and Afghans, the Sikhs became superb soldiers and the sword evolved into a symbol of both spiritual and secular authority. Guru Govind Singh (1675-1708), the tenth and last guru, devised two sacraments in order to create the idea of Militant Brotherhood; the first, a form of baptism with consecrated water stirred by a sword or dagger and the second, the communal partaking of a mixture of flour, sugar and butter, which broke caste. The brotherhood created by these rites, was called the 'Khalsa' or 'the Pure', and a member of the Khalsa observed the five Ks: i.e. his hair was unshaven, he wore a wooden comb in his hair, he had an iron bracelet on his wrist, he wore shorts and he carried a sword. In addition, the members of the brotherhood adopted the name of Singh or Lion.

The Sikhs became a military as well as a religious power. In 1799 the leader, Runjit Singh, captured the city of Lahore and became Raja. Twenty years later, in 1819, he forced the Afghans to relinquish their hold on Kashmir, and Runjit Singh became one of the greatest leaders of India during the period of transition between the fall of the Mughals and the establishment of the British Empire.

Travellers into the Punjab during the time of Runjit Singh were fascinated by the Sikh ruler. Those who had the rare opportunity of meeting him invariably recorded the interesting impressions they had felt. Runjit Singh was a short man with a terribly disfigured face ravaged in his youth by smallpox. In addition, he was blind in the left eye. The effect of this disability was awesomely enhanced due to the fact that his piercing right eye was unusually large (see Plate 14). His passion for horses was unequalled and his ability in swordsmanship was admired.

Sir Lepel Griffin, a Victorian biographer, on the other hand, wrote 'His moral being seemed at a superficial glance as dwarfed and distorted as its physical envelop. He was selfish, false and avaricious; grossly superstitious, shamelessly and openly drunken and debauched. In the respectable virtues he had no part; but in their default he was still great. With him, as with the most illustrious leaders of men, from Caesar and Alexander to Napoleon, intellectual strength was not allied to moral

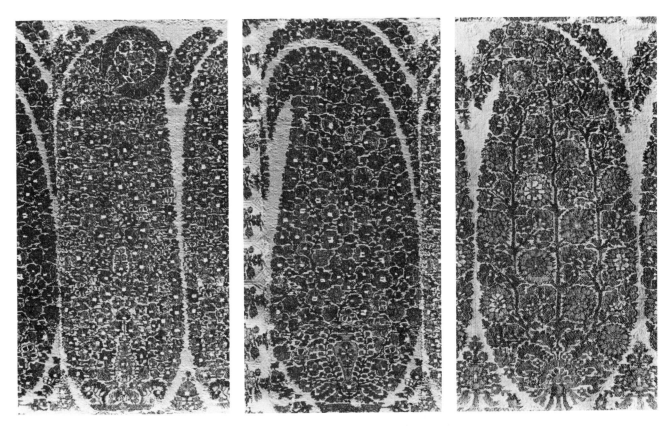

Plates 12a, b and c. Boteh details of Colour Plate 43, p.263. Afghan period, 1800-1815.

Plate 13. Kani dress cloth (fragment). Afghan period, c.1815.

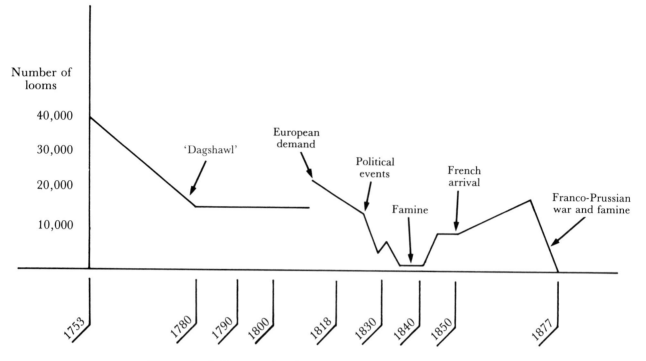

Figure 1. A diagram showing Kashmir's shawl production based on statistics recorded by visitors to Kashmir during the 18th and 19th century. For monetary values recorded during the years 1850-1865 see Watson, appendix B.

rectitude. He was great because he possessed the qualities without which the highest success cannot be attained. He was a born ruler with the natural genius of command. Men obeyed him by instinct and because they had no power to disobey. The control which he exercised over the whole Sikh people, nobles, priest and people, was the measure of his greatness.'[11]

The Sikhs ruled for only twenty-seven years. During that period they were preoccupied with military expeditions and therefore devoted very little time and thought to ameliorating the sad condition of the people. Baron von Hugel, who visited Kashmir in 1836, wrote: 'the dreadful cruelties perpetrated by their earlier rulers who, for the smallest offence, punished them with the loss of their noses and ears, make the poor Kashmiri well satisfied with their present, comparatively mild government.'

Kashmir was frequently hit by natural calamities. In 1827 a severe earthquake caused a heavy loss of life and property. The tremors lasted for three months and, to make matters worse, an epidemic of cholera broke out. The number of dead was so great that there was not enough cloth to shroud the dead bodies. Just five years later, in 1832, a terrible snowstorm ruined the rice crops just before the harvest, resulting in severe famine. Thousands died and thousands more emigrated to the Punjab plains of Northern India. The population of the Valley was reduced from eight to two lakhs.[12] Another famine devastated the region in 1838.

---

11. Archer, p.XX.

12. A lakh equals one hundred thousand.

Plate 14. A drawing of Runjit Singh, described as 'King of Lahore'.

Few clues exist, at present, which might establish whether Sikh influence directly affected the style of the Kashmir shawl. It is true that its style underwent a vast, if not dramatic, transformation during the reign of the Sikhs but perhaps this was coincidental rather than that a valid association can be made between the Sikh way of life and the weaving industry.

Pictures from this period tell us little. Sikh portraiture occurred rather late, since Runjit Singh did not like to be painted, obviously because of his own personal appearance. There is no evidence that he liked or even encouraged the activities of painters. The first time he ever sat to an artist was in 1832, when he was visited by the Governor-General, Bentinck. In fact, he was amazed that the Europeans should attach importance to drawing at all. The Hungarian painter, Schoefft, illustrated a few shawls in paintings of the Sikh military court based on notes made in 1841. But here their prosaic used as curtains and saddles do not directly further our knowledge of style.

Until the second quarter of the nineteenth century, no painting that is truly Sikh can be said to exist. Miniature painting as practised for the Mughals had expired and it was only in the Punjab hills that artists painted for the local Rajput princes and their courts. A review of Sikh portraiture does not offer any revealing discovery about style or about the type of shawl preferred by the Sikhs. Neither is there any detail in other aspects of their paintings, including the boteh itself, which might be associated with some of the common motifs often found in contemporary shawls. Similarly, the contemporary Qajar paintings of Persia must be excluded although they show us that the Persian nobles, especially the women, admired the Kashmir shawl greatly.

The weaving industry was regulated by Runjit Singh's loyal governors who once attempted to entice the Maharaja to Kashmir, a region in which he never set foot. One day a silk carpet of extreme beauty was placed before him which depicted all the wonders of Kashmir's luscious gardens and rainbow colours. Overwhelmed by its magnificence, it is said that he literally threw himself on the carpet, and in rolling on its rich velour, Runjit Singh vicariously tasted the sweet pleasures of Kashmir.

The labour employed by the 'karkhandars', or proprietors, of weaving factories had begun to be regulated by the dagshawl system (see above, page 25) which was created under the Afghans. As taxes became heavier, the rich karkhandars found more and more ways to shift the burden on to the shoulders of the weavers. The proprietors complained that as soon as a man learned his work and some of the employer's trade secrets he rose in value on the labour market, and every effort was made by his employer's rivals to secure his services. The practice of luring away a weaver was, therefore, made punishable by law. The weavers were now completely controlled by the karkhandars, a situation which amounted to little more than slavery. Furthermore, their survival was dependent on the allotment of rice that weavers were forced to purchase from the proprietors. The weaver, whether he worked or not, was obliged to pay.

These oppressive laws did not go unchallenged. Many weavers were said to have cut off their thumbs to escape the tyrannies of the karkhandars. The last Sikh governor, Sheikh Imam-ud-din, gave them a little relief in 1846 by setting the shawl weavers free from the bondage of the karkhandars. This revived the industry and during the rule of Gulab Singh there were 27,000 weavers working at 11,000 looms. But the wages paid to the workmen were miserably low and, moreover, in actual practice, the karkhandars managed somehow to keep the workmen under perpetual bondage.

Shawls manufactured in Kashmir during the Sikh regime were bought by Persian merchants and sent to Persia. Next came the Hindu bankers who brought them directly from the karkhandars and exported them to Lahore and Amritsar for Punjabi consumation. Runjit Singh distributed many of them as presents, as did several members of the Sikh hierarchy who imitated their ruler in their own small courts.

Jacquemont, a French botanist who travelled in Kashmir in the 1820s, pointed out that the officers under the Maharaja were careful to keep an agent in Kashmir to look after the shawls which were woven each year. This was obviously necessary to assure that the goods be delivered to the Sikhs in spite of the strong European demand where clients were paying exhorbitant prices.

According to Schoefft and the Russian prince, Soltykoff, the Sikhs probably made the Kashmir shawl more a part of their daily lives than their predecessors. 'The tents were doubled with Kashmir shawls', wrote the awestruck Soltykoff, who entered Amritsar in 1842. 'We only walked on Kashmir shawls and while sitting down I perceived that all the alleys, ceilings and streets, as far as the eye could encompass were covered thusly of superb shawls — even the horses were prancing on them.'[13]

During the reign of Maharaja Runjit Singh the Sikh interest in the shawl, and its symbol of the cone boteh, found expression in mural painting. The interior walls of the Golden Temple of Amritsar display a liberal use of the cone and bent cypress tree as purely decorative motifs. Apparently, it was not until about 1835 that the Maharaja was able to order the embellishment of the temple's interior. Another example is the 'baradari' or open pavilion of the Lahore Fort where Runjit Singh held court, and built possibly at the end of the eighteenth century. From what remains of the pavilion's mural, we can see a painted mihrab, the centre of which contains a large medallion on a sky-blue field in which prominent botehs appear 'floating' in scattered directions.

---

13. Soltykoff, p.158.

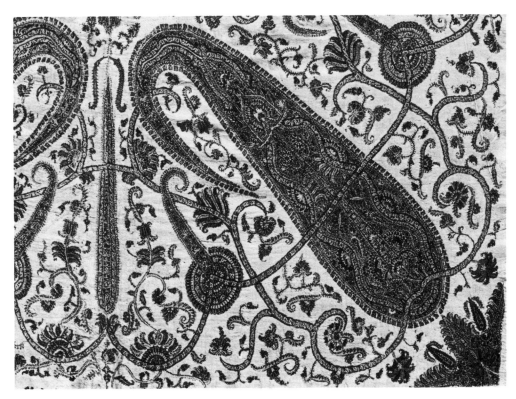

Plate 15. Embroidered shawl, Sikh period.

In contrast with the Afghan period, the shawl in the Sikh period, with its boldly sweeping curves, was more grandiose in design than ever before. It was a period of creativity unprecedented in the history of Kashmir, perhaps triggered by Runjit Signh's conquest of Kashmir in 1819, which had united it with the rest of the Punjab where his court was renowned for its splendour and magnificence.

Beautifully illustrating these ideas of pomp and grandeur is a vivid description by W.G. Archer:

'As Western missions, travellers and explorers traversed the Punjab, visited the Sikh court or watched the Sikh cavalry riding and drilling, all succumbed to the glittering dazzle of their dress, their handsome appearance, their great beards and turbans, above all, to the sheer sensuousness of Sikh colour. Ranjit Singh himself might consciously affect a wilfully drab attire but his troops and courtiers exuded feverish brilliance. So strong a love for flashing, almost gaudy hues inevitably influenced the artist and it is hardly surprising that in evoking the splendours of Ranjit's 'public image' they adopted a gay and dazzling palette. Confining pallid greens and misty blues to backgrounds, they employed colours as bold and loud as the great scarlet areas so common in certain types of Guler painting. Rich blues and deep greens, blazing orange-reds and piercing yellows imbued their portraits with clamant gusto and by a strident heightening of tones, gave the Sikh community a vivid impression of Sikh majesty.'[14]

This love of colour can be clearly seen in the shawl industry. During this great era shawl manufacturing transcended the mere decoration of a woollen ground and became the true vehicle of the technique of tapestry. At the same time the amli or embroidered shawl gained prominence. Although some authorities state that this technique began in about 1803, the shawl pieces themselves belie this theory. Up

---

14. Archer, pp.39-40.

34

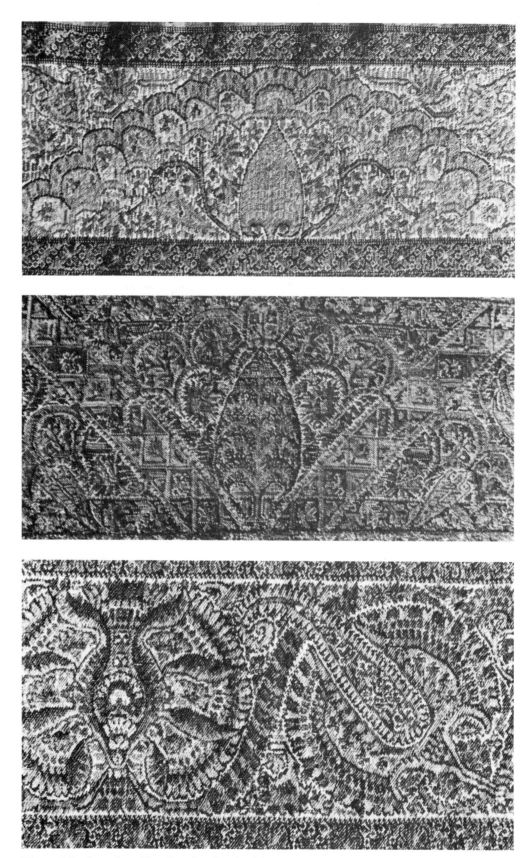

Plates 16a, b and c. Details of a shawl with spectacular 'art deco' patterns. Sikh period.

to now no embroidered pieces have ever been seen which might show pre-Sikh characteristics. As a matter of fact, shawls woven before this period are devoid of any such amli technique; even the corners of the central field (matan) are undecorated.

During the Sikh period although Kashmir was the centre of attraction for so many surrounding countries and provinces, each vying for a share of its commercial activities, its weaving industry appeared to remain predominantly in the hands of Persian merchants. Jacquemont remarks that 'for the most part, Kashmir shawls were bought by a small number of very wealthy Persians who export them to their native country via Bombay and Bouchir.'

Alongside the strong presence of Persian shawl merchants and the markets they represented, there was also the presence of Europeans, engaged in the service of Runjit Singh. From this point on, Europeans were to play an increasingly important role in the kani shawl industry. Tales of Napoleon's military exploits were widely known and admired, particularly by a militaristic society whose symbol was the sword, and when two of his former generals, Allard and Ventura, rode into the camp of Runjit Singh in 1822, the Rajah quickly recognised the advantage to be gained by having them in his army.

Other foreign officers followed; Colonel Henry Court, a French nobleman who later organised the French Legion, and Paolo de Avitable, an Italian by birth, whose dramatic career brought him to the governorship of Peshawar. But it is without doubt due to General Allard that the first direct link between Parisian shawl manufacturers and those of Kashmir was achieved.

Allard (see Plate 17) had been an aide-de-camp to Marshal Brune and, having miraculously escaped death in 1815 following the fall of Napoleon, he sought refuge in Egypt before going on to Northern India. There he gained the confidence of the Sikh ruler; he organised his troops and ultimately became his 'conseiller intime'.[15]

Allard visited Paris in 1835, after an absence of twenty years. He spent about six months there and was received by King Louis Philippe (1830-1848) several times during the course of his stay.[16] He was the centre of attention of many shawl manufacturers, each attempting to entice him with various business propositions and to profit from his lucrative situation in Lahore and Kashmir. One businessman even proposed the importation of Kashmiri weavers and their looms.[17]

It is known that the General took advantage of at least one situation, with the prestigious firm of the Gagelin Shawl Company, who gave him instructions on 'ways of *ameliorating* the Indian shawl industry'. On his return to Lahore he immediately arranged the export of eighty shawls chosen among 'the most beautiful fabrics of Kashmir and Lahore' and shortly afterwards, another very large collection of four hundred shawls was sent by his successor, General Ventura.[18]

Besides his status as commander of Runjit Singh's army, Allard was also appointed 'political agent of the French government at the court of Lahore' by Louis Philippe. He remained in close communication with French manufacturers and often sent the latest ideas in Kashmiri styles to Paris.[19] He also sent the Minister of Commerce in Paris the complete colour sample and warp-number designations stamped by the Syndicated Weavers' Corporation of Lahore. This proved very helpful to the wool spinners and shawl manufacturers of Paris.[20]

---

15. Cuvillier-Fleury, *Voyages et Voyageurs,* pp.294-5.
16. Expo 1867, illustré, Poitevin, pp.172-5.
17. Cuvillier-Fleury, *Notes historiques...,* p.89.
18. Poitevin, op.cit.
19. Expo 1839 vol. 1 p.145, J.L. Arnould received the public's admiration for a long shawl completely designed and coloured from a sketch sent by Allard from Lahore.
20. Deneirouse, *Traité,* p.38.

Plate 17. General Allard, described as chief commander of the armies of the King of Lahore.

A few years after Allard's return to India, the nature of the instructions he received from Paris' shawl manufacturers became apparent in a letter drafted by the Corporation of Kashmiri Shawl Trade Experts. A French translation of the letter was found in the report of the 'Exposition des Produits de l'Industrie Française' in 1839. A further translation into English follows, hopefully still with some of its Persian flavour.

'The weavers point out that a long shawl (dochalla) with large cones and borders, of the finest quality and sought after on the market can be constructed in the following manner: a pair of long shawls mounted on 12 looms can be woven within six or seven months and they would contain 20 seams. Now the question was: could a long shawl, unique (without a pair) be constructed on one loom without any seam in the body of the shawl.

It is for this reason that the Syndicated Experts Corporation of Long Shawl Manufacture has been convoked and after consultation, all things considered and weighed, they declare that if the shawl is established on two looms it is necessary that the warps and the wefts be of a superior quality to that of ordinary shawls and that in such case the design and colour mélange be in every way of rare perfection. Under these conditions a long shawl without seam would require three years to make during which time one would fear the alteration of colour and harm from insects.

The price of a shawl of commercial quality woven on 12 looms demanding six or seven months of work would cost according to its beauty 1,200 to 2,000 rupees. Such is the information that we can submit to Mirza-Ahad.

Now from a common accord between the said manufacturers it is agreed that unless superior orders are given, the manufacture of a long shawl, in the best ateliers, will be based upon the following:
1. Four large cones, on four looms with head of large border on six looms.
2. The middle with the large border, scalloped edges and small exterior border on two looms.

In one word, in the centre of a unique shawl (without pair) there are always two seams the latter handled exclusively by the seamster (rafugar), who performs this task with a perfection impossible to perceive by the average person.

Plate 18. Kashmir shawl with Maltese cross, Sikh period, c.1830. Except for a few details and the matan, this design is identical to one in a long shawl at the Yale University Art Gallery, with the Sacred Mountain pattern in the matan and sharp lunar crescents.

    In these conditions a long shawl would require a full twelve months of work day and night. We will wait for orders from Mirza-Ahad before starting.

    A square shawl with cones and open centre with large borders is made on four looms according to antique usage. On the demand of Mirza-Ahad, manufacturers have engaged themselves to make a square shawl (roumal) on one loom and this would require about eleven months of work.

    Written in Persian and faithfully translated into French, First Secretary Interpreter to the King, (signed) Jouannin, Paris December 21, 1838.'

The letter suggests that Allard's instructions involved the important and puzzling question of why the Kashmiri weavers were no longer producing shawls made in one piece (see Counterfeit or Kashmir, page 130). This report confirms the weavers' intransigence against making such a shawl. Taxes on kani-woven shawl goods were extremely severe (see page 32). As soon as a small piece of fabric was woven, the

Plates 19a and 19b. 19a (above) is a detail of Colour Plate 56, p.317, and the 'fan' tree on the left is similar to the palm trees found in Couder's work (see Plate 60 and Colour Plate 18, p.154). 19b (below) is a detail of Colour Plate 8, p.89.

tax collector saw to it that it was cut from the loom and physically brought for public examination and taxed according to its quality.[21] The consequences of the dagshawl system were far-reaching and shawls were later on constructed by the patchwork method.

Although it has been assumed that the first French agents arrived in Kashmir about 1850,[22] it is now understood that the two generals Allard and Ventura were acting as agents as early as 1835, and they were probably responsible for the publication of Chavant's design book, 'Album du Cachemirien' by the Kashmiri editor Kel-Avak-Oghlou, in 1837. The album was composed of detailed tracings of Kashmir shawls and rug designs which appealed to French taste (see Chapter 7, page 162). The generals' desire at the time was not to impose French taste, but rather to ensure that French merchants were receiving an above-average and high quality product based on the tastes to which Parisian fashion had become most accustomed. They were also trying to break the monopoly of the East India Trading Company.

After the death of Allard, just a month after the report was written, Ventura picked up on both the military and business affairs left by his colleague. A year later in 1839 Runjit Singh also died but Ventura continued in the shawl-trade business. 'During the last 10 or 15 years', wrote Baron Schönberg, who was in Kashmir in the middle of the nineteenth century, 'a brisk trade in shawls has been greatly promoted through the influence of the French gentleman resident at Lahore, General Ventura. He took a very active interest in this trade and during some years kept an agent in Kashmir.'[23]

The Baron also refers to a Monsieur Francis Le Boeuf, whose name often appears scattered among the shawl literature of the early nineteenth century. Honigberger mentions him as a travelling companion to General Ventura.[24] But by far the clearest evidence of Le Boeuf's role in this highly competitive fashion industry lies in Hajji Mukhtar Shah's manuscript.

Le Boeuf established himself in the shawl business in Srinagar under the guidance of General Ventura. Mukhtar claims that he introduced *designs of French taste* to the Kashmiri craft, and in particular the date of 1838 is mentioned for at least one special design. Unfortunately, this adds little to our knowledge since the date of many of Mukhtar's sketches is unknown. Nevertheless, it could be supposed that it was the 'bent-tip' boteh that was suggested by the sketches, in which the end of the boteh 'sprouted' another design device in the form of either a type of lance or a small thin cone, otherwise called 'buti-tip' cone (see Figure 27, page 100).

Shawl activities in the Punjab

Even before the arrival of French generals in Lahore, repeated attempts had been made at establishing a prosperous shawl industry in the Punjab, but Lahore witnessed many sieges and wars and the emigrant weavers were frequently forced to flee back to their native lands. Sufi cites from an anonymous report dated 1820: 'A rich banker, Shoogun Chund, of a respectable establishment and treasurer to the residency, has within two years made up several shawls under his own personal supervision, getting material and workmen from Cashmere; but the expenses are much beyond the saleable value of the manufacture, nor is it equal in any respect to the kind of article made at Cashmere. The colour is particularly defective and this, it is said, is a particular property of Cashmere itself. No article washed [sic]

21. Jacquemont, vol.3, p.285.
22. Baden-Powell, p.44.
23. Sufi, p.567.
24. Honigberger, p.92.

even in its neighbourhood attains to the same superior perfection in this respect. Runjit Singh tried similarly to manufacture shawls at Lahore but failed just as Chund did.'[25]

Following the great 1834 famine in Kashmir, however, the centre of the shawl industry shifted to Amritsar in the Punjab plain. Amritsar specialised in embroidered shawls which copied the kani ones. The Kashmir weaving industry slowly recovered, yet there were still advantages in shipping the unfinished woven product to Amritsar for bleaching, additional embroidery, fringes and borders.

The beginning of the shawl industry in Amritsar was due possibly to English initiative. A report written by Richard Strachey on the manufacture of the kani shawl at Srinagar, confirms that at the early date of 1812 in Amritsar 'shawls are better washed and packed than in Kashmir'. Strachey also travelled with Baron Elphinstone, as his secretary, when the Baron established an English embassy in Kabul. Elphinstone wrote in 1815 that 'Mr. Strachey made many inquiries on this subject and had some shawl stuffs made under his own inspection of wool procured at Amritsar. The manufacturers were pioneers belonging to the embassy and they worked in a common tent.'[26]

During his trip through Hindustan in the years 1838-9, C.J. French confirmed the presence of a shawl industry in Amritsar. 'The local manufacturers are limited to coarse woollen and other stuffs, while some fine textures are produced by the loom under the superintendence and by the manual labour of the poor Cachemerians who, driven from their mountain homes, are forced to come hither for a livelihood, such as the tolerance of the Sikhs will allow them to earn. The unbleached shawls of Cashmere are frequently brought here for the express purpose of being dyed and having their borders put on, the work of embroidery being very successfully carried out in this town.'[27] Still, much of the bleaching work was abandoned and, as a result, Westward-bound shawl products were poorly neglected and often went unwashed. Indeed, on some shawls found in western collections, bits of crusty rice paste can still be seen stuck between the woven fibres of the wool.

Other towns of the Punjab also developed their own 'Kashmir' shawl industry, due to the emigration of Kashmiri artisans who were forced to flee the Afghans. Jacquemont noted that 'since about 1810, Loudhiana has been the site of a new industry' employing 'over a thousand specialised workers and 400 looms', and in Islamabad there were '360 looms in activity as compared to 800 in the old days'.

While Lahore was still under Sikh rule the English government attempted to bring Kashmiri weavers to Loudhiana. According to the historian Sufi, 'a large bazaar was built for them and shops and houses were erected for workmen apparently to feed the supply for England.'[28]

Apparently, in spite of the fact that such new industries were developing far from Kashmir, they were nevertheless, closely supervised. The eighteen-day walk to say, Loudhiana, was frequently undertaken so that Srinagar's merchants could assure the smooth production of their products.

This carefully guarded control of the weavers might have annoyed the English and prevented them from controlling the manufacture or distribution of the shawl. The French of course were very influential in this domain, due to the presence of Allard and Ventura, and it appears that the first half of the nineteenth century was marked by a continuous economic tug-of-war between the two colonial powers, each trying to establish its own separate shawl industry, independent from Srinagar.

---

25. Sufi, p.567.
26. Elphinstone, p.508.
27. French, p.72.
28. Sufi, p.567.

Plates 20a, b, c and d. Jamawars or gown (long) shawls. Dogra period, late 19th century.

The Dogra Period (1846-1877)

With the death of Runjit Singh in 1839 the Punjab fell into a state of anarchy. By 1844 many foreign officers and residents, previously engaged in the service of the Maharaja, had wisely left the area for fear of losing both life and property. It was not until the British, after a fierce battle against the Sikhs, consolidated their domination of India that Kashmir came within their direct sphere of influence. The Dogra[29] prince, Raja Gulab Singh, was given the rule of the Kingdom of Kashmir by the British under the Treaty of Lahore in 1846.

Conditions prevailing in Kashmir at this time were deplorable. Baron Schönberg, who visited the valley, gave a sad picture of the people:

> 'The artisans and the weavers of shawls were in...miserable condition. The daily wage of a shawl weaver was 4 annas (16 annas to the rupee) of which half was taken by the governor in taxes and for the remaining 2 annas he was paid in kind...from the government depot at a higher price than that prevailing in the open market. A shawl weaver was forbidden to change his employer, the Karkhandar.'

The weavers' endurance reached its limit and on June 6th, 1847, they assembled and went on strike. In their demands to the Maharaja they asked for a permit to emigrate in a body to the Punjab. The threat was a success and the Maharaja conceded that the weaver should now be paid only according to the actual work found on the loom and could change his employer at will. However, it was not long before the weavers again fell slave to the oppressive tax system. In fact, the account left to us by the American visitor John Ireland tells us that the system remained in full force as late as December 1853: 'The Maharaja and his agents keep watch on every shawl made to get the 33% tax; and as soon as finished the shawl is shown to them and the Maharaja's name marked in thread in one corner of all Cashmere shawls.'[30]

In the Dogra period, as during the Sikh period, shawl style was influenced by foreign events but even more directly. Through the constant demand and increasingly sophisticated imitation-shawl techniques developed in France, Kashmir's industry was quickly gearing its production to satisfy European taste.

Just how much exposure Kashmir had to European designs during the beginnings of the Jacquard loom (1818-1830) still remains a rather obscure question, although there are, without doubt, early Kashmiri patterns of this period which evoke definite overtones of English and French influence (see above, page 39). The Jacquard loom did not advance technically before Deneirouse's innovation of 1825 (see Deneirouse, shawl maker and inventor, page 123) which revolutionised the machine and the imitation shawl. And it was not until well into the 1830s that the resulting designs of increased dimensions became widespread and fashionable.

When French shawl agents arrived in Srinagar, the loom's 'art-nouveau' designs (see, for example, Colour Plates 64, 65, pages 326, 327) were automatically adopted by the Kashmiri. They revived the stagnant shawl industry with patterns which completely covered the shawl's ground, and left practically no open centre (matan). The Kashmiris were already geared up to this type of work as a result of their development of the large patterned 'tapestry' shawls of the Sikh period. The effect would have been the same if the agents had come with cartoon designs similar to those used by Gobelins or Aubusson.

Shawls of the Dogra period should thus be viewed in the context of French influence. The 'tapestry' shawl was a practical and rugged fabric employed for

---

29 'Dogra' is a corruption of the sanskrit 'Dogirath', meaning two lakes. The name was originally applied to the inhabitants of the Jammu province.
30. Ireland, p.415.

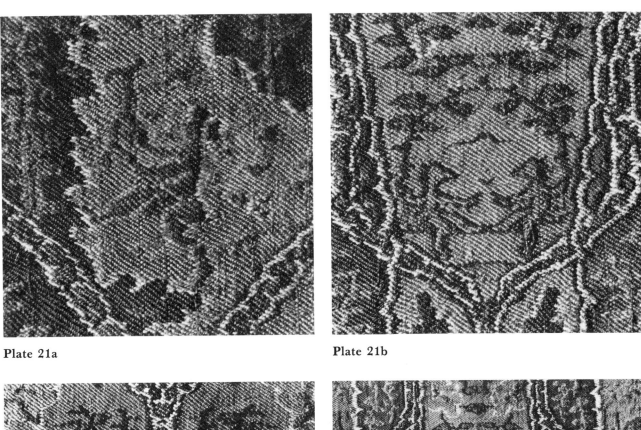

Plate 21a

Plate 21b

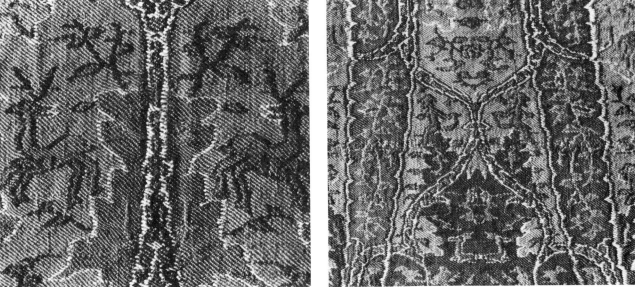

Plate 21c

Plate 21d

Plates 21a, b, c and d. Details of Colour Plate 63, p.325, showing woven animals and people. Plate 21a shows a man dressed in turban and knickers, climbing a mountain with a pickaxe in his hand. Plate 21b shows two anthropomorphic creatures sitting on a bench facing each other under an arch of flowers. Plates 21c shows a pair of reindeer. Plate 21d shows a pair of devil-like creatures with long tails in the centre. Just below them are a pair of seated reindeer. Above, to both left and right, are two mounted horsemen and below the horsemen have strange wings.

costume dress as well as for horses' saddles, tents, tent hangings and decorative curtains. It had become a necessity among the Sikhs.[31] The vast majority of these fabrics came from Amritsar and other surrounding areas of the Punjab such as Loudhiana, Lahore and Pathankot. But their wool was of a coarse quality and the designs were vulgar imitations of those of Kashmir.

This period was also marked by the discovery of more rapid ways of completing a kani shawl. Due to the large areas of design to be woven, the pattern was broken down into fragmented parts, each woven separately, at times on separate looms. These were sent to the rafugar, a shawl tailor or joiner who would work out which pieces went where. The Kashmiri people no longer know how such work was performed, or how the pieces were able to be fitted with such masterful perfection.

The designs brought to Kashmir by French agents represented various fashionable European styles. For example, the Jacquard shawl's central field was frequently made of two distinct colours to give the impression that, when folded, there were two separate shawls (see Colour Plate 64, page 326). An Englishman, R.W. Chapman, working for the French firm of C. Oulman of Paris, actually received first prize for a design of this type at an exhibition of Punjab manufacturers. Thus, after the second half of the nineteenth century, the shawls of India were basically patterned after the French imitation — particularly the Jacquard shawl. This did not belittle the design creativity of the Kashmir weaver for he was continually inventing new ways to assert his Indian heritage. French designs in Indian shawls were in fact, an Indian interpretation of a French conception.

Although all foreigners had been expelled in 1844, they returned once political stability was achieved in Northern India, especially during the period following the Great Exhibition of London in 1851. Anand Koul offers a list of the French agents who came to Kashmir during successive years between 1856 and 1882, including the number of years each agent remained on duty and the company he represented. Included among them, for example, is the company Uhlan.[32]. Koul also names Khwaja Amir Ju Gangu as one of the chief shawl traders of Kashmir.

A contemporary anecdote recounted by Ireland visiting Kashmir in December 1853, vividly exemplifies the bustling activities which the French shawl market created.

> 'Most of the people were at work on a magnificent shawl for the Empress Eugenie of France, a white ground or center and it will be the most elegant one he [Hajji Mukhtar Shah] has ever made. He says thirty men have been steadily at work on it for 6 months and it will require three more months to finish it. The price when finished will be about 1,300 rupees or 650 dollars, and such a shawl as would sell for about 4,000 dollars (!) in London or New York...my shawl took 15 men, 7 months to make. The workmen only receive one and one half annas (4.75 cents) a day.'[33]

Doruka (the reversible shawl)

In the 1860s a new type of shawl was created which used a different weaving technique from the interlocked kani shawls. The 'doruka' or reversible shawl enjoyed a tremendous success during the later part of the nineteenth century. According to Koul, 'it was in the time of Maharaja Ranbir Singh (1856-1887) that the ''doruka'' shawls or shawls with ''face on both sides'' were made. The inventors were Mustafa-Pandit and Aziz Pandit. These ingenious men also invented the ''Zamin past qul bala'' — shawls with raised floral work.'[34] This last term, 'Zamin past qul bala', recorded by Koul in 1915, may not, per se, imply embroidery at all

---

31. Soltykoft, p.32.
32. Probably the French company MM Oulman fils.
33. Ireland, p.409.
34. Koul, p.32.

Colour Plate 3. Dorunga fragment, c.1870, showing contrasting colour change between the front and the back of the same shawl.

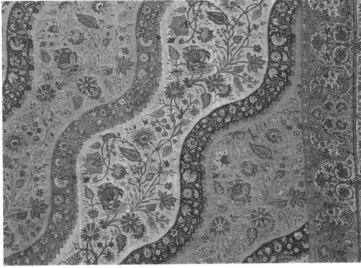

Colour Plate 4. Detail of a long shawl, c.1890.

Colour Plate 5. Detail of a long shawl showing the 'Khatraaz' pattern, c.1890.

Plate 22. Doruka (fragment). Dogra period, c.1870. 28cm x 35cm. In all probability the last word in dorukas are those rare pieces which are entirely woven and without any embroidery at all. In this unique sample, the right half has no embroidery, but the left half is fully decorated by it, and we can clearly see how much the additional needlework becomes mandatory. Most dorukas were woven with embroidery in mind.

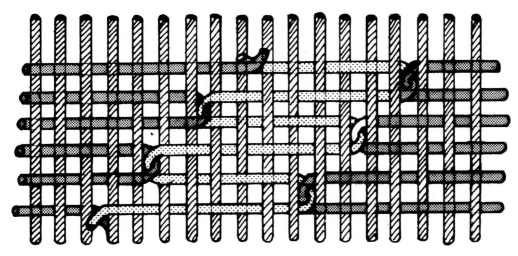

Figure 2. Single-interlock weave of a doruka, a completely reversible shawl. Drawing by G. Vial.

but may refer to what has now become India's most prized collector's item, the 'dorunga', meaning literally two colours.

On elaborate 'jamawars' or gown pieces woven in the doruka technique, certain colour areas or often the whole ground of one side of the shawl were meticulously covered by a different coloured yarn of pashm using a couching stitch which followed exactly the direction and imitated perfectly the 'ribs' of the shawl's twill (see dorunga, Colour Plate 3, page 45). Such work is astonishing, for not only is it difficult to imagine but it is also almost impossible for the naked eye to discern such subtle contrast except by the use of a magnifying glass. In general the cheaper weaves required more embroidery to correct the defects in design expression. The weaving technique of both the doruka and dorunga are exactly the same. The dorunga is created from a doruka by adding the couching stitch to one of its sides.

Because of the doruka's high cost and its late arrival on the shawl market almost none of them were shipped to the West. The occasional piece today which does crop up at auction here and there, was probably brought back by its owner personally from India. Therefore it is only recently that interest in this 'micro' weave has come about. The flat smooth appearance of the woven fabric is achived by a single interlocking of the wefts' colours — a technique which eliminates the ridges on the reverse side (compare Figure 2 with Figure 15, page 66). This technique may be compared to those shawls woven in France or Russia in the early 19th century. It is very possible that agents from both of these countries encouraged its use in Srinagar.

The doruka shawl was known for its special design, which rarely resembled the large tapestry shawls (see Colour Plate 6, page 64, and Plate 23). In the latter part of the nineteenth century, however, a technique was invented by which an 'imitation' reversible shawl was made, and this 'imitation doruka' became very popular. It was made by taking a kani shawl woven in such a manner that the pattern did not leave a mess of criss-crossing and hanging threads on the reverse. The embroiderer then outlined both sides of the shawl simultaneously by passing his needle from one side to the other, making sure that the ridges on the reverse were carefully concealed. By running the hand over both sides of the fabric, it is easy to feel the difference in texture. In the same manner, the perfection of an authentic doruka can be determined by the delicate way in which the skilled embroiderer has cleverly embellished his design.

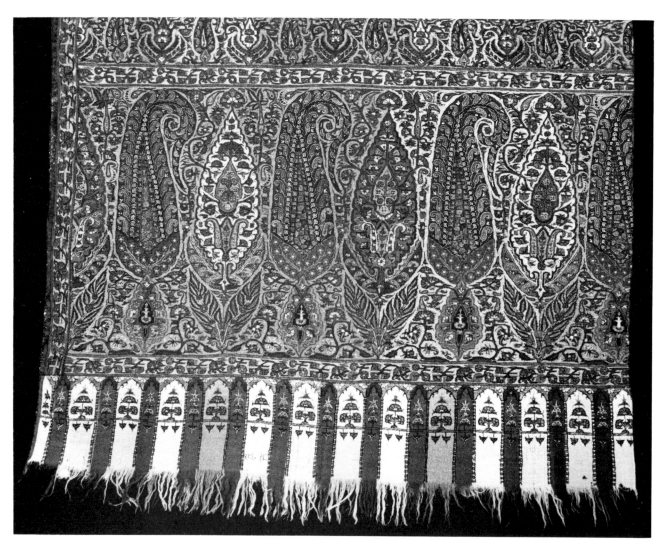

Plate 23. Doruka, reversible shoulder mantle. Dogra period, c.1870. 142cm x 330cm.

Decline of the Kashmir shawl

The shawl industry began to decline with the institution of the dagshawl tax system during the beginning of Afghan rule in Kashmir. The warring Sikhs sustained this sytem, perhaps not in name but in practice, if only to support their military exploits. The natural calamities of the 1830s caused the weavers to emigrate en masse to the Punjab, leaving their homeland. Finally, the master weavers refused to teach young apprentices their trade. As Jacquemont wrote in 1831, 'not one white beard was seen throughout the karkhandars'.

The arrival of the French agents gave the industry a tremendous lift which lasted for twenty years. The moving eulogy of Hajji Mukhtar Shah's narrative shows the Kashmiri's deep recognition of the French, who did so much to spur creativity and employment in a depressed industry. The Franco-Prussian War of 1870, along with a sudden change in European fashion, ended the European popularity of the shawl. Kashmir's shawl industry crashed brutally as a result, and received its final coup de grâce from the decimating famine of 1877. A prolific and rich era came to an end; the kani shawl had passed from a thriving, historical actuality to the domain of legend.

Chapter Two
Structure and Composition

It is important to understand the construction of the Kashmir shawl, not only for a basic appreciation of its aesthetic qualities, but also in order to date it within a particular historical period. Throughout Kashmir's history the shawl represents the numerous ups and downs experienced by the peaceful populace of Kashmir. Under Mughal rule the Kashmiris enjoyed a freedom of expression brilliantly mirrored by the arts and crafts in which they excelled, but with the arrival of the Afghans in 1753 and the Sikhs in 1819 political turmoil, oppressive policies, and excessive taxation began to tear away the basic fibre of this stoic race of people. Because it was a rich source of revenue, the weaving industry avoided being stifled completely, as is demonstrated by the many fine shawl specimens of the later period. By the beginning of the nineteenth century, however, radical changes in construction began to take place.

In spite of these changes, certain styles in design remained constant from the beginning of the seventeenth to the early nineteenth century. Such consistency was sustained by a ready market among people of conservative taste. Due to this, certain patterns often existed for many years before they came to be considered 'classic', and caution should be used when attempting to assign a specific date to a motif which developed possibly over a period of up to fifty years. The Kashmir shawl thus attests to the continuity of standard in fashion, and expresses the rich, elegant tradition of the Orient.

After the iconographic study of any given pattern and motifs, the next significant criterion for placing a shawl within a particular historical period is its basic construction. How the border (hashia) is attached, how the centre field is woven or twilled, how the design patterns are displayed, how the embroidery is applied, how many differently woven sections form the complete shawl, and lastly, what kind of dyes are used; all these give us clues regarding a shawl's origin.

There were basically three kinds of shawls: the dochalla or long shawl, the patka or waistband and the rumal or square shawl. It is possible that the patka may represent the earliest form of kani weaving; the decorated rumal did not come into prominence until about the middle of the eighteenth century.

The Dochalla and Patka — Mughal and Afghan periods

The dochalla, or long shawl, underwent a gradual evolution. The continuation of motifs over long periods makes it difficult to break down its development, but one can nonetheless divide it into the four main phases. Dochallas of the pre-Afghan period display prominent characteristics which clearly set them apart from later examples. In addition to the colours, which were usually of subtle and exotic tones, the ornamentation was strictly reserved for the extreme ends or pallas, and for the narrow borders or hashias which ran the length of the shawl. The matan or centre field of the shoulder mantle was always devoid of additional decorative weaving.

Because many shawls were made to special order for dignitaries of the Mughal court, their sizes may have varied. In 1668, Bernier commented that shawls measured about 114cm by 170cm with a palla of about 30cm high, and were decorated by weaving. His observations do not appear correct and at the moment there are no existing shawls which support his statements. In general, it has been found that shoulder mantles of the period measure about 129cm by 280cm

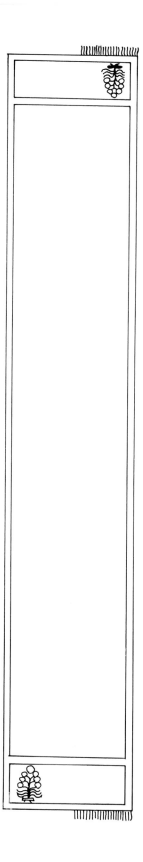

Figure 3 (above). Dochalla. Mughal period. Approx. 129cm x 280cm. Scale 1:200. Border 1cm wide.

Figure 4 (right). Patka or Turban. Mughal period. Approx. 70cm x 460cm. Scale 1:200 Border 3.5cm wide. Palla 20cm high. The patka went out of fashion c.1810.

(Figure 3), with a palla of about 18cm high at each end. Shawls falling outside these dimensions were recut for one reason or another. These early shawls are rare indeed and it is always very interesting to discover them when two identical ones have remained sewn back to back (from the original idea of a dochalla or twin shawl). This reinforces the theory that during Mughal times it was the fashion for shawls to be worn in this way.

Although shoulder mantles were devoid of additional weaving (i.e. ornaments outside the pallas), this is not necessarily the case for the patka or waistband. Occasionally a patka may be found decorated with various overall patterns of small designs such as floral sprigs, stripes, or wavy lines, which further demonstrate the kani technique. Usually its size is approximately 70cm by 460cm (Figure 4). The waistband, probably the oldest type of kani weave, died out around 1810 (see Chapter 4).

The Afghan invasion of Kashmir in 1753, had a drastic effect on the Kashmir shawl industry. As we have seen, the taxes levied caused the quality of the Kashmir shawl to deteriorate. Subtle nuances, such as whether the shawl's hashia was inter-locked or woven with the entire shawl, became increasingly significant. Shawl-makers often attempted to escape the watchful eye of the tax collectors by manufac-turing a shawl in several pieces in several ateliers and then fitting the pieces together. Such a technique however, often had a negative effect on quality. Richard Strachey recorded in 1812, for example, that 'at most of the shops [at Srinagar] shawls containing much work are made in separate pieces at different shops and it may be observed that it very rarely happens that the pieces when completed correspond in size'.[1] It may be inferred then that fine shawls of this period which were permitted to remain on the looms until final completion came most likely from the royal ateliers which were immune from taxes. In other words, the way a shawl was pieced together or woven depended directly on the severity of the contemporary tax system. In contrast shawls of the pre-Afghan period possess a rare diaphanous texture and were often woven in one piece with the finest of shah tus. Most of them were royal pieces carefully preserved and stored away as heirlooms to be passed on to future generations.

At the end of the Afghan period the Englishman, Moorcroft, explained that a silk warp was employed to weave the hashia, which offered the advantage of a more prominent contrast of the dyed weft colours than could be achieved when just using plain 'pashm' yarn. This added strength and supported the rest of the shawl, which was disproportionately heavy. Although he claims that narrow hashias were woven with the shawl, there are actually few dochallas of Moorcroft's period which would make this claim a general rule.

Dochalla — Sikh period

There are two basic types of long shawls which characterize the Sikh period: the 'classic' and the modern. The 'classic', demanded mostly by conservative taste, is defined by a continuation of earlier motifs which retained the appealing characteristics of eighteenth century shawl patterns.[2] But close scrutiny of the design composition reveals that significant changes came about. Besides the brighter colours, these shawls may often be distinguished by their 'modern' hashias. The graceful meandering vine composed of tandem repeats in the form of 'bent-tip' strawberries and 'pin-wheel' leaves, and the small flower buds of trefoils framed in hexagonal repeats, gave way to more abstract designs of meandering serrated leaves or branches alternating with sharply circular rosettes.

1. Strachey, p.80.
2. Plate 190, although classified here as 'late Afghan' is nevertheless an excellent example as a transitional piece of this type.

Figure 5 (left). Dochalla. Afghan period. Approx. 131cm x 304cm. Scale 1:200. Border 1.5-2cm wide.
Figure 6 (right). Tapestry shawl. Sikh period. Approx. 150cm x 320cm. Scale 1:200.

The 'modern' Sikh shawl on the other hand represents a clear break from traditional design. The important details of classic designs were suddenly subordinated to stylistic conceptions of a fanciful and fantastic nature. No longer was the shawl designer limited to just the narrow pallas with their rows of botehs, which permitted so little freedom of expression. The increasing height of the boteh meant that a larger surface area of the shawl was included in the design pattern. This had the effect of ushering in further abstractions to fill the newly developed ground space. A new type of shawl was created, the 'tapestry' shawl (see Figure 6).

The tapestry shawl was created by the 'modern' school of design. By 'tapestry' is meant those shawls which no longer illustrated simple boteh repeats on the palla, but often developed an underlying theme of abstract symbolism in which the sweeping boteh is reduced to a secondary role. The term also indicates a diminished matan or centrefield whose size is relatively small in relation to the remaining decorated portion of the shawl (Colour Plate 52-55, pages 314, 315). The hashias grew in size to about 10cm. On more elaborate shawls the palla design theme may invade the flanking hashias, but in general they were made separately and then sewn on. Such design intrusion was probably due to the Jacquard shawl's influence towards the end of the Sikh period. The term dochalla is really a misnomer when applied to these types of shawls because they were obviously much too heavy to be worn in pairs. Nevertheless they continued to be made in this way and the term dochalla became a general term for all long shawls. Today the Kashmiri will say jamawar (gown pieces) to mean long shawl.

In the rumal it is rare that we come across the same full elaborate patterns found on the tapestry shawl, even on a diminished scale. The tapestry shawl continued up until the end of the kani shawl period, or 1877. Chavant's album (see Plates 75-78) permits us to date its early beginnings at least before 1837, and many of them are certainly contemporary with Jacquemont's visit to Srinagar in 1831. Last but not least we have Moorcroft whose 'Account of Shawl Goods' may date their real creative flowering at about 1820.

The 'jamawar tapestry' shawl was constructed of various borders, woven panels and embroidered fringes (see Figure 6). The central design of the pallas was usually made up of two or three rectangular panels which were then carefully meshed together. Often this was performed so perfectly that the shawl must be flipped over to locate the invisible seam. Finer quality and specially commissioned tapestry shawls are usually found with their main end panels woven all in one piece. The matan was always sewn in and then flanked by rectangular panels which exhibited a motif similar but subordinate to that of the end panels.

Occasionally some jamawars of the Sikh period are found with what appears to be a peculiar type of construction. At first sight one would be tempted to say that the shawl was made upsidedown. But this can easily be explained from the knowledge of how the Sikhs utilised shawls. In this instance the pallas are reversed, i.e. instead of the botehs standing up where the hooks from the end of each pallas are facing each other, the opposite is true. The answer for this is discovered in a painting by the Hungarian, Schoefft, of the Sikh Military court which illustrates the many uses of the Kashmir shawl. Here the shawl was employed as a curtain under the arches of the 'baradari' or open pavilion at the Red Fort in Lahore.

Dochalla — Dogra period

During the Dogra period, which began in the 1840s, the method of construction remained basically the same but was modified slightly due to the sweeping designs generated by the Jacquard loom. The pieced panels, formerly of a geometric nature, were now often composed of all kinds of shapes, including circular forms. They ventured boldly and protruded frequently beyond the confines of the main panels. A tapestry shawl during the Sikh period was made up of ten or eleven parts (see Figure 7); during the Dogra period it was often made up of dozens or more.

To this must be added the embroidered fringes, which were normally taken from standard stock and therefore required no extra time for their manufacture. During the second quarter of the nineteenth century, the town of Sealkot, about 200km (125 miles) south of Srinagar, became known for the weaving of hashias only. This accounts for the obvious differences in colour tones between the wools used in the main part of the shawl and its borders. Sealkot borders were often of a very coarse

Descriptive names of the shawl's decorated surface

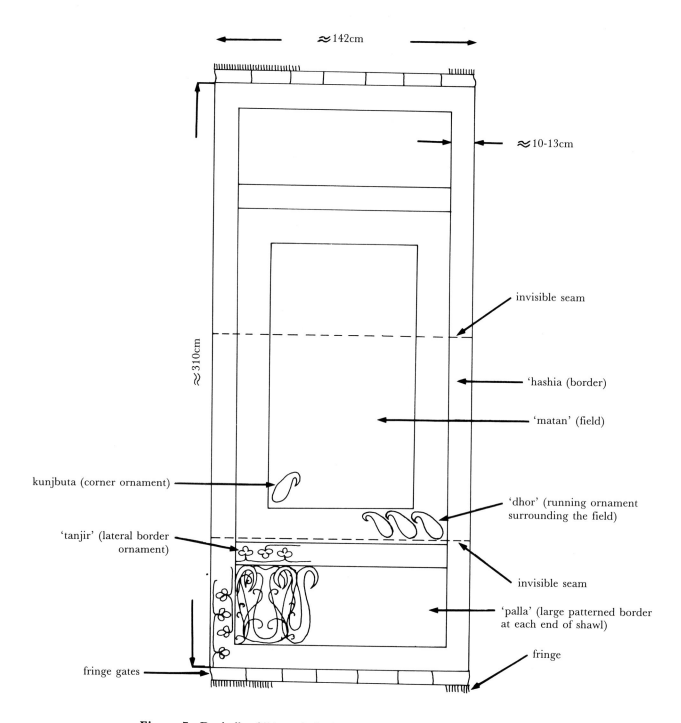

≈142cm

≈10-13cm

≈310cm

invisible seam

'hashia (border)

'matan' (field)

kunjbuta (corner ornament)

'dhor' (running ornament surrounding the field)

'tanjir' (lateral border ornament)

invisible seam

'palla' (large patterned border at each end of shawl)

fringe

fringe gates

Figure 7. Dochalla. Sikh period. Approx. 142cm. x 310cm. Scale 1:200.

Figure 8. Dochalla. Dogra period. Approx. 140cm x 330cm. Scale 1:200.

and cardboard-like texture, and the colour was usually of a pale green which rarely matched other parts of the shawl.

The Rumal

The popularity of the rumal appears to have increased during the late eighteenth century, while Kashmir was ruled by the Afghans. This popularity was probably due to the newly created markets in the Near East that had opened in 1753. Later, Europe also began its demands upon Kashmir's shawl industry, resulting in a rebound in popularity of not only the 'rumal' but all types of shawl goods. The rumal was cheaper in price and often took less time to weave and was, therefore, easier to

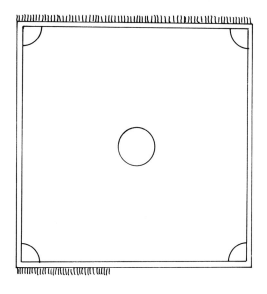
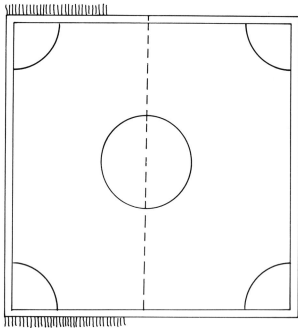

Figure 9. (left) Chandar. Afghan period. Approx. 130cm x 130cm. (Patka hashia standard.) Scale 1:200. Border 3.5cm wide.
Figure 10. (right) Chandar. Late Afghan period. Approx. 160cm x 160cm. Scale 1:200. Border 3.5-4cm. wide.

sell than the 'dochalla'; at the same time it represented many of the fine decorative features and qualities of the expensive court shawls of legendary Mughal times.

Square shawls manufactured prior to about 1815 are almost exclusively of the chandar type, also known as moon shawls. There are few extant pieces which illustrate the boteh prior to this date. The centrefield contains a large circular motif filled with flowers and often centred on an open field of repeated buti (sprigs of small flowers), birds, or the checkerboard squares which were made for the Persian market.[3] Repeated motifs, in accordance with Islamic vernacular, were arranged in orderly transversal rows running across the matan or field. Each corner of the matan was ornamented with quarter circles of the same design theme as the central medallion (Figures 9, 10). At present, hardly any examples of the chandar exist which may be attributed to the Mughal period, but there are many of exceptional beauty from the Afghan period.[4]

During the Sikh period, as design dimensions grew, the rumal developed a new format. Four separate kani panels were carefully joined together to form a square, the middle of which was usually filled with plain black or white 'pashmina' measuring less then one square metre. Of the four panels the sides containing the two smaller panels were normally woven with the hashia included within their design pattern, while the other two panels usually had their outer edges sewn to separately woven hashia strips. Finally, a fringe composed of multi- coloured strips of plain pashmina without ornamentation, was added to two ends of the shawl, a traditional convention on shawls of the Sikh period (Figure 12).

The most frequently found rumal today is that of the Dogra period. It is composed of many pieces, each piece containing a part of the total design. If the pieces have been joined well the shawl should lie perfectly flat without any buckling

3. Jacquemont, p.289.
4. The finest collection of early moon shawls can be seen at the Benaras Hindu University Museum.

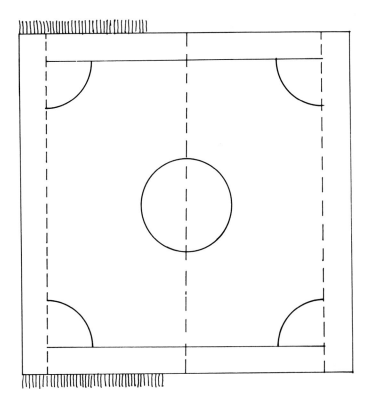

Figure 11. Chandar. Sikh period. Approx. 160cm x 180cm. Scale 1:200. Border 14cm wide.

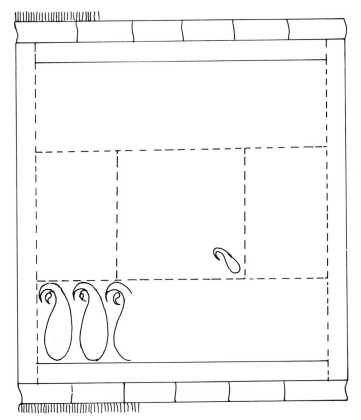

Figure 12. Rumal. Sikh period. Approx. 180cm x 180cm. Scale 1:200.

Figure 13 (left). Rumal. Dogra period. Approx. 180cm x 180cm. Scale 1:200.
Figure 14 (right). Rumal. Dogra period. Vase shawl. Approx. 180cm x 180cm. Scale 1:200.

and its various motifs should match up perfectly. It is not difficult to find shawls of this type containing literally hundreds of pieces. These 'patchwork' shawls were made in great quantity after 1850. The traditional fringe of this period was made from many small pashmina strips of a variety of colours, each measuring about 8cm in length. Each was embroidered with a mihrab-type motif.

Another type of rumal found in abundance during the latter half of the nineteenth century was the 'vase' shawl (Figure 14). Void of the usual sweeping botehs, its busy design was composed of leafy vases or urns arranged in a complicated fashion and entangled with all sorts of strange botanical forms. This gave the shawl an over-charged aspect, as any fraction of the ground which might have remained plain was completely filled in with tiny, nondescript sprigs. The shawl's tiny centre normally was expressed by a sunburst medallion as the design's foliage merged from all corners towards the central axis. Another characteristic of the vase shawl is the special fringe which was manufactured expressly for it. It was made up of hundreds of small pieces of finely embroidered pashmina sewn together in an overlapping fashion and then embellished with additional embroidery which ingeniously hid the seams.

The last type of rumal commonly encountered is the 'foldover'. A European innovation introduced in Kashmir, it was made with two narrow adjacent borders (sewn design side up) and two larger adjacent borders (sewn design side down). All four were of the same design. When the corner linking the two narrow borders is folded over diagonally, all four borders are aligned in the form of a chevron.

It is thus possible to discern the period when a shawl was made by examining the method of its construction. The general tendency as the shawl developed through the late eighteenth and nineteenth centuries, was toward an increasingly fragmented construction as compared with the single-piece shawls made in Mughal times.

Chapter Three
Manufacturing Techniques up to the Present Day

Wool

Traditionally, Kashmir shawl weaving employed a fleece derived from a Central Asian mountain goat. 'This type of goat is probably the most beautiful of all wool producing goats,' wrote S. Turner, England's ambassador to Tibet in 1783. 'I find it superior in beauty to the Angora goat. The colour of these animals varies. They have straight horns and are not as tall as the smallest sheep from England. The wool which serves to make the shawls is extremely fine and short. It is covered by other long and hard hairs which envelop the animal and conserve the delicateness of her first dress.'

The Angora goat mentioned by Turner derives its name from the city of its origin, Ankara, and it produced a greyish-yellow fleece. Similar species of goats were found in other locations such as Erzurum, Eastern Turkey, and Northern Persia. The Kirman province also produced great quantities of goat's wool which were exported along the caravan routes.[1] Vigne wrote in 1842 that 'goats producing the shawl wool are common in the countries west of the Caspian and excellent shawls are made there also.'[2]

Due to the varying political situation of the Northern regions surrounding Kashmir, the pashm (unwoven goat's wool; woven goat's wool is called pashmina) came from different places at different times: Yarkand, Khotan, Sinkiang, Lhasa or sometimes the Kirgiz steppe-land region all supplied wool.

The ancient custom has not changed very much today, since wool is still brought down from the Eastern regions of Ladakh via the capital city, Leh. Even at the altitude of Leh's 3,500 metres (11,500ft.), among the scattered green, oasis-like hamlets of the Indus valley and where newly arrived tourists gasp for breath during their first week of acclimatisation, the local goats are incapable of producing the fine underfleece. The pashm cut-off point, below which the goats do not produce the special wool, appears to be at 4,500 metres (14,750ft.) in the Himalayan region known as Chang-Thang. This rugged and remote mountain region lies just east of Leh and runs north and south to cover a vast area of about 50,000 square kilometres (32,000 square miles). Approximately one half of Chang-Thang is controlled by Chinese Tibet. The legendary lake of Pangong, located at the centre of this region, is also divided in half by the Chinese Tibetan frontier.

The people who supply the goat fleece are known as Changpas, nomads whose livelihood depends on the herding of yak, sheep, horses and, of course, goats. Although some of the 'lena' (pashm in Ladakhi) slips across the border from Tibet, the greater portion of all the fleece supplied to Kashmir and the hill towns of Himachel Pradesh (Kulu, Manali, etc.), comes essentially from the Changpas of the Ladakhi side of Chang-Thang.

A tall robust race of herders, of whom 85% are Buddhist, the Changpas live in black yak hair tents called 'rebos'. Chang-thangi 'lena' merchants begin arriving in Leh by mid-July depending on the altitude at which their merchandise originates:

---

1. *Dictionnaire Universel de Commerce etc.* 2 vols., 1805.
2. Vigne, p.126.

the warmer the region the sooner their arrival; the colder the later. In any case, Leh receives a more or less continuous flow of lena up to about mid-September. According to Ladakhi dealers in the area of Lal Chowk, Leh's main boulevard, the annual quantity of raw, unclean fleece varies between 14,000 and 15,000 kilos (30,000 and 33,000lbs) per year. But of this seemingly large amount approximately one half finds its way to Himachel Pradesh through the Kulu and Manali dealers who journey to Leh in order to supply their own weaving centres. The bulk of the remaining fleece is bought up by a few Kashmiri dealers who in turn resell it to the shawl manufacturers of Srinagar.

Jammu and Kashmir residents can enter fairly easily the area of Chang-Thang but Indian residents, although not necessarily prevented, require special permission from the Deputy Commissioner. All other outsiders are formerly restricted from entering and the recent Indo-Pakistan military clashes have, unfortunately, condemned this beautiful nomadic land to possibly many more years of isolation.

Not all prospective pashm dealers seek purchases through Leh. Some will go directly to Chang-Thang where a free and open market thrives. The best quality of fleece is derived from goats fed off the greenest pastures. In general, a Changpa dealer goes around collecting the pashm from the variously scattered areas where sometimes the herds amount only to a few goats. Once he has amassed a fair quantity he will offer the whole lot for sale. The buyer carefully inspects the wool by extracting several different samples, depending on colour. The quality is quickly observed by his experienced touch and usually the finer the fleece the whiter it is. After the buyer has determined the various grades that he will end up with, an agreement is made on the final price. Thus the deal concludes very simply and honestly over a friendly cup of 'solja' or butter tea.

Lena comes in several shades: off-white, grey and sometimes black. In Leh, first quality sells for about 450 roupees a kilo; after cleaning, 400 grams remain. Second quality sells for 350 roupees a kilo, leaving only 300 grams cleaned.[3] The cleaning removes the longer wiry hairs which go into making 'namdas', embroidered floor mats manufactured in Kashmir.

Supply and demand and even the political situation can greatly affect the open market price. The Jammu and Kashmir government has established a price support system to provide Chang-Thang with economic stability. Since 1981, for a unity of standard exchange, or two kilos of pashm, 520 to 540 roupees is government guaranteed. Twenty years ago the price of fair quality lena was as little as 24 roupees.

Since 1975 when Ladakh opened its doors to tourism, the local shop owners of Leh and the local farmers have enjoyed a prosperity which make many of them take a rather blasé attitude toward trade in general.

Pashmina shawls are also one of the woven products of the handicrafts centre of Leh. The Jammu and Kashmir government is trying to promote artisan industries. In 1984 a Pashmina shawl measuring one by two metres could be bought for 550 roupees but although its warmth may equal that of those of Kashmir, visually it will never equal the work of woven art for which the Kashmiris are famous. The women in Kashmir are responsible for spinning the fleece and the quality of their hand spun yarn remains to this day unrivalled throughout the world. In 1984 Mr. Ali Raza[4] pointed out that two spinners from Srinagar were officially invited to Leh in order to show the Ladakhi women their fine technique. After only two months the project was abandoned and the women returned to Srinagar. It appears that the Ladakhis were incapable of adapting themselves to the tediousness of the work involved.

---

3. Summer 1984.
4. The development manager of the Crafts Centre of Leh.

Many nations and regions have imitated the Kashmir shawl, but in general those woven outside of Kashmir have rarely been made of the silky fleece from the Tibetan mountain goat and as a result have rarely been as fine in quality. From time to time, France and Russia have had access to a type of Oriental wool which greatly resembled that of pashm and they copied Kashmir shawls, often achieving a startling similarity. Persia and Afghanistan also imitated this style. Some of the most important imitations came from India's Punjab region, where large quantities of shawls were quickly woven by the Kashmiri weavers who settled there during the early part of the nineteenth century.

In their haste to supply shawls to the European markets, the Punjabi weavers were forced to import Kermani wool from Persia and blend it locally, either with cheap goat or sheep wool. This is because Kashmir exercised severe control over its coveted pashm and did not relax this control until around 1860. By that time, however, it was too late, as the fashion market for such luxury articles had begun to draw to a close.

Nevertheless, the fashion market for shawls in India has endured as an elegant dress tradition, and among wealthy Indians a pashmina or shah tus (pronounced tooch) shawl is still considered a symbol of opulence. The seductive salesmanship of the Kashmir merchant is a sight to behold as he caressingly unfolds his billowing fabrics with an indescribably proud condescension. The old custom continues in which the client is permitted to take home a few shawls for a day or so before making his final choice, in much the same way as when buying a rug. Confidence between buyer and seller is an absolute must; the shawl represents more than just a fashionable purchase, it is an investment.

There are three main categories of natural wool used in Kashmir: rafle, pashmina and shah tus, and many variations exist in the quality of each. Today almost all common woollen shawls are woven from rafle, a machine spun wool derived from merino sheep.

The standard size for a modern woman's shawl is one by two metres. One of top quality pashmina (plain woven goat's wool) sells at the Government Arts Emporium of India for about 200 dollars. But by far the world's rarest and most expensive wool is shah tus (king's wool). It comes from the ibex, a wild Himalayan mountain goat which grazes at extremely high altitudes. In the warm spring time the Ibex rubs itself against rocks, thus shedding the fine short hairs which grow close to the animal's skin. The fallen fleece is then collected from the rocky slopes, from where it is packed and carried to the various weaving hamlets and towns. At present, the tus trade is controlled by Nepalese merchants who receive it from Tibet. Most of this trade is black market and with 1984 prices at 14,000 roupees a kilo (the equivalent of 1,000 dollars also on the black market), various clandestine methods must be devised to move the wool into India and on to Srinagar for resale. In Srinagar small measured mounds of the precious fleece are carefully weighed each morning on a jeweller's balance and then distributed to the few local women who are permitted to spin it by hand. Colours vary from charcoal grey to dark brown, and the price of the finest of the shawls made of this rich wool easily approaches ten times that of pashmina shawls of the same one by two metre size.

In 1823 Moorcroft made a brief reference to 'asli' tus, which simply means genuine wool. A minute portion of the shah tus collected each year invariably contained a few white hairs, which were stored away and saved year after year. After perhaps ten or fifteen years of hoarding, it was possible to weave an all-white shah tus shawl. Because it was pure white, it was considered the world's rarest wool and accordingly its price almost inestimable. It is now for all practical purposes extinct.

Modern woven shah tus has an incredible warmth-giving quality, which is felt immediately upon contact with the skin. In the traditional demonstration, the

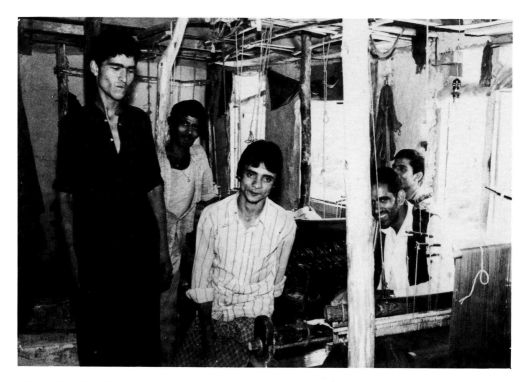

Plate 24. Shawl weavers of Kanihama.

Kashmiri merchant, squeezes it into a little ball, then tosses it up into the air; when he does so, it billows out suddenly to its full dimension. Shawl dealers refer to the shah tus as the ring shawl because in demonstrating the wool's amazing characteristics to the client the dealer takes great pleasure, in accordance with the ancient custom, in slipping the entire shawl through a finger ring. As shah tus ages it acquires a shiny lustre, and if it is white ibex dating back a few centuries, the fleece develops a golden patina.

Most Indians will purchase this kind of shawl only from a Kashmiri, since the shawl's authenticity might otherwise be called into question. In addition, only the well-seasoned connoisseur would be advised to undertake this selection unless the purchase is conducted through a reputable shawl dealer. This is because there are numerous qualities which might fall under the heading shah tus or pashmina and therefore a certain amount of caution is necessary. The dealer will never have his shah tus cleaned to perfection, for to observe a few extraneous hairs within the weave is considered absolute proof that the shawl is genuine.

Weaving technique

Since the unfortunate collapse of the kani-shawl industry in the late 1870s there has been no real attempt on the part of private industry to revive the ancient tradition. During the last one hundred years, the intricacies of the weaving technique have not only been lost but the numerous families who had once been deeply involved in making the shawls, have also long since taken up other means of livelihood, often totally unrelated to their families' heritage. The last person reputed to have held the precious knowledge of many of the weaving techniques, Gulam Qadir Rangriz, died in 1979.

One cannot help feeling a certain compassion when listening to the conversations of Srinagar's inhabitants as they reminisce over the kani shawl's past and the once thriving industry which so enriched the culture of Kashmir. But in spite of the

Plate 25 (left). This shawl, of rather coarse quality, a product of Kanihama, will probably be sold at the Government Arts Emporium.
Plate 26 (right). Preparing a 'hubble bubble' or hooker bowl with embers from the 'kangri' (small basket heater) for a moment of relaxation for this weaver from Kanihama.

sincere efforts on the part of the villagers of Kani-Hama, under their present director, Ghulam Mohammud (who goes under the title 'technical cum marketing and production manager'), a lack of motivation is clearly apparent. The necessary stimulus might come about through demand and the financial backing of a free enterprise system, drawn from the weaving industry's private sector.

Furthermore, an almost insurmountable obstacle still remains: the guiding patriarchal heritage of the old weaving gurus, who were once able just by their living presence, to convey the ancient tradition to 'children of the loom', and provide thereby an unbroken link with the past, is no longer there. The strong feeling remains that only they could ever offer the stimulation required to achieve success.

Today the specialists are gone, their work abandoned to the realm of legend. The 'naqqash' who wedded golden fleece to flower and colour, the 'rafugar' whose seams vanished, the dyer whose brilliant hues transformed texture into a chromatic scale of magic colours, and the master weavers whose dexterity baffled the onlooker, such craftsmen exist no longer. Only their woven masterpieces remain to echo sadly the legacy of a glorious artistic past. The weavers paid a heavy price for excercising their skills. Jacquemont had noted that almost all chalbates (weavers) were either crippled or blind before the age of fifty.

This loss of the traditional skills illustrates why it is necessary to pay careful attention to the eye-witness accounts of weaving by travellers to Kashmir in the nineteenth century. Moorcroft sojourned in Srinagar in 1823, and he provides us with one of the most valuable accounts of the overall kani technique:

'Having ascertained the kind of pattern most likely to suit the market, the weaver applies to persons whose business it is to apportion the yarn according

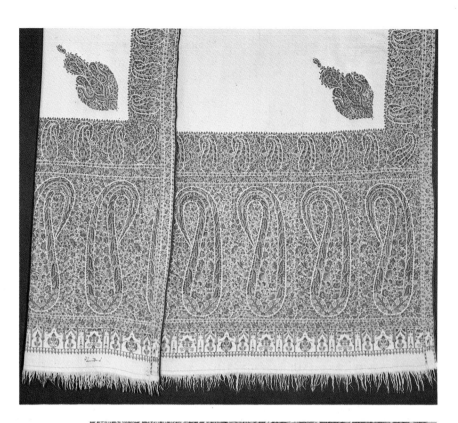

Colour Plates 6a and 6b. A doruka or reversible shoulder mantle (see p.44). Dogra period, c.1865. 145cm x 325cm.

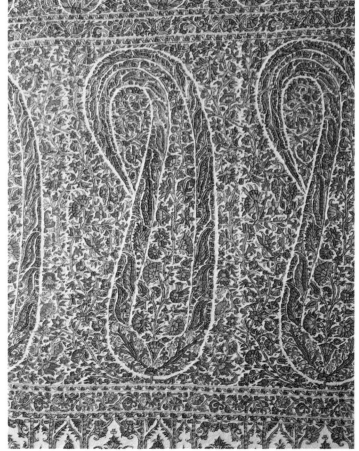

Plate 27. Young Kashmiris weaving a modern kani shawl in Kanihama, 1981.

to the colours required, and when this is settled, he takes it to another, whose function it is to divide the yarn into skeins accordingly and each skein is delivered to the dyer. Weft yarn is single but a little thicker than the double yarn or twist of the warp. Its weight is estimated at one half more than that of the warp. The nakatu receives the yarn in hanks but returns it in balls and in one day he is capable of preparing the warp and weft for two shawls (dochalla). Next the warps are stretched and dipped into a hot rice water solution which stiffens each length and sets it apart from the others.'

(It should be remembered that these yarns are being prepared for a manufactory process lasting as long as one year or more (cf. Allard's letter), depending on the elaborateness of the shawls. Here the yarn is given added strength and protection against fraying in order for it to withstand the constant friction due to the manipulation of the tojis.)

We can also learn much about the technical construction of the shawl through an important discovery by the English linguist and cryptologist, G.W. Leitner, in 1870. His invaluable account provides important insights into the technical aspects integrating weave and design.

'The warp of "kani" is of three dimensions: 1) the smallest of 700 pairs of thread (a pair is technically called "nal", 2) the middle size of 1300 nals, 3) the largest size of 1900 nals. These are the only three dimensions of which a warp can consist. Some fine extant shawls contain over 2200 nali. The warp is generally red although sometimes it is black or white.'

'A plan (naska) of the specimen of the shawl required is first drawn upon paper, and flowers of various colours are depicted. From this plan the number of nals required for the warp is estimated and spread on the loom. The specimen plan whose length and breadth are equal to those of the warp, is then fixed underneath so as to allow the drawing to be seen through the warp. Keeping constantly in view the plan on the paper, the head of the manufactory (ustad) goes on repeating with marvellous rapidity in the language of shawl weaving the different colours and their quantity which he thinks would be required in the several nals in order to produce in the shawl the flowers and colours upon the paper. The other workmen, in accordance with these directions, take up the needles bearing the several colours and put them in where required. A clerk (talim nawis) is also present there and puts down upon paper, in the *shawl alphabet,* one after the other, the words as they are uttered by the head of the manufactory. The *shawl numerals* indicate the number of the nal, and certain fixed signs which are placed on the right or the left of the numeral, the name

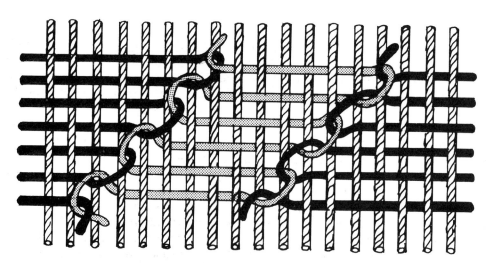

Figure 15. The 'kani' weave. Twill tapestry woven shawl, reverse side. Drawing by G. Vial.

of the colours. The plan of the shawl can be easily reproduced from this writing which clearly shows what colours are used in the different nals at any particular stage. Thence the great importance of obtaining as many of the older of these records as possible, if any serious attention be made to revive the good old patterns.

'Talam or talim is the name applied to the paper on which the process, as repeated, is put down. Each line of the talim is a clear representation of each stage (raftar) of weaving. The increase or decrease of colours, or the changes in their places necessary to produce the required flowers, are exactly represented upon the paper. The aggregate of the number of nals, however, in each line remains invariably the same, being the total number of nals in the warp — this number is for remembrance sake put down on the top of the talam. Any mistake which might have occurred is corrected by a comparison of the parts woven with this paper.'

Moorcroft had observed that:

'The workman prepares the ''tojis'', or needles, by arming each with coloured yarn of the weight of about four grains. These needles, without eyes, are made of light, smooth wood and have both their sharp ends slightly charred to prevent their becoming rough or jagged through working.

'Under the superintendence of the ''tarah-guru'', the weavers knot the yarn of the tojis to the warp. The face or right side of the cloth is placed next to the ground, the work being carried out at the back or reverse on which hang the needles in a row, and differing in number from four hundred to fifteen hundred,[5] according to the lightness or heaviness of the embroidery (woven-pattern). As soon as the ''ustad'' is satisfied that the work of one line or woof is completed, the comb is brought down upon it with a vigour and repetition, apparently disproportionately to the delicacy of the material.

'Silk is generally used for the warp on the border of the shawl and has the advantage of showing the darker colours of the dyed wool more prominently than a warp of yarn as well as hardening and strengthening and giving more body to the edge of the cloth. The warp differs in breadth, the narrowest consisting of twenty and the broadest consisting of fifty threads. The operation of passing the yarns through the needles is performed precisely in the same way as in Europe.

'Three men are employed upon an embroidered (woven) shawl of an ordinary pattern for three months, but a very rich pair of shawls will occupy a shop for eighteen months. The weavers are all males and begin to learn the art at the age of ten.'

---

5. Jacquemont has recorded as many as 3000 tojis.

The dyes

In addition to being known for the exquisite lustre of the goat's wool, the Kashmir shawl is famous for its beautiful colours. Pashm and natural dyes are two inseparable entities which, when properly prepared and combined, radiate remarkably brilliant colours. The whiter and finer the fibre of the wool, and the finer the yarn into which it is made, the more easily it receives a bright colour. This is one of the main reasons why the goat's fine white wool is preferable to that of sheep.

Hajji Mukhtar Shah claimed that the first shawls employed only red, saffron yellow and indigo blue. The colours, according to the earliest extant shawls, which date from the Mughal period, do indeed display few colours, but the tints used show a greater sophistication of dyeing techniques within the available chromatic range, than existed in later periods. The subtle and exotic hues exude a colourful charm which harmonize closely with the Mughals' deep appreciation of nature. Moorcroft mentioned, for example, that over three hundred tints were used during Mughal times. Although this seems to be an exaggeration, unsupported by the extant woven fabrics of the period, nobody can deny that India had long been the home of ancient dyeing techniques such as 'resist' and 'mordant', which held colours fast in spite of repeated washings — well before other nations were aware that such techniques existed. But again, this is India; Kashmir remained a fairly isolated region for a long time.

The Mughal hues appear to have remained in vogue until the first half of the eighteenth century. At this time, strong indigo blues and bright bold reds from cochineal began to become increasingly evident in the 'transitional' shawl pieces of the period. Yellow was used sparingly.

With the arrival of the Afghans in Kashmir and the opening of new foreign markets, the shawl's popularity necessitated a larger scope of contrasting colours. But this did not mean that new dyes were invented. In 1823 Moorcroft mentioned that sixty-four tints were in use and that all were fast. At this time the dyer's art had already begun to decline. At the beginning of the nineteenth century a definite change is noticeable in the colours. Persia and Afghanistan not only demanded special shawl designs but also required particular colours. Among the kingdoms of Central Asia, for example, and especially in the markets of Kabul, a deep madder red was a traditional colour among the inhabitants. The ground colour on the Sikh tapestry shawls employed this madder red profusely and often it tended to drown the overall design of many of the more elaborate pieces. This gives one the impression that many of the bright colours used before Moorcroft's time had disappeared.

Jacquemont arrived in Srinagar in 1831 and observed that 'very mediocre dyes' were being used; and he pointed out especially that yellow was not very fast. By the time Vigne arrived, about ten years later, the situation was not much changed, except for the fact that a new craft had been created to compensate for the earlier deficiencies. 'The colours of a shawl after it has been washed,' wrote Vigne, 'are often renewed so well as to deceive any but the initiated by pricking them in again with a wooden pin, dipped in the requisite tint.'[6] This supposes that yarns were uselessly dyed with full knowledge that their colour would fade drastically immediately after a first washing. One wonders why shawl makers even bothered to use them at all.

Moorcroft makes no mention of any defects in the quality of dyeing, but following his departure from Srinagar in 1823 many curious changes occurred within the shawl industry. In particular, one popular type of shawl represents a good example

---

6. Vigne, p.131.

of this 'pricking' technique: the Sikh dochallas containing the bizarre hooked-vine motifs. Their wool was of a coarse nature and their normally dark muddy colours were a bit crude, compared to the bright colours known in Kashmir. They might have been made in Lahore, the military capital of the Sikhs. If so, their singular design may have been related to the fashions of the court.

One possible cause for this decline in the dyeing techniques is the fact that many expert dyers emigrated to the Punjab, taking the secrets of their trade with them. Dyeing techniques are intricate processes which require carefully controlled conditions, and colours may be modified if the techniques are used elsewhere than in the original geographical region.

Reports of Kashmir and the Punjab of the early nineteenth century are filled with accounts of various towns which competed with each other for the manufacture of the 'Kashmir' shawl. The English and the French also vied with each other in this domain, luring away from Srinagar both dyers and artisans of the shawl trade.

By the close of the Sikh period dyeing techniques had improved and methods of making colours fast were rediscovered; as one enters the Dogra period with its large designs, one rarely sees any of the 'pricking' which appeared all too frequently among the mid-Sikh period shawls. According to Hajji Mukhtar Shah, these improvements might have come about through the instigation of a Russian merchant from Kabul, one Yusuf Armani, who taught the local dyers new techniques in colour shading. Consequently, indigo was used with purified sulphuric acid while red was used with nitric acid. The Farahan rugs of the second half of the nineteenth century illustrate particularly well the effects of sulphuric acid dyeing, which gives the wool a greenish-blue colour.

The following list provides a general description of the colours in use and their sources, as recorded by the various visitors to Srinagar during the first half of the nineteenth century:

Crimson to violet: cochineal, kermes, logwood or any mixture thereof, promegranate skins. Inferior tints were obtained from kermes.

Green: English baize (broadcloth). Green was extracted from this cloth and reused in the shawl.

Blue: indigo.

Black: iron filings, iron sulphate, wild pomegranate skins.

Light brown: wild pomegranate skins.

Orange and yellow: carthamus and saffron.

Drab (dull brown-yellowish grey): walnut skins.

Alum (mordant): used for all dyeing.

Only Vigne ventured to record how a special tint was obtained:

'The fine pale yellow colour of a new shawl is given by means of sulphur fumes. A hole is made in the floor about a foot in diameter and six inches in depth. Over this is placed a small square chimney of poplar-wood, open of course above. Some lighted charcoal is put in the hole and over it is sprinkled a small handful of bruised sulphur. Around the chimney and about two feet distant from it is placed a horse or framework about five feet six inches in height upon which four shawls are suspended and the external air is further excluded by another drawn over the top. When the sulphur is consumed the shawls are withdrawn and others are subjected to the fumes of fresh sulphur. They are kept until the next day, then washed again in water, dried and pressed several together between two boards.'[7]

---

7. Vigne, p.131.

Chapter Four
Symbolism and the Boteh

The key to understanding basic shawl design is to realise that its history is developmental. There is no fundamental break between say, the high traditions of Mughal classicism and the work of the 'modern' artist of the Sikh period. To understand one artistic period of the shawl's history, it is necessary to work through the others, much as a painter learns the important techniques of varying styles. The methods of weaving remained the same; the materials did not change; the colours varied slightly in their chromatic range. The slow and subtle evolution of the shawl's motifs can thus be understood by looking at the component parts of the shawl design itself, by carefully examining many shawl pieces.

Prior to the first half of the eighteenth century, shawls are extremely rare and this hinders the establishment of any firm theory for the various Mughal schools of design. However, there are many miniatures of the seventeenth and eighteenth centuries which clearly depict people wearing the Kashmir shawl, although extremely few in which a Kashmir boteh pattern may be positively identified. One magnificent example in the Rijksmuseum, Amsterdam, is a miniature of Nekman

Plate 28 (left). A portrait of Madame Rivière by Ingres, 1805.
Plate 29 (right). A portrait of the Empress Josephine by Gros, 1809.

Khan (died 1672), commander-in-chief of Carnatic. (See Varadarajan, *India in the 17th Century,* pp.35, 36.)

The many court paintings under Napoleon, such as Ingres' Madam Rivière (1805) (Plate 28), Baron Gros' portrait of the Empress Josephine (Plate 29) and Girodet's 'Revolt of Cairo' (1810) offer us a late but tentative perspective. We can glean further information from the records of the European travellers to Kashmir. Finally there is the wealth of designs in the albums left by the French artists such as Oberkampf and Petitpierre who incorporated the boteh motif into their design albums at the beginning of the nineteenth century (see Chapter VII). All these sources serve as invaluable guides to the evolution of various motifs and patterns.

For a long time the Kashmir shawl has been characterised by the boteh (or buta meaning flower in India), the principal motif with which the shawl is associated. This repetitive curvilinear shape has been known by many names since its first appearance on shawls in the eighteenth century including paisley, pine cone and mango.

The development of the Kashmir shawl is closely related to the development of the boteh motif; in fact, the motif's different forms express the different periods in the shawl's development. It began in the Mughal period as the flowering plant ('floral' boteh), evolved into a slightly abstract representation of flowers ('semi-floral' boteh) and then developed during the Afghan period into a more stylized curvilinear representation of foliage and flowers rising to a vertex at the top ('cone' boteh). By the middle of the nineteenth century, under the Sikhs, it had developed into an extremely stylized form of sweeping sinuous curves ('sweeping' boteh) far removed from any resemblance of nature's flora (see Figures 25-28, pages 98-101).

The shawls shown in the Illustrated Guide (starting on page 171) have been chosen to illustrate the development of the boteh; by examining them and comparing them, the origins and evolution of this important symbol may be studied.

Mughal Period

The Mughals adhered to a social structure ruled mainly by the laws of Islam, and their art, dependent to a large extent on Persian craftsmen, expressed a predominantly Islamic world view. It was a culture in which textiles held a significant place. Islam held a country's individual development within a unifying force, determining the themes and motifs which dominated its sacred and secular arts — arrangements of realistic flowers, abstract arabesques of geometric composition and calligraphic inscriptions — but eschewing the human figure.

The kani shawl of the Mughal period is marked by highly sophisticated woven patterns, a graceful, naturalistic rendering of the flowers of the boteh, and a carefully constructed hashia which served as a frame around the boteh itself. The remarkable artistic quality of the few extant pieces suggests the existence of a serious weaving industry centred around the court workshops of the Mughal emperors (see, for example, Plates 88-93).

There are difficulties, however, in interpreting the meaning of the realistic flowers identified with the Mughal period. The closer one approaches nature, the further removed one feels from anything abstract. Nevertheless, the Mughal shawl, despite the purity of its naturalistic motifs, has symbolic meaning. The boteh undulates gracefully as the leaves fold and twist gently about themselves in a play of light and shadow, while its peak culminates in a full bloom, which is often portrayed by a dominant flower blossom swaying at the top. The plant's reproductive organs are usually shown by the pistil which often protrudes beyond the top blossom. As the seed bearing organ, the pistil was a typical Mughal characteristic exemplifying the never-ending cycle of organic growth. On finer illustrations stamens can also be

Plates 30a, b and c. Royal souvenirs of the flowering plant exalted by delicate rococo mihrabs. Red Fort, Delhi. Built 1638-48.

discerned (Plates 88, 90). The open and semi-opened buds intertwining with the plant's sinuous stems provide a permanent reminder of the organic and regenerative forces of botanical life.

In the conventional Mughal boteh, which probably emerged during the last years of Jehangir's reign (1605-1627), the flowers were normally all of the same species freely spaced on a plain background. Although they were at times woven in ways suggesting various states of growth and positions of suspension, the total effect was always that of a very specific plant. We also often find leaf stems at the base of the plants. As the boteh evolved towards a more abstract style, the stem became a kind of forsythia branch or raceme (stalked flowers arranged singly along a common main axis); the foliage was composed of either flower buds or tiny leaves, normally with two branches placed at the bottom of the boteh opposite each other (see Plates 96-98). From here the boteh evolved in one of two ways: either as its outline became more formal with the racemes arched upwards, becoming the proper curves of the general form; or else, the racemes remained under the weight of the plant, still in the form of opposing leaves but taking the shape of a ram's horn curving outward and down. This effect is especially apparent on shawls which have multiple rows of small repeated botehs (or buti). The ram's horn or leafy fronds later appeared along with other flowers, pouring out of the base which had been added to the design. Finally, the motifs all blended together and eventually assumed the curvilinear shape of the vase which influenced greatly and set the pattern for the cone boteh of the Afghan period.

The hashia acts as a frame for the palla's row of repeated boteh. Often, and following strict rules, a key element of the flower was harmoniously incorporated into the hashia's meandering vine. In this way, the boteh's design was enhanced by the hashia which echoed and framed it. If the boteh's design was in itself aesthetically lacking, the hashia could compensate, and thereby preserve the overall aesthetic effect. The results were often surprising; the ingenious blending of rectilinear and

Figure 16a (above). Hashia detail of Plate 83, Mughal.
Figure 16b (below). Hashia detail of Colour Plate 20, p.173, Mughal.

floral movement in the high Mughal period demonstrates an acute awareness of the most subtle and delicate design techniques the rules of which may have been established by the court workshops.

Later, hashia designs lacked artistic harmony but rather blended in either by force of matching colour or increased frequency of their vine repeats. Such is the style often displayed by hashias of the early eighteenth century. The palla's top and bottom hashias differ only from the long flanking ones in that the tandem repeats of the latter are shown compressed. This phenomenon appears to be reserved only for shoulder mantles. See for example Plate 133.

There is reason to believe that certain floral forms of the boteh developed out of the Mughal social structure. For example, the Mughals' passion for flowers is undisputed and evident in their art. However, from time to time, certain strange leaves and flowers appear on shawls in ways which do not allow logical conclusions concerning their provenance. They seem enigmatic in much the same way as the bizarre geometric motifs found on nomadic tribal rugs. Besides the shawl's colour, the mixture of flower blossoms and severely laterally pointed leaves might well have reflected a special system of rank, indicating the owner's status within the hierarchy of a rigid society (see Plates 99 and 100). More specifically, the patka shawl most often displays lateral leaf displacement. The patka is a band wrapped and tied around the waist. Soldiers, especially, were required to wear them, and kings and emperors bestowed them on their officers and nobles in recognition of services rendered. During Akbar's time the waist band invariably displayed geometric patterns, while a change to flower designs became noticeable under the rule of his son, Jehangir.

Except through brief and unprecise chronicles scattered here and there, extremely little is known about the kani industry of the early seventeenth century. A recent and major find by the Jagdish and Kamla Mittal Museum of Indian art, has brought to light new evidence of this obscure period of shawl weaving. The find consists of six palla fragments, illustrating altogether twenty-two floral botehs from a shoulder mantle. They were woven of a rare and exceedingly fine-spun shah tus, finer than any other kani piece known, probably during the early seventeenth century. The Mittal fragments were obviously part of an exceptional royal piece and possibly also part of a king's 'toshakhana' (imperial wardrobe) as observed by a faint stamp attached to one of the fragment's corners. Their beauty, execution and feathery texture exudes an aura of technical sophistication which could only have been achieved through an industry developed over an extended number of years.

Plate 31. The cenotaph of Mumtaz Mahal, the Taj Mahal, Agra. Built 1632-53.

This find opens a new and early chapter in the history of Mughal art showing the existence of an elaborate and unmistakably rich industry yet to be surpassed in intricacy of weaving and flawlessness of design (see Plate 88).

Another of the earliest extant Mughal pieces known is composed of two palla fragments, one of which is conserved by the Calico Museum in India and the other by the Victoria and Albert Museum, London. Delicate flowers, captured in the process of blooming, form the motif. Here is the realism typical of Mughal shawls, achieved through the subtle play of undulating leaves and of frail curved stems. The buds and blossoms are slightly exaggerated in size, and the piece gives one the impression of the fragility of a perishable flower burdened by its overgrown flora. The plant's stem seems to grow right out of the ground, although there is a slight attempt to show root growth, a peculiarity of early Mughal court shawls (see Plate 89).

Plate 32. Flowers from the Dara Shikoh Album, c.1635. During Jehangir's reign, Western influence in the form of a flowering plant, naturalistic in appearance, became a favourite among Mughal patrons of the arts. Invading the upper flowers of this delicate plant is a menacing sky of grotesque Chinese clouds. This suggests how easy it was for the naqqash or shawl designer to re-interpret them into the scheme of Kashmir shawl patterns, where they eventually became part of the boteh.

Other extant shawls also demonstrate the subtle artistry of the Mughal period. Among the earliest surviving court pieces is a fabulous white shah tus shoulder mantle at the Boston Museum of Fine Art (Plate 90). The cut gem-like flower buds of the unidirectional hashia meander exhibit a characteristic free spacing in perfect harmony with that of the exquisitely drawn botehs to make this royal piece one of the finest specimens of the Mughal period. Although Chinese clouds (see Plate 32) are absent from this piece, the Chinese influence is possibly seen in the device by which the boteh's stem has been rooted in the ground; this resembles the Greek letter 'pi' or more probably the Chinese ideogram 'Ta' meaning great. Although there have been many contemporary variations of this idea in shawls, this one possesses an undeniable curvilinear stroke making the influence of Chinese ideograms seem the more believable. The botehs of the Mittal fragment also have ideogrammatic roots (Plate 88). It appears this was a particular characteristic of the seventeenth century shawl and has not been observed elsewhere. The discovery of further pieces hopefully will shed more light on this subject. Figure 17 shows some of the more interesting root-securing devices from the earliest known shawls, and some Chinese ideograms with which to compare them.

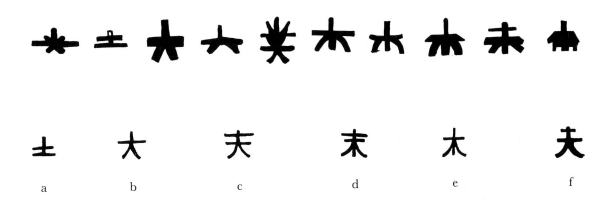

a   b   c   d   e   f

Figure 17. Top line: tracings of root securing devices employed on Mughal shawls of the 17th century. Bottom line: Chinese ideograms and their definitions: a) t'u: earth; b) ta: great; c) t'ien: heaven; d) mo: branches; e) mu: timber; f) fu: a master of craft. These root drawings and their close similarity with Chinese characters suggest the possibility that Mughal artists were conscious of their meaning. (They may be seen in other works of Mughal art: see, for example, the lobed Nephrite bowl, 17th century, at the Metropolitan Museum of Art, acc. no. 02.18.762.)

By the mid-eighteenth century, the Chinese root device took on various abstractions until the development of the mound after which time the vase and the dish came as additional non-botanical elements. One may speculate about the form which the mound takes. It is almost always stepped with heavy outlining, often in two tones, while spots decorate the mound's interior (Plates 102 and 111). Keeping in mind contemporary Mughal painting, we find that court artists were unsurpassed masters at creating oblique perspectives by which depth perception was often translated into a full foreground view. If we follow this theory into weaving, what we may have here within these mounds are actually tiny fish in a pond or basin.

In the Chinese cloud patka such as that in Plate 92, the top and bottom hashias contain an intentionally forced compression of rosebuds and cloud bands. Instead of the conventional oscillating design often reserved for the vertical hashias, here the clouds trail between the rosebuds and miniature clouds to connect them, all facing

Plate 33. Flowering plant on a marble wall of the Red Fort, Delhi.

the same way. On the other hand, in the vertical hashia bent tip 'roses' or 'strawberries' with appendages on the concave side, have whiffs of clouds attached to the base of the flower in a similar manner to the botehs of the palla. In all probability, the bent-tip strawberry (Figure 18) was a rose which by force of Mughal fashion moulded itself into the compelling bends of the classic vine of the hashia.

In the earliest examples, the meandering vine repeats almost always retained the same flower, while the later ones began slowly to incorporate as many as six different flowers, at the same time that the boteh developed floral variety. Where the blossom appears too large to be intelligently incorporated into the hashia in its entirety only a part, or in some cases just one half of it, was used to achieve the proper equilibrium.

There is no doubt that the Chinese cloud shawls strongly influenced future designs,

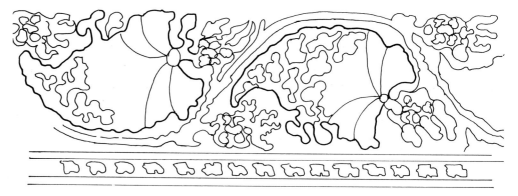

Figure 18. Vertical hashia detail of patka shown in Plate 92, with Chinese cloud band and 'birds in flight' guard border. A 'bent-tip' strawberry meander, Mughal.

most notably the 'rank' shawl of the early eighteenth century whose lateral leaves were probably a further, more abstracted development of the Chinese cloud patterns. Plate 99, although a 'rank' shawl, continues to retain in its top and bottom hashias the Chinese inspiration. Plate 100 is another good example of a continuation of the Chinese cloud-band idea. (For further discussion of rank shawls see pages 23, 24.)

In the Mughal period, the design of the patka differs in an important way from that of the shoulder mantle. Conventionally, the main floral vine of the patka's hashia is bordered on both sides by a fairly sophisticated geometric pattern, something which except for the chandar of the eighteenth century, is rarely found on the kani shoulder mantle. These guard border patterns usually further consisted of three rows of brocaded weaving on a common ground colour. The centre row often displays a kind of tiny rhomboidal pattern while on some specimens this angular shape actually takes the form of birds in flight (Figures 18, 19). Flanking the guard borders is either a solid colour line of weft brocading or one filled with a series of contrasting flecks. See for example Colour Plate 23, page 176. This angular elaboration peculiar to the patka suggests that it may have played a much more dominant role in kani weaving — possibly before the use of the flowering plant and perhaps as far back as the Sultanate period (1215-1526). Therefore the Kashmir shawl as a shoulder mantle may still have been something of a novelty, as suggested by Abul Fazl, Akbar's court chronicler, and thus its use as a medium for the art of kani weaving may have also been a recent innovation. This leads us to the more ancient brocaded patka whose similarities in format approximated the shoulder mantle.

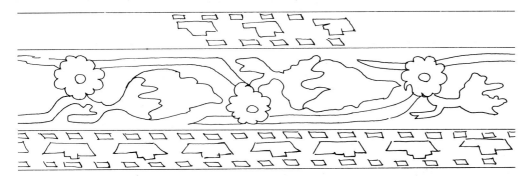

Figure 19. Detail of the hashia of patka shown in Plate 99 with Chinese cloud band and a 'birds in flight' guard border, Mughal.

Figure 20. A reconstructed hashia repeat of the patka fragment shown in Plate 86. Note the angularity of the repeat.

The patka designated the military or social rank of the bearer and it usually measured about .70m x 4 to 5m or longer. It was not until about 1640 that the flowering plant began to make its appearance on the patka.[1] Mughal painting of the first half of the seventeenth century shows that it was highly ornamented with geometric or Persian scroll-type patterns, often further embellished with gold covering large portions of the patka's ends and sometimes the whole piece. Apart from the brocaded ones and an exceptionally unique seventeenth century kani patka (Plate 85) however, no other kani patkas meeting this geometric or scroll description have at present come to light. Nor do we find large traces of arabesques or geometric patterns among the dozen or so extant patkas of the seventeenth century. Nonetheless, on closer examination of the kani patka one detects a conventionally wide border or hashia of about 3.8cm of which the guard borders are always composed of running specks and tiny rhomboids. Paradoxically although the shoulder mantle was much wider its hashia remained very narrow, less than two centimetres.

Figures 21a and b. Hashia details of Plate 93, Mughal.

Following the decline of the Mughal empire, the classic Mughal style was perpetuated by many provincial kingdoms. Mukhtar Shah cites the example of Hyderabad, a predominantly Muslim state ruled by a dynasty of Nizams, as being a continuous outlet for the old, traditional court designs. The flora of such provincial shawls often represented state emblems of various kingdoms removed from direct Mughal domination. One might also cite the kingdom of Lucknow, whose ruler Nawab Asaf-ud-Daula was a generous patron to numerous artists, musicians and writers who were attached to the city in the late eighteenth century.

In conclusion, the Mughal boteh stressed the realistic representation of nature,

1. Kahlenberg, pp.153-166.

Plates 34a and b. Details of sculptured marble interior of the Moti Masjid, built in 1699 by Aurangzeb.

along with an extremely delicate harmony of design. This emphasis was shared by the other impressive art mediums of the Mughal period, such as carpet weaving and even architecture. The Mughals, in fact, so venerated flowers that, even during the austere reign of Aurangzeb, they often used them for decoration. The mosque of Delhi's Red fort (Plate 34), for example, remains a dazzling testament to an empire whose art was rooted in an inspired appreciation of nature.

Afghan Period

With the arrival of the Afghans in Kashmir in 1753, a long and fruitful period came to an abrupt end. The Afghans were great admirers of the shawl, but the severe hardships they inflicted on the Kashmiri weavers brought about a decline in the shawl's quality.

Under the Afghans, the boteh became more stylised. Its flowers began to be formed into bouquets of almost nondescript foliage. Flowers were not always completely unrecognisable, and in some cases, the crocus, marigold, and rose, retained a semi-naturalistic appearance. Nonetheless, the boteh tended to move away from naturalism, towards more abstract forms. It was during the Afghan period that the cone buta first appeared, and its enclosing curvilinear walls (see, for example, Plates 124, 125) perhaps reflect the restrictions on political and creative freedom placed by the Afghans on the people of Kashmir.

However, the historical origins of this motif are not entirely clear. Indian culture prior to the mid-eighteenth century offers very few clues to the origins of the cone. The Red Forts in Delhi and Agra are both ornamented in the flora idiom (Plates 30, 34); even the sumptuous palaces of Rajastan, where no expense was spared, contain no motif resembling the cone. Nowhere in India had the cone been enshrined, ennobled or worshipped; and if it did ornament a few later monuments, miniatures or textiles it was never a major motif, but always a minor part of the general design. The cone boteh appeared frequently, however, in Persian architecture as early as the eleventh century. It can also be found in Coptic weaving and Byzantian jewellery of the sixth and seventh centuries and so it is probable that the cone motif was borrowed from the cultures of Persia, Egypt, or Byzantium. It is tempting to see it as an elemental shape representing the force of life itself and recurring in periods of cultural and artistic awakening.

Extensive analysis of hundreds of shawl designs strongly suggests that the cone boteh evolved as a result of the many stylistic changes in the floral boteh, especially in the important transitional period at the end of the eighteenth and beginning of the nineteenth century, though this does not necessarily preclude the notion of, say, Persian origins.

One of the most important features in the transition from Mughal to Afghan styles is the replacement of a single species of plant by a mixture of all different kinds of flowers(see, for example, Plate 102). Another related change is the appearance of a vase and a dish, which was undoubtedly abstracted from the Chinese ideogram root. This was the first time that objects other than flowers were represented in the boteh's design.

The vase served to support the large number of flowers, which otherwise might have upset the aesthetic harmony of the design. Later, the vase, often very small, became a purely ornamental feature, rarely in proportion to the huge array of flowers which was soon to develop. Such disproportion would never have been allowed in Mughal decoration, where harmony was considered as the primary aesthetic virtue.

The vase was an extremely important stage in the boteh's evolution (see Plate 113). It is believed that its appearance is contemporary with the emerging of floral variety. In addition, the vase's curvilinear form most likely encouraged the development of the cone boteh. The change toward a less specific representation of floral species had other effects as well. Towards the third quarter of the eighteenth century, flowers were no longer drawn naturally but as abstracted decorations. The boteh was no longer a representation of nature, but an intense collage of colours within a curvilinear form. This was the cone boteh in its pure form.

One of the earliest transitional patterns from the Afghan period is the 'Qajar' boteh (see Plates 124 and 125 and Colour Plates 28-30, page 210), so-called because of its similarities with a boteh pattern found in a pre-Qajar painting.[2] The significance of this painting lies in the fact that it is the only known eighteenth century source which portrays a typical Kashmir-shawl boteh. A glance at the illustrations in P.J. Falk's book, *Qajar Painting,* will demonstrate the importance of the Kashmir shawl in the Persian courts, especially the court of Fath Ali Shah (1798-1834). Although the Persians shunned its use as a shoulder mantle (see page 105), they were widely worn as patkas, gilets, turbans, and also cut into every dress accessory imaginable, including socks and gloves.

A frequent Mughal element forming the base of the boteh had been the raceme (see page 72) usually shown growing up at opposing angles. The addition of the vase changed all this and the racemes began to move upwards slowly either within the boteh or pouring out of the vase. In either case, if they remained at its base, they assumed the curvilinear form of the boteh. The important characteristic of the Qajar boteh is that the raceme has already worked its way to the top to 'sprout' forming an apex, the early beginnings of the pine cone. At the turn of the eighteenth century the popular theme was the sinuous protrusion of several racemes at a time forming the apex (see Plate 166). This style was meticulously captured in French painting by court artists such as Ingres (Plate 28), Gros, and Girodet.

Along with the Qajar boteh came the 'radial flower' technique in which small flower buds appear attached like spokes on a wheel, orbiting a floral rosette (Figure 22). This had the effect of freeing the floral stagnation which arose from the curvilinear constraints of the boteh and creating a new graphic dimension. In the Boston Museum of Fine Art there is a particularly fine fragment exemplifying this technique (see Plate 125). And in a later version in the collection of the Victoria and Albert Museum the radial technique can be seen predominating in an early nineteenth century shawl (see Plate 176).

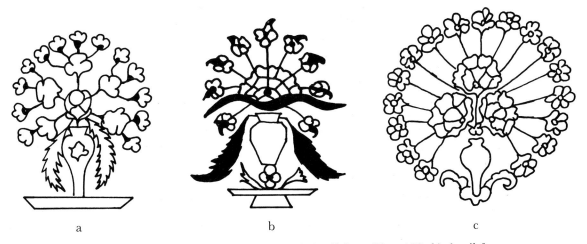

a   b   c

Figure 22. 'Radial' flowers of the Afghan period: a) detail from Plate 139; b) detail from Plate 125; c) detail from Plate 161b (millefleurs prayer shawl).

2. Falk, p.28, fig.9.

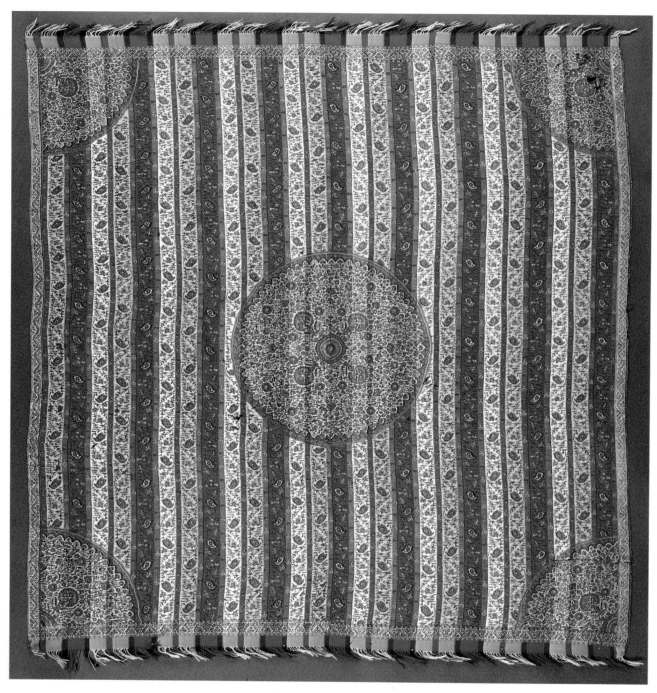

Colour Plate 7. Moon shawl (chandar), late Afghan style, c.1815. Medallions show typical characteristics of the flattened flower, 'radial' flower technique, the vase and dish, etc. The field is in 'Khatraaz' or striped style.

Another feature was added soon after. A curved branch detached from the boteh, but similar to the branches inside, was woven in an upward arch towards the top of the boteh. Occasionally it swept over the top. This 'coif' (Figure 26, page 99) was a clever ploy to balance the design of the repeated botehs which all leaned in the same direction. It was developed by the Kashmiri artists into a strong conventional form so much so that it often completely encircled the boteh (Plates 175, 176), representing the beginning of the ground embellishment.

Other concentric forms followed. Encouraged by the coif boteh technique, weavers added a new dimension to the cone boteh, as ornamentation appropriated more of the ground. The hardened shape which crystalised in the transition from the Afghan to the Sikh period is a direct result of the encircling branch.

The heavily filled ground which developed had the effect of a halo encircling the cone boteh; this added a floating dimension which caused the boteh to appear completely detached from the ground and set against a floral setting. This marked the beginning of a new far-reaching style which was once referred to as 'transparent', but was wrongly attributed to European influence. The transparent boteh became an artistic theme for many future shawl patterns both in India and Europe. Shawls of the tapestry type (discussed on pages 53, 96), with lavish designs, often display such scattered cones which are almost totally independent of the ground pattern (see Plates 215, 218).

Finally, the detached branch was added back to the tilted rose at the top of the boteh, sometimes hanging over it, sometimes ending with a small flower. Branches inside the boteh also evolved toward increased abstraction. Early examples of the shawl portrayed slightly curved branches growing up almost vertically; later, they began to cross over each other in a snake-like fashion. The branches eventually crystallised into two solid curved lines representing perhaps an abstracted form of heavy vines. (See Figure 24, page 90.)

Under the Afghans, then, the boteh became more stylised and abstract. It no longer focused on a realistic representation of nature, but rather attempted to portray an intensity of colour within a curvilinear form. The central theme of the Afghan period was the evolution of the boteh into a cone-like shape. At the beginning of the Sikh period, this form crystallised even more when the effect of underlining was created by the fully ornamented ground. This had the effect of drawing a smooth, unbroken line completely around the boteh. The colour of the line depended on the ground dye.

During the Afghan period, the laws of Islam were graphically and repeatedly expressed within two dimensional Euclidean space throughout the diversity of design patterns. Afghan shawls possessed a unity which enlarge one's perspective creating a sense of harmony by the geometric play of light and shade. The chandar, or moon shawl, was one of the main forms for such expression, especially through the tiny duplicate floral sprigs of the chandar's field. The moon shawl was especially important since the central medallion played an important role in creating the illusion of a third dimension (Plates 128, 129, Colour Plate 7).

To conclude, the Afghans imposed severe exactions on the people and especially on the weaving industry from which they reaped huge financial gains. This in turn took its toll over the years upon the magnificent Mughal style which eventually degenerated into a confusion of packed flowers held within the confining walls of a new type of curvilinear boteh. The natural growth and development of the flowering plant slowly disappeared. The new stylistic convention was to more or less fill up the cone shape, cramming the flowers in wherever a free space permitted. Acting as catalysts to the development of this new shape were the vase and the dish. (See Appendix I for 'A Brief Review of French Painting: The Empire Style'.)

Sikh Period

As the Sikh period began, design features reflected the influence of Western fashion, brought about in part by the influx of the French and the Industrial Revolution in Europe. There was a sudden decline in Islamic influence; the patterns which had represented the high point of Indo-Muslim exploration of the subtle symmetries of space began to decline. The Kashmir shawl reflected new and changing fashions. Napoleon's return from Egypt left an indelible impression in the Middle East that the Orient, including England's India, was not completely immune to military conquest. In addition, the lavish fashion of the Napoleonic empire left a clear mark on the fashion of the East.

Napoleon's fall coincided with the rise of another monarch, Runjit Singh. Although Singh's conquests lacked the elegant glory which the Western mind attributed to Napoleon, he was no less revered by a people who identified greatly with those who are courageous and cunning in war; Runjit Singh (Plate 14) became the great Maharaja of all the Punjab and the Kingdom of Kashmir in 1819.

The Sikhs broke all the sacred shawl-design rules; they pronounced the might of an indigenous race, emphasising their genuine Indian heritage. The bold features of the Sikh Kashmir shawl do little to conceal the fervent militarism behind Sikhism. Such symbolism is not always defined in the form of a simple design component but, rather it is often suggested by the image of the total composition. It is for this reason that the denomination of 'modern' art can be justly applied to those shawl-designs created with the arrival of the Sikhs in Kashmir in 1819.

The artist, whether his designs are woven in wool, carved on stone or painted on canvas, has at all times been the instrument and spokesman of the spirit of his age; consciously or unconsciously he gives form to the nature and values of his time. The shawls we find during this period of 'modern' art reflect the military bravado which moulded Sikhism. True to the teachings of the Sikhism's founder, Guru Nanak (1469-1529), the eclectic Sikh influence incorporated a rich variety of abstract images from all walks of Oriental culture.

This is one of the most fascinating transitional periods (1815-1820) in as much as one can see clearly the new infusion of Indian blood injected by the upsurge in symbolic content of the nascent shawl patterns. The pomp and splendour of the rich court of Maharaja Runjit Singh forms the background for this renaissance. Although his patronage of the arts remains obscure, and little is known of his encouragement of the weaving industry (a few interesting references, however, do exist) the underlying theme of Hindu influence cannot be denied.

Besides the Golden Temple of Amritsar and a few building additions within the Red Fort of Lahore, the Sikhs left no resounding monuments which serve to stamp their esoteric culture with a personal style. Unlike the great Mughals, they never left any personal written accounts or autobiographies despite the omnipotent force their presence signified in Northern India.[3] But all this tends further to stimulate our curiosity in the search for the cultural outlets of an impressive race of people and to cause us to delve deeper into the expressive and prolific weavings of the Sikh period.

The earliest clearly-dated reference to some of the styles of the boteh during the Sikh period are Moorcroft's designs, which he sent to England in 1823. Apparently, Moorcroft sent back thirty-four drawings from Kashmir to England, but apart from eight which were acquired by the New York Metropolitican Museum of Art in 1962, little is known of their whereabouts, and so it is difficult to isolate the exact beginnings of important features which appear to have been introduced at the time of Sikh conquest of Kashmir in 1819.

---

3. Archer, p.xviii.

Plate 35. Shawl pattern sent to England by Moorcroft in 1823. 40cm x 16cm. Inscribed verso 'Turquoise Colour by order of Mahummud Azeem Khan, Indian'.

Moorcroft's eight boteh designs (shown as Plates 35-38) nonetheless offer us a rare opportunity to visualise cone-styles popular in India, Persia and Russia in 1823. They contain important details which reveal some of the design ideas which became increasingly popular on later shawls. These show Indian — as opposed to Afghan — influence, and this influence accords logically with the ending of Islamic rule in Kashmir.

Plate 35 is probably the most important of Moorcroft's designs. It represents a vase, created by flowing cupped ferns whose neck and rim have been drawn in to define the top. Growing out of the vase is an exotic, flattened display of various stylised roses. Some appear to be in the process of blooming from buds surrounded by small leaves; others appear in full bloom but partly hidden by a strange array of what looks like unusually long 'lotus flower' leaves, of the type often seen in Indian miniature painting. The roses resemble a type of shield or perhaps an open fan (see Figure 23, overleaf).

The rose itself is composed of neat concentric circles of rows of equally sized and spaced minute petals. Sometimes the leaves are so large that they dominate the rose

Figure 23 (above and opposite). A series of drawings showing the development of the fools cap: a, b and c are taken from Moorcroft's drawings; i is a detail of Plate 207. The other tracings are from various shawls.

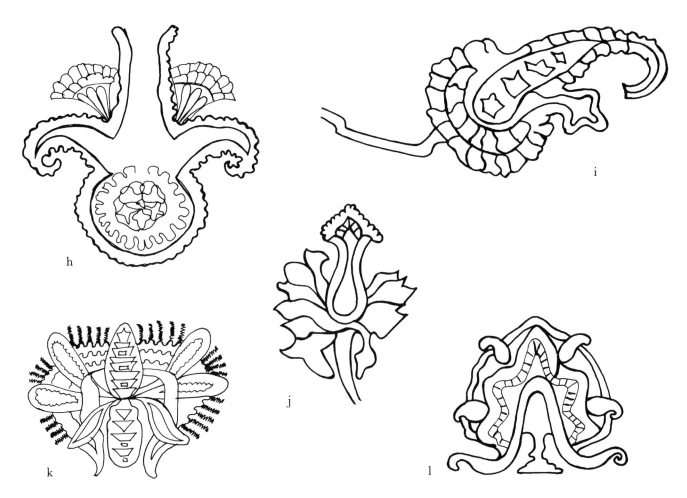

h

i

j

k

l

and are arranged in such a way that they could be taken for a flower themselves — perhaps a lotus flower.

The lotus-like rose was adopted as a convention of design, and variations were often employed in the meandering floral motif of the shawl's hashia until the very end of the kani shawl's history. It appeared especially on the Sikh tapestry shawls. Sometimes the rose splits apart to form a kind of stretched peacock's tail. Turkish velvets of the sixteenth and seventeenth century frequently portray a similar type of abstract design, often described as a carnation. At other times the 'lotus' leaves appear to grow directly out of the middle of the rose. In this case the leaves are either fanned out or grouped together in a kind of narrow cone boteh, similar to a type of Anthurium flower.

This drawing suggests how the ubiquitous 'tilted-top' rose evolved into the lotus-rose which has by this time become integrated into the new langauge of the Sikh style. In all its forms, the rose, symbol of love and passion, appeared in every period.

The narrow cone boteh eventually detached itself from the mother lotus-like rose and broke away to become a separate and independent motif, retaining a small cluster of 'rose' petals at its base. The motif looks like a fool or clown's cap[4] but it has a striking resemblance to the jewelled ornament worn by the Indian and Persian nobles, called a 'jigeh' or 'aigrette', attached to the front of turbans as part of traditional court costume (see Figure 23i).

---

4. Vigne, Vol.2, pp.133-4. Vigne confuses this subordinate motif with the major cone motif itself.

Colour Plates 8a and b (opposite and above). Shawl. Sikh, c.1825. 140cm x 330cm. The tall botehs seem almost superfluous against the background of architectural paraphernalia which became fashionable at the court of Runjit Singh. The mihrab, with its spandrels round three scalloped circles, is Islamic in flavour. Other design features are an eight point star and a shield surrounded by spears. A close inspection of the fine detailed work which embellishes almost all the curving elements reveals a fascinating admixture of shawl school styles. Compare this with Chavant's drawing, Plate 76.

Another important design development was that of the hooked vine. This derives from an evolution in organic growth. Popular boteh themes of the late Afghan period displayed an increasing use of first vertical and then interlaced branches. The vine can be seen in its nascent form in Colour Plates 41 and 42, pages 259, 262 (see respective details in Figures 24a, c, below) in which the boteh's inner structure has been built around the rising ogival pattern of leaves and tiny blossoms. Within a short time the vine hardened (see Plate 36 also Plates 190 and 191 with respective details in Figures 24d and e, below). In the National Museum, Delhi, there is a superb transitional shawl in which the vine is seen composed of pointed hooks menacing the restraining walls of the boteh's curvilinear form (Plate 190). One can almost feel the pent up energy and the need to break away that is generated by the bold visual impact of this revolutionary pattern. It radically underlines the unconscious social changes which took place. Furthermore it shows an absolute mastery of the synthesis of Mughal and Afghan styles. The lower flower clusters recall those of the 'Qajar' boteh while the radial flowers have been placed towards the middle. Cradled by the first hooks are two smaller vases while the small isolated floral ornaments (butis) lying between the coif botehs enhance the Mughal touch through the graceful arching of winged leaves. Although the raised dish appears slightly truncated, its chevron pattern combined with the cross-emblasoned vase effectively support the thick hooked vine which rises in an ogival fashion to dominate the boteh.

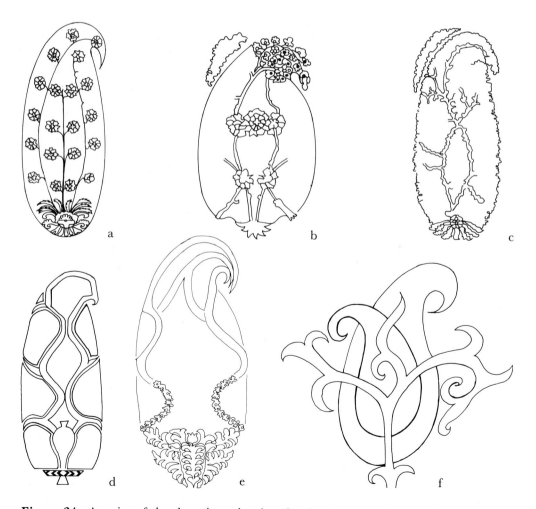

Figure 24. A series of shawl tracings showing the development of the hooked vine.

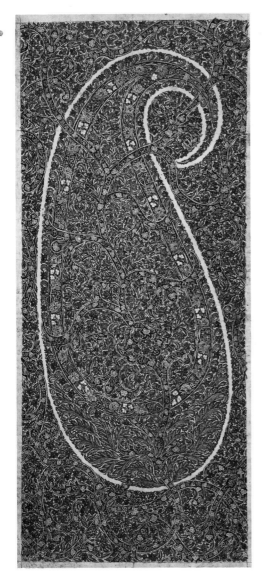
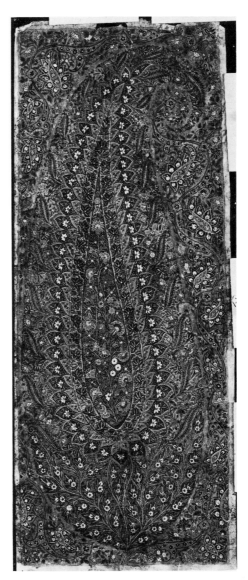

Plate 36. Shawl pattern sent to England by Moorcroft in 1823. Lacquered tempera on paper, 36cm x 15cm. Inscribed verso 'Yellow and betel colour by order of Mahummud Azeem Khan, Russia'.

Plate 37. Shawl pattern sent to England by Moorcroft in 1823. 35cm x 14cm. Inscribed verso 'Verdigris colour, by order of Mahummud Azeem Khan, Russian'.

In another of Moorcroft's drawings, the boteh's inner cone is seen outlined with leaves arranged in the form of scales (Plate 37). This is seen on many shawls woven during the 1840s and later, the 'sweeping boteh' also assimilated this idea. We see here another detail not often found on Kashmir shawls; the arabesque which winds around the boteh as part of the ground décor. For centuries the Persians artfully employed this design on the elegant rugs of Ispahan and Shiraz. Classical rug designs such as the split arabesque, 'gul', leafy palmette, etc., found their way into Kashmir's rug weaving industry — an industry which enjoyed a success concurrent with that of the shawls. Yet, oddly enough, this motif is never seen on shawls. Perhaps the naqqash or designer felt that the use of such motifs would confuse his wealthy clients, who preferred not to mix the two design mediums. Or perhaps the idea of someone walking on rug designs and then weaving them into delicate shawls

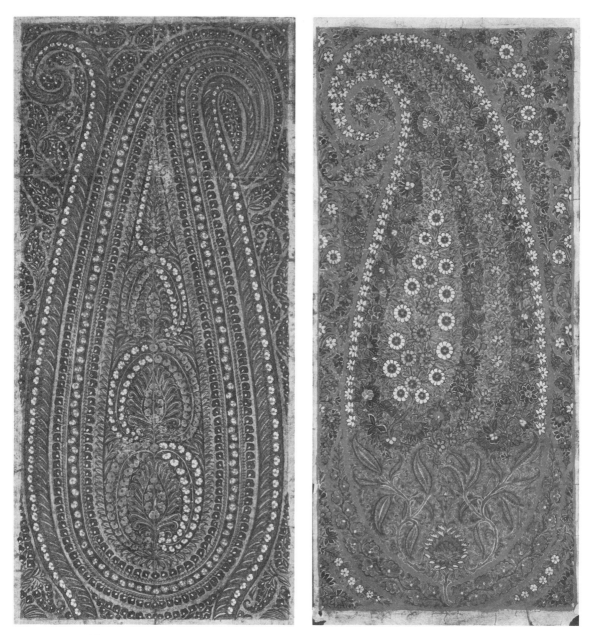

Plates 38a-e (above and opposite). Shawl patterns sent to England by Moorcroft in 1823. **Plate 38a** (left). Tempera on paper, lacquered. Inscribed verso 'Hindustan'. **Plate 38b** (right). 35cm x 16cm. Inscribed verso 'Pomegranate colour, Hindustan'.

seemed almost blasphemous. Whatever the case may be, the unusually rigorous separation of these weavings further validates an art which developed within its own strong and independent sphere.

Plates 38a-e show further designs recorded by Moorcroft. Plate 38a is rather less elegant and interesting than the others; we see here a decline from the rare and exotic to the commonplace design abstractions which permit cheap imitations. In this drawing a snake-like form curls in the opposite direction from the boteh's tip — a variation of the earlier coif boteh technique. The boteh's centre is filled with three superimposed medallions above which is a kind of cypress tree or spear. The evolution of this ubiquitous, phallic element seems appropriate as a symbol of the

 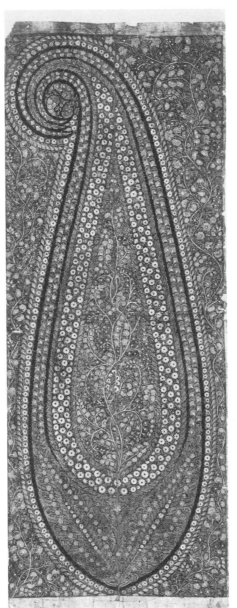 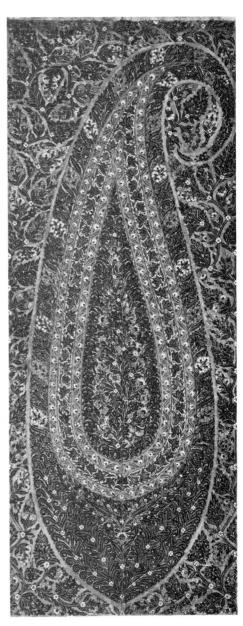

Plate 38c (left). Gouache on paper, 33cm x 13cm. Inscribed verso 'Elephant colour, by order of Shooja ool Moolkh, Persia'. **Plate 38d** (centre). 35cm x 14cm. Inscribed verso 'Lapis-Lazuli colour, for Shah Zuman, Persia'. **Plate 38e** (right). 37cm x 15cm. Inscribed verso 'Dusty colour for Shah Zuman, Persia'.

Sikh force piercing through and melting away Pathan opposition. This motif demonstrates the declining influence of Islam on designs.

It is curious that pieces of such contrasting quality come from the same period, yet one realises when one tries to date textiles, that such disparities are anything but rare. In addition to his drawings, Moorcroft left among his correspondence and notes a list of over eighty shawl fabrics, along with their corresponding descriptions and prices.[5] For example he describes certain pieces as 'ornamented with flowers

---

5. Irwin, 1955, pp.37-45.

either in the corner or running all around the shawl between the border and the field', or 'green sprigs on a white ground', or 'large grounds of flowers somewhat in the form of the cone of a pine with the ends or points straight or curved downwards'. From this it may be implied that the bent-tip boteh was in vogue as early as 1822.

Finally, we come to a curious remark concerning the shawl fabric called 'hashiyadar Kunguradar'.[6] Moorcroft says: 'This has a border of unusual form with another within side, or nearer to the middle, resembling the crest of the wall of Asiatic forts furnished with narrow niches or embrasures for wall pieces or matchlock, whence its name.' This appears to be the first mention, from any source, of architectural ornamentation on shawls. The idea of forts, parapet openings and guns certainly coincides not only with the divergently 'modern' shawl styles but also with the Sikh's obsession with war. Vigne refers to a pair of woven shawls commissioned by Maharaja Runjit Singh representing his victories.[7] Perhaps in the future shawl pieces will be discovered that will shed more light on the early appearance of architectural motifs in Sikh weaving.

In the 1830s, Chavant, the well-known publisher and designer, published a drawing of a shawl made in 1825 (Plate 78). The drawing gives us valuable information concerning the boteh's development in the period immediately following Moorcroft's departure. We can see that around 1825 a new style of cone came into being. Instead of the curled-tip characteristic of Moorcroft's cones, the new boteh displays a stretched-out body. Instead of the tip curling about itself, it assumes a kind of folded aspect with a sharp lance-like tip reaching perhaps half-way down, barely touching the side. This reflects the increased tapestry work which then began to cover a larger area of the shawl.

With this came a subordinate form of leaning botehs. They were reduced-size models of the lance boteh and were used for decoration of the 'dhor', the area surrounding the centre field of the shawl. Shawls at the beginning of the Sikh period show that the lance or folded boteh was clearly non-existent before this time. The lance boteh marked the last significant design innovation until twenty-five years later when French agents arrived to impose their style — the sweeping or zoomorphic boteh (see Figures 27 and 28, pages 100, 101).

Our knowledge of Sikh style is further expanded by the erudite Victor Jacquemont (1801-1832) (Plate 39), a botanist sent by the French government to visit India. His clear description of the shawl trade in Loudiana, Islamabad and Kashmir offers us an intimate account, not only of the techniques of production, but also of the political situation and slave-like oppression suffered by the poor Kashmiri weavers.

Jacquemont arrived in Kashmir just eight years after Moorcroft, a timely arrival since just one year later Kashmir suffered a terrible famine which devastated the whole region. His stay in Srinagar provided some enlightening details about changes in style which took place during this important period (1823-1831). The measurements of the new boteh tend to corroborate the evidence found in Chavant's drawing relating to the increase in the boteh's size. His comments also suggest that a decline in quality had occurred by this time: '. . . the open field (matan) diminishes to almost nothing', wrote Jacquemont, 'by the enormous height of the palms (cones) which are now 0.70m to 1m long, and furthermore the designs today do not have anymore the agreeable bizarreness of those in the past; they are baroque. Those that the European taste would condemn the most severely are the most sought after in the Orient and the ones held in the highest esteem today represent indelicate figures of flower vases, houses and even animals.'

---

6. Irwin, 1955, p.28.
7. Vigne, vol.2, p.124.

Colour Plate 9. Long shawl, French, 1865-70. 340cm x 146cm. This unique shawl exhibits a very rare weaving technique about which very little is known at present. It appears that the weft had been woven utilizing special brocading shuttles which completely eliminated the floating threads on the back, thus avoiding the post-weave cutting procedure ('découpage'). The shawl is woven all in one piece (see p.129 for further discussion of this technique), cf. *Le Châle Cachemire en France au XIX siècle,* p.90.

Plate 39. Victor Jacquemont.

We see here Jacquemont's nostaglia for the earlier style of fine, delicately woven shawls so magnificently portrayed by artists such as Ingres and Baron Gros; the rare shawl of subtle woven fleece which fell in smooth, undulating folds, enveloping the feminine figure in voluptuous curves, now seemed to belong to the past, if not to the realm of legend.

The Sikhs' arrival, ending the Afghans' tyrannical rule, saw a veritable creative explosion. On the one hand, new designs flourished, and the decorations on Kashmir shawls became more ornate than ever before. On the other hand, the curvalinear boteh became less essential to the organic unity of these new, more abstract design patterns.

Under the Sikhs, the design of the boteh focused on the aigrette or fool's cap, the serrated leaf, the lotus-like rose, the 'leaning' and 'stubby' boteh (with lance tip), the hooked vine, the spear or cypress tree, stacked medallions, concentric cones, and certain unidentified architectural ornamentation (see Plate 74).

Moorcroft's drawing shown as Plate 38a suggests that certain aspects of these changes had already started as early as 1823. However, the boteh had become but an echo of the past, a hollow skeletal form whose presence was necessary for economic reasons only, as a symbol without which the shawl could not be sold in many markets. There is thus little doubt that by the early 1830s, the Industrial Revolution in Europe creating an ever-expanding consumer market, and the influx of European fashion had combined with the years of foreign domination to alter the classic tradition of the kani shawl.

To conclude, the principal weaving associated with the Sikh period may be known as the tapestry shawl. The huge size of the sweeping botehs and the multitude of large architectural and curvilinear patterns began quickly to invade the whole surface area of the shawl. Hollow botehs detached themselves from the increasingly dominating ground designs to evaporate through scattered directions across a roaring sea of new images, exotic and enigmatic. The riotous agitation of the boteh's flora swept away practically all botanical reality in its path. It appears that in one fell sweep the Sikhs obliterated all graphic souvenirs which recalled the hard struggles against their Mughal and Afghan rivals to vindicate their rights to Northern India. The close look into this boteh microcosm provides a clear distinction of the evolving key elements which eventually emerged, fused and even re-separated to form the churning symbolism of the Sikh period.

Dogra Period

Few design innovations developed within the boteh style during the period which followed the death of Maharaja Runjit Singh in 1839. Raja Gulab Singh took over Kashmir in 1846 and within a few years French agents arrived there in large numbers with the latest Parisian shawl patterns. The abrupt change in political climate brought with it many foreign visitors, including a well-known English watercolourist, W. Simpson. He came to Srinagar to paint shawl weavers and embroiderers and the comments he made concerning the changing artistic scene are worth quoting:

> 'The great estimation in which Cashmir shawls are held in France, and the consequent demand for them, have induced some of the large houses in that country to keep agents in Srinugger [Srinagar]. One result of this is that the French design patterns in Paris and send them out to Cashmere for execution. Although their designs are all in the Oriental style, they are no improvement on the old work of the natives. . . [the French patterns] were perhaps purer than the old; they contained more free and sweeping lines, but they wanted the medieval richness of the native taste. It may be described as the difference between a piece of rococo ornament and what an artist of the thirteenth century would have produced. There was a distinguishing character about the original style which is being rubbed out by this foreign influence.'[8]

The Dogra period is indisputedly intermingled with the sweeping all over patterns generated by the Jacquard loom. Practically all the kani shawls were of the patchwork kind, pieced together with sometimes as many as a hundred separate pieces, like a jigsaw puzzle (this was a feat in itself). Nevertheless, there are many surviving shawls which belie the idea that the kani industry deteriorated completely during the middle of the nineteenth century. On the contrary, the French presence in Srinagar greatly encouraged the kani weaving industry and was responsible for its revival. But the Franco-Prussian War of 1870 and changing European fashions virtually ended the shawl industry until and including the present day (see Figure 1, page 30). The style of this period is further discussed in Chapter 6, Shawl Weaving in France.

The shawls such as in Colour Plates 54, 58 and 60-66, pages 315, 318, 322-328, represent the kani master-pieces of the post-Runjit Singh period, the period 1840 to 1877 when French influence dominated the weaving industry of Srinagar. Their design expression is often removed from the Islamic vernacular that patterns displayed before the arrival of the Sikhs in Kashmir in 1818. This is to say that as the import demands of European markets increased, there was a corresponding decrease in the Islamic elements of design, either through abstraction or direct elimination.

French shawl designers of the nineteenth century such as Couder and Berrus left a profound imprint of their creative styles both on the industry of France and Kashmir. Indeed, Srinagar was, in a sense, the 'Gobelins' atelier for France's tapestry shawl market. At the time of the Great Exhibition of 1851 and onward, the Kashmir weaver rarely began his days work before consulting the design and pattern books brought to Kashmir by Parisian agents.

---

8. Simpson, p.5.

Pictoral development of the boteh

The following boteh sketches do not necessarily demonstrate the evolution of the naturalistic flower boteh into the curvilinear cone, but rather clarify some of the working vocabulary employed in the text and captions. Research on the Kashmir shawl is still in its infancy, so it is difficult to be absolutely positive about a rigid chronological sequence of the boteh. Prior to the late eighteenth century, pictorial evidence is lacking. The drawings here are from pieces which in the author's opinion represent the artistic high points of Kashmir's weaving industry and thus express stylistic developments which one may associate with archetypal pieces.

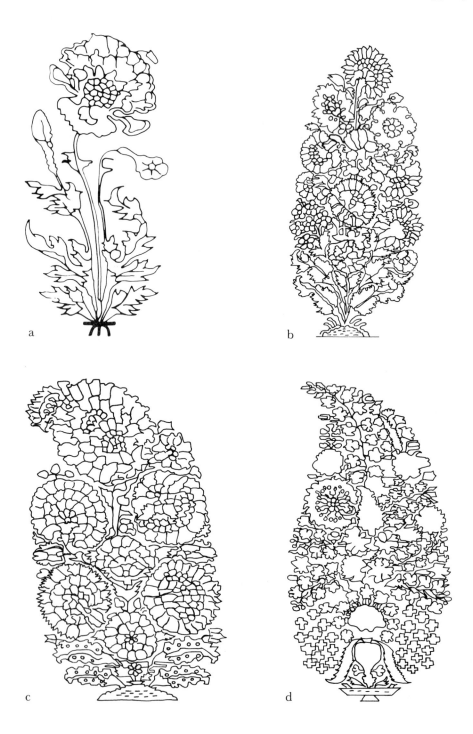

a

b

c

d

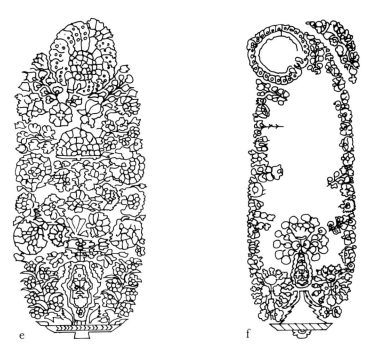

e   f

Figure 25 (opposite and above). a) Flowering-plant boteh with ideogram root, Mughal, mid-17th century; b) Multi-flora boteh with mound, Mughal, early 18th century; c) Large top-rose boteh with serrated-edge pistil and mound. Stylistic exaggeration. Mughal, mid-18th century; d) Qajar boteh with radial flower technique. Afghan period, c.1765; e) Large top-rose boteh, freely spaced flowers, millefleurs, with vase and dish, Afghan period, c.1775 (Mughal transition); f) Mosaic coif boteh with large radial top rose. Afghan period, c.1800.

a   b   c

Figure 26. Arching raceme coif botehs. Tracings from: a) Ingres 1805; b) Baron Gros 1809; c) Girodet 1810.

Figure 27. a) Tea-pot boteh, 1800; b) hooked-tip boteh, 1820; c) bent-tip boteh, 1820; d, e) buti-tip cone, 1825; f) 'sweeping' boteh, 1825.

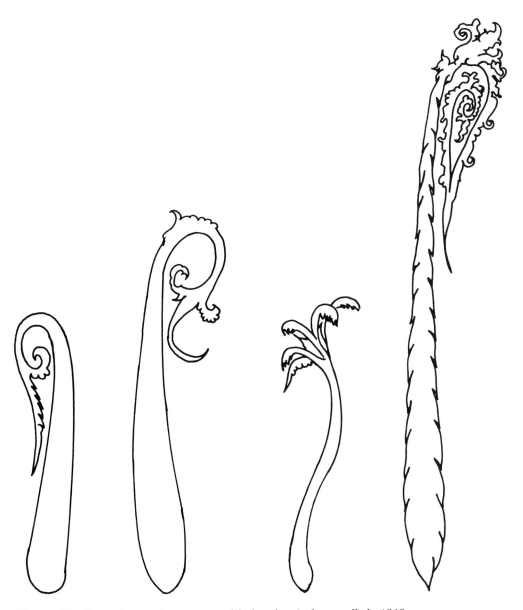

Figure 28. Berrus' sweeping zoomorphic botehs, 'celery stalks', 1848.

Conclusion

The original impetus behind the design of the shawl came from Mughal India. The Mughals' emphasis on the realistic imitation of nature in all forms of art was responsible for the early forms of the boteh being a natural representation of flowers, hence the cliché of the flowering plant. Following the Afghan invasion in 1753, however, the boteh began to evolve towards an increasingly symbolic style, first with the cone shape of the late eighteenth and early nineteenth century, then with the more elongated forms that emerged following the Sikh invasions of 1819. By this time the boteh had become the trademark of the Kashmir shawl in the new markets opened by the Industrial Revolution; it represented for the Occidental buyer the epitome of elegance and the shawl became increasingly popular in the West.

Chapter Five
Shawl Trade and Shawl Fashions in the Orient

The Persian Shawl Industry

Persia played an active role as intermediary for the lucrative commerce of Kashmir shawls but the date of the exact beginnings of her own shawl industry has yet to be established. Apart from what is known about shawl commerce, and various scattered references to Persian shawl weaving of the early nineteenth century, much of the industry's history remains in the dark. Travellers to the Orient, bent on finding out about the shawl-weaving industry, often focused on Kashmir, whose unsurpassed reputation was worldwide, and ignored Persia almost entirely. The modern textile historian is, therefore, left with few sources of information regarding Persia's indigenous shawl weaving.

Some sources do exist, if not for the shawl at least for other textiles. One of the most valuable is the Frenchman Tavernier, who made many trips to the Orient in the middle of the seventeenth century, and who commented in some detail on the Persian textile industry. He was quick to discover the value of goat fleece and went to great efforts to export it to France. During his fourth voyage, in 1654, he was informed that such wool is not dyed and that it remains in its natural colours of clear brown, ash grey, or rarest of all, white. In addition to being very costly, the white wool was reserved for the muftis, mullahs and others of the law who wear only white, both for their sashes and for the veils with which they cover their heads during prayer. He also noticed a twill weave of a special type of wool so fine and delicate that the fabric was more beautiful and expensive than if made of silk.[1] Although Tavernier often mentioned rare wool being worked at Kerman, Yezd and Alep, nowhere does he use the word shawl.

The Persian nobility was, however, very fond of sashes (patkas), which they wore wrapped around their waists with the brocaded ends conspicuously displayed. The sash represented an important dress accessory to the court costume and, therefore, few were exported. Hanway observed in 1753 that 'even in the presence of Kings the Persians wore their sashes as turbans which were made of costly Kermani wool. Finer ones were valued at one hundred crowns compared to ones selling between eight and ten.'[2]

The Persians also wore a robe called 'cabaye', which fell just below the knees, and was made of very fine toile quilted with large stitches in order to hold a batting of cotton. Tavernier explained that such toiles would be a bargain if not for the fact that they did not hold their colour; as soon as a drop of water fell an embarrassing stain developed. The sleeves were long and hugged the arms down to the wrists. Similarly, the robe hugged the body just to the waist from where it fanned out. With the robe a beautiful silk sash was worn of which the ends were ornamented with flowers in gold. On top of this, they again wore another sash made from the fine wools of Kerman. The richest sometimes wore three sashes of which the first two were silk, and the third wool.[3]

---

1 Tavernier, vol.I, p.172.
2 Hanway, vol.I, p.331.
3 Tavernier, vol.II, p.268.

From the Oriental travels of G.A. Olivier in 1794-98, we learn for the first time of an active shawl industry in Persia. Commissioned by the French government, Olivier, like many other learned emissaries, was sent to collect information on the Orient before Napoleon's incursion into Egypt. 'One million piastres worth of Kashmir shawls', noted Olivier, 'arrive each year in Bagdad by caravan and are distributed throughout Turkey. Sent by the Pacha, they often go to Constantinople by way of the Tartares [probably Turkestan]. Persia also exports Kermani shawls which have neither the beauty nor the fineness of the others.'[4]

Many shawls in the past have been perfunctorily, but probably correctly, attributed to Persian origin simply because of their coarser wool and inferior colours compared with those of Kashmir origin. The dyes, wool and even the designs appear conspicuously different. In spite of Olivier's criticism, however, some Kermani shawls did achieve a fair degree of quality. They were woven from the fleece of baby goats which grazed on the mountains surrounding Kerman. Olivier wisely remarked that the Kashmir shawl was woven from the fleece of the Tibetan mountain goat; a fact of which few people were aware at the time, especially in Europe where shawls were just beginning to become fashionable.

That valuable artifacts were made at all in eighteenth century Persia is especially amazing when one considers the hardships of daily life. It is difficult to imagine an atmosphere less conducive to the weaving of rich textiles than a country which witnessed incessant political turmoil, frequent wars, and absolute rulers who thought their survival depended on fratricide. Kerman was the scene of terrible slaughter in 1747 when Nadir Shah plundered the city, decapitated thousands, and employed their heads in the construction of a tower. He left Persia in a state of devastation and left behind a legend of cruelty that spread throughout the world. Adrian Duprés of the French embassy wrote in 1807: 'The Persian Empire, one of the most beautiful in the world, has become more or less a vast cemetery since the death of Nadir Shah.' This ghastly image describes accurately the prevailing conditions at the end of the eighteenth century.

Duprés also carefully surveyed Persia's trade and left an illuminating account of the state of shawl commerce. It appears that Bagdad was the main entrepôt for foreign merchandise coming from Persia. Besides shawls made in Bagdad itself, others were imported from Kashmir, Kerman and Kashan.[5]

Duprés noted that Yezd also manufactured shawls, but they were a far cry from the rich brocades which had in the past dazzled the eyes of the courts of the Orient as far away as China. For example, Marco Polo had visited Yezd and was awed by the incredible silks and gifted weavers of the city's flourishing industry.

By the early nineteenth century, however, all that seems to have disappeared, for Duprés observed that shawls woven in Yezd were 'of an ordinary quality'. They were composed of different colours, solid or striped. Those made of long, yellow and red stripes, in a rough-quality wool, were sent to the port of Bander Abbas. These were shipped in turn to Máscate and re-exported to India where they found a 'very active and competitive market'.[6]

While Kashmir shawls offer rich and varied shapes and designs, there is almost no such variety in Persian shawls. The earliest seem to date from just before 1800, and usually consist of variegated stripes of simple sprigs and other unrecognisable, small flowers.

During the Sikh period, however, design patterns became more pronounced. The Sikh style greatly influenced the numerous shawls of nineteenth century Persia. The

4 Olivier, *Voyage dans l'Empire Ottoman, Egypte et la Perse,* vol.4, p.446.
5 Duprès, vol.I, p.196.
6 Ibid, vol. I, pp.126, 252, 400; vol.II, pp.160, 375.

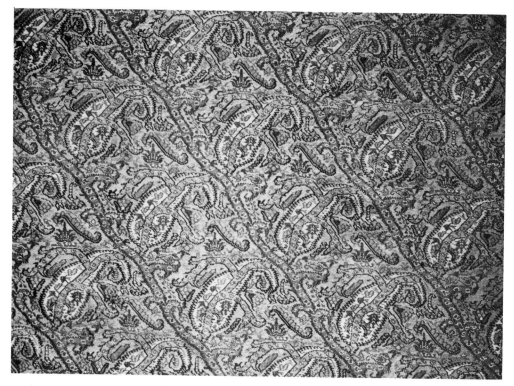

Plate 40. Persian kani shawl, Sikh period.

lance-like bent-tip boteh, the boteh resembling a stubby hook with occasionally angular sides of a geometric nature, or the boteh in the form of a teapot without handle, are all found on the Persian shawls. These are the same styles which were initially popular in Kashmir in the second decade of the nineteenth century.

The design details popular with Kermani shawls of Persia are often blurred by the rather coarse weave of their wool. Nevertheless, they retain important features of Sikh abstract designs: the concentric cone, the stacked array of rose medallions; and the rustically hooked vine instead of the forked arabesque found in Persian court carpets. It is interesting that among kani Persian weaves probably made before the Sikh period, practically no designs emerge which may be compared to the contemporary style of Kashmir. Between the simple sprig and the bold Sikh designs, we find no transitional development in Persian shawls of the boteh forms which were prevalent in Kashmir.

Persian shawls from regions other than Kerman also show strong Sikh influence. Kashan weavers used whole-component motif ideas such as leaning reciprocal botehs interspersed with tiny cone botehs resting on leafy fronds. These were widely used on carpets later on. Botehs were generally very small, rarely exceeding ten centimetres in height and almost always scattered over the field.

These observations strongly suggest that the Persian shawl industry came to life during the Sikh period. The natural calamities which devastated Kashmir during the 1830s, had caused mass emigration of the shawl weavers to the Punjab, and it is possible that Kashmiri weavers in need of work found employment in Kerman, in both the shawl and the rug industry. At the same time Kerman became a prominent supplier of goats' wool to the Punjab plains.

The study of the Kashmir shawl is aided by several sources of information. Not only do we have the rare sample pages of dye swatches found in the books of Watson (1877) or Leitner (1882) as a testimony to the chromatic past of the Kashmir shawl, but even today many an old shawl-weaving family in Srinagar still harbours, with great pride, the worm-eaten pages of a sample book containing early shawl fragments. Unfortunately, nothing of such nature has come to light concerning Persia's shawls. Chavant's *Album du Cachemirien* (see page 162) published in 1837, tells us, however, that in certain parts of Persia designs were not solely limited to the simple repeat patterns found among shawls assumed to be of Persian origin. This important document provides us with a few invaluable tracings of carpets from Teheran and Kabul, disclosing the early use of sophisticated Kashmir shawl designs. More important, however, is the disclosure of a large-patterned Kashmir-shawl design woven in Teheran (Plates 76, 77), disproving the notion that all Persian shawl designs must be of small patterns.[7]

Vigne, who travelled in the region in 1842, records that excellent shawls were also made in the Caucasus.

Style and fashion

The Persian shawl was used differently in Europe than it was in the Orient. From a noble shoulder mantle for men in the Orient it changed to a fashionable article of female attire in Europe. In Persia, its use was more as an ornamental fabric while in Europe it gradually shifted from high fashion to a more prosaic use: to keep warm in the cold winters and unheated houses.

Depending on the country and customs, the donning of the shawl had various symbolic meanings. In the Orient, however, it was a luxury article reserved only for the noble and the rich, and was considered an indispensable part of their wardrobe. By royal decree 'Princes by blood and great persons only shall be able to wear them as belts'; another edict required that narrow (Kashmir) shawls formerly worn around a bonnet (according to court etiquette) be replaced by the 'new fabrics now being manufactured in Kachân'.[8] This reveals a certain patriotism toward Persia's indigenous products, and at the same time hints of the existence of a weaving industry that was still quite young.

Persian patriotism was also described by Baron Elphinstone. Dispatched to Kabul in 1809, he established an English embassy there and wrote: 'The shawls exported to Persia are of a pattern entirely different from those seen in India or England. They were universally worn till lately when the king of Persia forbade the use of them with a view to encourage the manufactures of his own country.' The Baron was well acquainted with the industry of Kashmir shawls. His secretary who accompanied him to Afghanistan, Richard Strachey, had made 'many inquiries on the subject'.[9]

Elphinstone also describes a 'shawl carpet', found in one of the Kabul homes he visited:

> 'Carpets of highly wrought shawls are also used but this piece of magnificence must be very rare, from the enormous expense. Moolah Jaffer of Seestaun had a shawl carpet of great size, with separate pieces for sitting on, which was bespoke for Shauh Mahmood, and which was bought for a quarter of its price after the prince was dethroned. Moolah Jaffer asked 10,000 pounds for it which he said was far below its value: he intends to try and sell it at the courts of Persia and Russia and if he fails, to cut it up and sell it in pieces to the Turks.'[10]

Another type of shawl greatly admired by the Persians was the Kashmir 'khatraaz' which simply means 'straight lines' in Kashmiri. Khatraaz (Plate 41) was a striped cloth of different colours containing either tiny repeats or a type of

---

7 Chavant. *Album du Cachemirien,* pp.2-3.

8 Duprès, vol.2, p.395.

9 Elphinstone, p.290.

10 Ibid, pp.268, 269.

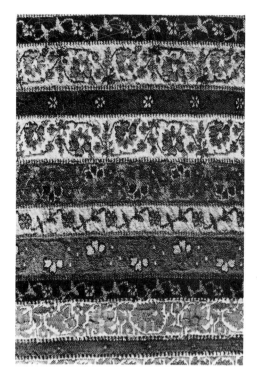

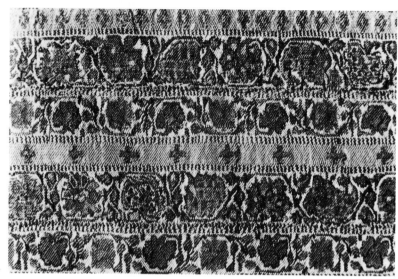

Plate 41 (left). 'Khatraaz' or striped kani cloth using hashia motifs. Afghan period, c.1800.

Plate 42 (above). 'Khatraaz' or striped kani cloth using hashia motifs. Afghan period, c.1800.

meandering floral design which ran the length of the stripes. It was normally woven in one piece, in the same dimensions of the standard long shawl, but rarely worn in the same way. The well-to-do cut it up and used it for vests, coat linings, stockings, and in general as a soft fabric worn close to the skin. 'The Persians seldom wear shawls thrown around the shoulders like the people of India' wrote Fraser.[11]

Fraser also recorded other styles popular in Persia at the beginning of the nineteenth century in his informative 'Account of the Commerce of Persia'. He wrote:

'Those which they chiefly admire are richly flowered all over, or spotted with pines [botehs] of great or less size on a rich ground, as black, blue, green, yellow, crimson or scarlet. A few of the striped patterns are liked but the former are the best.' In commenting about another type of shawl he alluded to the chandar or moon shawl: 'Square shawl-handkerchiefs are also required for the ladies; these should have a handsome centre ornament with a border to match.'[12] (Colour Plates 40, 43, pages 259 and 263.)

Arabia and Turkey had also coveted these rich fashion articles long before Europe; and their taste for the finest specimens was without equal. The Count of Modave, while travelling in the Orient in 1775, noticed their extreme popularity. He related that '. . .there is not a son of a good mother, as the saying goes, who would not want a few [Kashmir] shawls at his disposition', though he considered that the Persians did not care in the least about wearing them. The Turks thought highly of the Kashmir shawl, which they required to be richly ornamented and of the best quality. Wearing it became an important event, especially during an outing through town which of course was never accomplished on foot; walking was considered a degradation. The nobles went about Constantinople for example, on horseback, accompanied by a numerous group of lackeys and servants who attended them on foot.[13]

11 Fraser, 1826, p.369.
12 ibid.
13 Bibliothèque National, *The Costumes of Turkey*.

Plate 43. The corner detail of a fragment of a moon shawl kerchief, mid-18th century. One of the earliest kani pieces illustrating an Anglo-Mughal pattern. The chunky flower rosettes, the heavy stem and the saw-tooth leaves point to a mid-18th century style. This is the only known chandar of this period that does not illustrate a purely Islamic style. Notice the atypically narrow hashias.

During the Afghan rule of Kashmir, Jacquemont offers us a clue to the design origins of those checker board shawl patterns often seen on late eighteenth or early nineteenth century shawls (see Plates 139 and 140). He describes a pashmina cloth of which the ground is always striped in length and breadth and divided into small squares. He noted, however, that its manufacture, although very popular under Afghan domination, was practically abandoned by the time he visited Srinagar in 1831. This pattern, called 'longui' was often woven in the same dimensions as a standard long shawl. It was the Afghans' favourite turban in the winter and it was frequently woven as a belt too. The longui's colour was generally a dull dark blue, striped with red.[14]

European Textiles in the Orient

Even before Kashmir impinged on Persia's weaving industry, the country was beginning to feel the first effects of Western design products such as fine printed goods. Western textiles were already enjoying an international reputation and France especially was on its way to establishing firm political and commercial ties with the Orient.

Fraser described the impact of French textiles such as chintzes and printed cloths, on Persia in 1821-22:

'The French and the German manufacturers have been much more successful than the English in hitting the Persian taste; no doubt because they took care to have the best information upon the subject; and every bazaar had a full display of their rich and glaring chintzes, while many of our more sober English

14 Jacquemont, vol.3, pp.289-290.

goods lay neglected on the inner shelves unasked for and unseen. It would not be easy to convey an idea of the kind that would suit the eastern markets, but novelty, united with rich and well-blended colours, seldom fails to please.'[15]

The Persians were extremely fond of printed goods and manufactured large quantities. They were not equal in quality, however, to those imported from Mazulitpatam and other parts of India. French, German and English printed goods were in 'great measure' replacing those of Indian provenance. Fraser commented:

'The success of this branch of the trade depends very greatly upon the pattern sent, for fashion in this respect in Persia is to the full as capricious as in Europe, and the inhabitants will reject an excellent article merely because the pattern does not please them while they give extravagant prices for goods of a very inferior description merely because their gay colours happen to suit their fancy; for want of attention to this material point, there were hundreds of chests of printed cottons, that had been sent from Bombay, lying at Shiraz and Isphahan, totally unsaleable.'

Fraser noted that French and German patterns were 'often preferred' to those of English origin. High luxury items such as silks, brocades and embroideries, chiefly supplied by the French, also captured the Persians' fancy.

From the Paris Exhibition of French National Products in 1819 we learn that French shawl manufacturers were enjoying new markets in Germany, Italy, and the Orient.[16] Constantinople, an entrepôt for European merchandise to the East, was renowned for shrewd and capable merchants accustomed to travelling exceptionally long distances. They represented trading companies across Turkey, Persia, Afghanistan and India. The French retained company agents in these countries and as many as twelve 'maisons' were being represented in Alep (Syria) in 1804.[17]

We have no account of just how France's exact imitation shawls were received in the Orient. Unusually fine shawls, featured at the national exhibitions of French products, were often exported and the exhibit reports often describe how exquisite specimens were 'en route' towards Constantinople. These prized products represented France's highest artistic achievements, and were officially offered as cordial gifts in recognition of various political and economic agreements.

The English also sent shawls to India and although they were of inferior quality, their low price did attract a certain clientele. Fraser purchased two English imitation shawls in Bombay, at 40 rupees each, with the intention of selling them in Persia. They were of the turban type and measured 10 yards by 43 inches. From previous trips he had an idea of Persian taste, but he appeared dismayed when he was able to sell them for only 100 rupees each. The Persians, it happened, objected strongly to the rough and ragged appearance of the shawl's reverse side. Fraser conceded '. . .if this could be made more to resemble the real shawls, it would tend greatly to increse their sale.'[18]

During the same period, Moorcroft also recounted how English shawls were received. In his letters from India he explained that 'they gave great credit to British artists for their close imitations, but considered them inferior to the Kashmeeree original.'[19]

Trade Routes of the Orient

Kashmir shawls were exported, of course, first throughout the Orient, and then throughout Europe. Moorcroft has left an account of how the shawls were treated

15 Fraser, 1826, pp.367-369.
16 The French Consul Duprès along with the new ambassador, General Gardance, were dispatched to Teheran in 1805.
17 Olivier, vol.4, p.181. See also Hanway, vol.1, p.48.
18 Fraser, 1826, p.369.
19 Irwin, 1955, pp.24-25.

for export. The shawl was taken from the loom, inspected, washed and dried, and prepared for shipment.

> 'The packages are of various dimensions but they are formed on one principle: the shawls are separated by sheets of smooth, glazed and coloured paper, and they are placed between two smooth planks of wood with exterior transverse bars which, projecting beyond the planks, offer a purchase for cords to tie them together. The whole is then placed in a press or under heavy weights for some days, when, the planks are withdrawn and the bale is sewn up in strong cloth. Over this a cover of 'tús' [?] or of birch bark is laid and an envelope of waxcloth is added and the whole is sewn up as smoothly and lightly as possible in a rawhide, which contracting in drying, gives to the contents of the package a remarkable degree of compactness and protection.'[20]

The packages, or 'bedris' as they were sometimes called, exported to Afghanistan, Persia, and other destinations using overland routes, were subject to heavy taxes. In their journey towards Peshawar, north-west of Srinagar, and twenty days by caravan, the terrain was so rugged and mountainous that the route was nearly impossible, even by mule. At each resting station a toll was fixed, depending either on the bedris's weight or on just a cursory glance at the bundle. As a result, a shawl, when it arrived in Peshawar, had already been taxed up to twenty rupees. From Peshawar, shawls went on to Kabul where they were again subject to a new toll of 2½%. Following this, they proceeded to Meshed where the same fate awaited them.[21]

Information on road taxes was given by the English traveller, George Foster, who published an account of his travels 'Journey from Bengal to England' in London in 1790. Forster had concealed his Western origins by disguising himself as a Turkish shawl merchant in order to slip unobtrusively into Kashmir, unvisited by any Western traveller since Bernier in 1668. Forster noticed a large number of duty stations, thirty in all, where goods were taxed between 3% and 4%, between Lucknow and Srinagar. 'This charge', noted Forster, 'with the expenses necessarily incurred in the course of a tedious and distant land conveyance, largely enhances the price of the shawls in the lower part of India'.[22]

In addition to these cumulative custom-duty taxes, the high cost of transportation was also a problem. It varied greatly according to the route. Furthermore, strict precautions had to be taken to avoid being attacked by marauding bandits. Jacquemont informs us, for example, that 'commerce had been practically annihilated by the state of anarchy devastating the countries to the north and west of Attock (between Peshawar and Srinagar) for the past twenty years, whereas formerly it was quite considerable between India, Afghanistan, Bukhara, etc.' The brigand Turkomans, a purely nomadic tribe similar to the Kirghiz, who found easy prey among the poorly armed caravans, were a constant threat.[23] Protection was necessary; ironically the Indians often had to pay four rupees per shawl to the chiefs of the robbers themselves. On the other hand, certain areas were well guarded; in the direction of Herat, Persian troops were stationed to assure the safety of the routes.[24]

A sophisticated level of finance supported this vast movement of merchandise, showing how important the shawl industry had become. Merchants conducted their affairs through a system of credit, loans, promissory notes and money lenders. Passing through Ispahan in 1650, Tavernier recorded in detail the way in which the more than ten thousand 'banians', or money lenders, operated.

---

20 Wilson, p.186.
21 Duprès, vol.2, p.395.
22 Forster, vol.1, p.223.
23 Klaproth, 1829, vol.1, p.48.
24 Duprès, vol.2, p.395.

'They are all bankers and very adept especially in the knowledge of money. The majority of money invested by the important merchants of Isphahan is in the hands of the "banians". When in need of a large sum, a fair collateral will suffice for obtaining a loan the following day, provided a large interest is paid — sometimes up to 18%. But payment is made in secret due to the laws of Mohamet which forbids interest. . . . Normally, loaned money is amortized in three months at an interest rate of from 6% to 12%. Merchants not actually residing at the place of their purchases are required to take out new loans to pay off the old. The new money is paid off at the city of their destination. For example money from Erzerom is refunded at Bursa, Constantinople or Smyrna. Money from Bagdad is paid at Alep.'[25]

Other travellers' accounts also describe the money lenders. Mir Izza Tullah, in his travels in 1812-13, found the 'wafarush' financing shawl manufacturers and the 'mugims' appraising shawls and observed 'All merchants made their purchases through the mugims.'[26]

Victor Jacquemont wrote:

'Loudiana is the most frequented city between the Punjab and the countries to the North of Attock and India. A banker is never missing and they have their first correspondents in Amritsar, Lahore, Djeaodri, and Delhi; their relations stretch from Calcutta, Bombay, Kashmir, Attock, Peshawar, Cabul and Hérat.'[27]

The Kashmir shawls were exported by a number of different routes. Nearly all the imports and exports to and from the Punjab and other parts of India passed south through the Pir Panjal and Banishal passes, because the Jhelum Valley route was often closed to all trade during the early nineteenth century due to political disturbances. The Northern shawl trade with Tibet and Russia passed along the Ladakh and Gilgit routes (see end papers).

The earliest account of shawl commerce and activity comes from a learned French military man, the Count of Modave, who travelled in India during the years 1773-76, about half a century before Moorcroft's detailed report of the same subject. According to Modave, most bedris taking the southern routes passed through the large depot at Lahore, then descended to Tatta near Karachi, by the Indus River. The 'banians', at times merchants but most often usurers, shipped them abroad via the Red Sea.

In their descent towards Tatta they also passed through the famous trading city of Multan, from where many of the Kashmir shawls were diverted to new overland routes to Persia. Multan enjoyed great prosperity during the seventeenth century as a strategic and key city of the Mughal Empire. In 1752 it was annexed to the Kabuł kingdom and from 1771 was repeatedly attacked by the Sikhs before being taken by Runjit Singh in 1818.

Multan was renowned as a trading city; it was composed mainly of merchants and contained a larger number of factories than its rival city, Lahore. The Multanis controlled almost all commerce west between Hindustan (India) and Persia, their city being the point of reunion for caravans between the two.[28] Shawls shipped from Multan passed through Kandahar to Bagdad, joining Persian shawls woven in Kerman, Yezd and Kashan. From Bagdad they were sent on to Constantinople.

About 65 Multanis established a small colony in Astrakhan, under Afghan rule: it was witnessed by Count Jean Potocki who travelled through the Caucasus in 1797.[29] Kashmir, of course, at this time was also under the Afghan domination

25 Tavernier, vol.II, p.155.
26 Sufi, p.562.
27 Jacquemont, vol.3, p.33.
28 Deloche, p.336.
29 Klaproth, 1829, vol.1, p.50.

and their leader, Zaman Shah, resided in Kandahar. After passing through Multan most merchandise from Hindustan was sent to Turkey, South Arabia and Persia via the cities of Surat and Tatta.

John Grose, in his voyage to the East Indies in 1757, noticed that Surat, in addition to shipping shawls also manufactured them, but remarked that there were 'but few and not many of the finest sort'.

Modave explains that the Kashmir shawls arriving in Tatta were practically the only article of merchandise transported to the Western countries. This was carried out by Indian merchants who, from the sixteenth to the seventeenth century, had established a series of colonies stretching from the Persian Gulf to the Caspian Sea, from Shiraz to Astrakhan and from Kandahar to Isfahan.[30] Basra, at the western end of the Persian Gulf, was the principal port-of-call for shawls arriving from Tatta and Surat. Quetta, situated between Multan and Kandahar, was also a principal shawl market. Apparently, the latter city contained a shawl-weaving community as early as 1794.[31]

On the north-west routes, the shawls that left Kabul for Bokhara were eventually traded by Khivan merchants in Russia by way of Orenburg and Astrakhan. These merchants resold some of the shawls in their hometown of Khiva and the remaining ones were carried into Russia. In addition, Bokhara, Meshed, Kabul and Andijanin all had their own shawl-weaving production centres.

Bokhara, in spite of the political upheaval at the end of the eighteenth century, enjoyed a very active commerce under the influence of an impartial and calm government. It was situated on the great caravan route. Fraser remarked: 'There are two, not more, caravans per year which pass between Bukhara and Russia, but each consists of from 4,000 to 5,000 camels in a journey lasting three months.'

Shawls sent via the northern routes continued their journey to Tiflis, Georgia, located mid-way between the Black Sea and the Caspian Sea. This important city was the major stepping-stone for Oriental goods departing for the great cities of the north: Amsterdam, London, Saint Petersburg, and Moscow. During the nineteenth century, the famous fair of Niji-Novgorod attracted quantities of rare merchandise which were purchased by merchants of all nationalities including many French who came from Paris.

France received her shawls through resident agents in Constantinople or Moscow; Marseilles received shipments coming from Alexandria, Smyrna and Constantinople. The Rhine frontier near Strasbourg gave entrance to shawls arriving from Marcarieff via Moscow and Vienna while Bordeaux's trade was limited to Bengal. The major French companies however, imported directly from Kashmir.

Honigberger, in 1852, suggested that shawl transportation should not be by the long route round the Cape of Good Hope, but by the Red Sea and the Mediterranean, or if possible entirely overland because unless shawls are hermetically sealed they invariably suffer from the sea voyage.

In general, however, most shawls shipped to London went from Bombay via the 'John Company' or East India Trading Company. In London, auctions of the merchandise would take place for three days twice a year, in December and June, attracting dealers from many countries.

Through this variety of land and sea routes, then, the Kashmir shawl was brought to world-wide markets.

---

30 Deloche, p.339.
31 Singh, p.95.

Chapter Six
Shawl Weaving in France

In previous chapters the exposure of the Kashmir shawl to foreign influences has been discussed but the argument has been confined to shawls made in the Orient. In this chapter French attempts to manufacture a shawl which could compete directly with those arriving from the East are considered.

It has been suggested that the popularity of the shawl first began in England, and that it may have been the English who first began copying it. However, recent studies of the European shawl do not mention whether England ever employed the Indian weaving method. This chapter, therefore, discusses not only France's distinguished development of the kani shawl, but also France's great mechanical invention, the Jacquard loom, which eventually provided all of Europe with an efficient means of manufacturing the 'Kashmir' shawl.

When Napoleon returned from Egypt, the generals and officers who had served under him brought back mementoes of the Orient. Among these were Kashmir shawls which they wore wrapped around their waists as belts, and which had been plundered from the Mamelukes, the soldiers of the Egyptian Army. Contemporary artists vividly captured France's oriental exploits through portraiture, often depicting a subject dressed in full military uniform with a Kashmir shawl worn as a belt, as in the colossal painting by Baron Gros, where Napoleon is shown walking

Plate 44. A caricature mocking the Kashmir shawl's high fashion, 1795.

among victims of the plague ('Napoléon visitant les pestiférés de Jaffa', Louvre Museum).

Napoleon's return also brought important new trends in fashion. Feminine fashion simplified itself and women began wearing sheer white décolleté dresses. This caused a need for warmer outer garments, and the Kashmir shawl was an ideal solution in terms of beauty, warmth and texture.

The most important factor in the growth of the shawl's popularity, however, was the Empress Josephine (Plate 29). She lived in a most creative period of female fashion and her clothes deserve to be studied as representative of the social history of her era. She was the first to adopt the 'robe de simplicité', and the triumph of the revolution made the fashion of a simplified dress universal. Endowed with infinite charm rather than beauty, Josephine was the paragon of the well-dressed woman. Her extravagance in clothing and jewellery was legendary; she changed her dress ten times a day and never wore the same pair of stockings twice. Her wardrobe contained hundreds of the rarest of Kashmir shawls. When buying, she was reputed never to ask the price.

At that time England, with its virtual complete control of the seas and its mighty East India Trading Company, maintained an almost complete monopoly over goods coming out of India. Not only was France ruined financially by the Empire wars, but in 1786 she had signed a commercial treaty with Britain which turned out to offer many more advantages to the British than to the French. Despite the Continental Blockade of 1806 by which Napoleon had sought to isolate the British, much foreign merchandise continued to enter France as contraband. The silk manufacturers of Normandy and Picardy were completely crushed by British competition.[1] Much of the silk weaving was therefore phased out and their looms began the weaving of woollen 'Kashmir' shawls. Picardy was the major region for shawl production after the shawl prototypes had been designed in Parisian ateliers.

First French shawls

The French shawl during this transitional period was born out of the industry of ladies' scarves made of silk gauze with a plain weave. The borders were narrow, the botehs thin, slender and brocaded in silk in one or two colours. They were made on the drawloom and the wefts were left uncut on the reverse side.

In 1805 the first shawls with trimmed reverse sides (découpés) were wefted in wool on silk warp with five or six colours. The use of more colours necessitated the operation of trimming as the shawl began to accumulate extraneous weight and lose its softness. The weave was not strong enough to prevent the wefts from falling out — a dire deficiency which had to be immediately rectified. Out of this urgency a system of heddle play (jeu de lisse), operated by the foot of the weaver, was invented to consolidate the weave. The method was called 'pas de liage'. Although this strengthened the wefts, the pattern suffered becuse the warp covered half the point forming the flower.

In view of these technical difficulties and the very high demand for Kashmir shawls, dealers were thwarted in their attempts to satisfy the market. It is not surprising, therefore, that French manufacturers set about finding new ways to fabricate their own 'real' Kashmir shawls: first, exact imitations of the Indian original, and then new styles which followed French ideas of design and innovations in production technology.

In 1806 the production of shawls of silk warp and wool weft necessitated the need for looms of a more complicated nature. The common drawloom contained four hundred pulleys arranged in eight rows of fifty each. Even with two warp threads

---

1 Martin, vol.3, p.319.

Turban fait avec un fichu de Mousseline Brodé.

Caricatures Parisiennes.

Les Modernes. N.º 2.

A Paris, chez Martinet, Libraire, rue du Coq N.º 15 et 15.

Plate 45 (left). A First Empire shawl, 1804. The laurel wreath was then a popular theme in ornamentation.

Plate 46 (above). A contemporary fashion illustration, c.1805, entitled 'the Modern Woman', a study in ostentation.

assigned to each pulley it was impossible to make the design larger than twelve to fifteen centimetres. In view of this limitation, a way was found to augment the number of pulleys to 1,200 in order to copy the Indian shawl. This became a complicated and expensive method since a second drawboy was required to handle the tremendous increase in drawstrings.[2]

The exact imitation shawl

The 'exact imitation' shawl was made either on a real Indian loom, or a similarly constructed French loom, called 'à espouliné' using a twill-interlock weave. These shawls were so well made that they were often sold, not as imitations, but as bona fide Kashmir.

The person credited with having first woven one of these shawls was Bellanger, a wool maker from Rouen, who was associated with Dumas-Desolme.[3] Since the

---

2 London Universal Exhibition, 1851.
3 Bellanger died in 1829 whereupon his company was absorbed by the Ternaux family.

first public exhibition of an imitation Kashmir shawl occurred in 1802,[4] we must assume Bellanger produced his shawl somewhat before this time. Subsequent national exhibitions of French industrial products often refer to him as having made and 'revealed the shawl to the commercial world'. It appears that he was sent a beautiful Oriental shawl by a far-sighted general of the Expeditionary Army, and he immediately prepared a drawloom with a special harness invention and weave composition in order to copy it.[5]

Deneirouse, considered doyen of the French shawl industry, pointed out that Bellanger was a 'man who knew how to predict and prepare the future of an industry. He succeeded in producing a natural flower shawl conserved by his family with religious care, in perfect conformity to the most beautiful shawls of India.'[6]

Héricart de Thury, who followed closely the early developments of shawl weaving remarked: 'The Maison de MM. Bellanger Dumas and Descombes is one of the oldest in Paris. It is to this company that France owes her first "shall" of silk and cotton with fringes, and they were the first having tried to imitate Kashmir shawls with silk and wool, with such success that France produced shawls worth 20 million francs during several years of which a large part were exported. This was achieved before Lyon's shawls in 'bourre de soie' or silk floss, came into favour.'[7]

There had, however, been a possible precursor although whether Bellanger knew of it or not is open to conjecture. It appears that in 1785 there was an attempt to establish Indian weavers in Thieux, France. It is not known from what part of India they came or whether they were knowledgeable in kani shawl techniques, but it would appear that their work involved the weaving of toile or linen cloth.[8] A Monsieur de Montaran, Master of Petitions and Intendant of Commerce, was charged by the government to oversee and record the daily expenses of these weavers. The attempt was short lived as the work proved unprofitable.

Bauson and Girard

The Indian technique, called 'châle espouliné', received its name because shawls made in this manner were woven with 'espoulins' or tiny wooden needles similar to the tojis used on the Kashmiri loom. Although Ternaux and a few other wool manufacturers had a small fraction of their shawls woven by this method, Bauson, a former associate of Bellanger, was the first to come up with the idea of establishing an atelier uniquely devoted to this type of weaving. Bauson's atelier received much public attention because he employed young orphan girls. He developed special weaving techniques using a loom of the Indian type. M. de Thury, in reporting his findings to the Interior Minister, described Bauson as being the 'inventor of certain processes which are particular to himself and not used in any other of the numerous ateliers which I visited and studied'.[9]

Bauson started his atelier in 1808 in Sèvres, and entreated the French government to give him financial aid on the grounds that his company 'contributed to the progress and perfection of industry'. His requests were not met and in 1815 he offered his company to the state in order to be made a National Industry, similar to the tapestry manufacture at Gobelins. Bauson argued for this in a letter addressed to the Duc de Duras:

'If the atelier is given the title of "Manufacture Royale", several weaving establishments of this type would be formed in various orphanages in Paris, an

---

4 Rézicourt, Jobert and Lucas and Co., Reims, were the first to exhibit an imitation Kashmir shawl. They were associated with the Ternaux brothers.
5 Bellanger employed the same weaving technique as in India. Expo. 1839.
6 Deneirouse, *Traité. . .*, p.10.
7 Expo., 1819, p.10.
8 National Archives Paris F12-2414, letter from Héricart de Thury.
9 ibid.

establishment which would have much in common with that of Gobelins, the only difference being that it takes a long time to train a weaver at Gobelins but very little for the Kashmir; the weaving is done mechanically without art and only two to six months are necessary for an apprenticeship.'[10]

It became clear at this point that the government was turning a deaf ear, not only to Bauson but also to a great many anxious and industrially creative entrepreneurs eager to embark on new ventures. Financial aid was very scarce and the government was fiscally ruined by the costly Napoleonic wars. Furthermore, the Restoration of the Bourbons brought with it a large influx of foreign merchandise and the English took advantage of this opportunity with low-cost products resulting from their head start in the Industrial Revolution.

Bauson remained, however, obstinate in his demands to the Interior Minister, Le Comte de Vaublanc, since he felt that it was highly unjust that his company should not be nationalised. Finally in January 1816, the following year, he was asked to sketch an outline of the types of shawls he proposed to offer.[11] He supplied the following estimate of shawl prices:

Shawl, 2.5 x 1.5m, white ground and large cones and borders according to the fineness and richness of design: 900-1,500 francs

Shawl, 1.5 sq. m, flowered ground without borders: 390-550 francs

Shawl, 1.5 sq. m, striped with flowers, without border: 480-700 francs

Shawl, 1 sq. m, striped without borders: 400-500 francs

Shawl, 1 sq. m, flowers, without borders: 330-450 francs

Bauson then decided not to solicit any further subsidies either from the King or from the French government, but to attempt simply to obtain the privileged title of 'Fabricant de Cachemire de Son Altesse Royale Madame La Duchesse d'Angoulême'.[12] In this way his merchandise would receive preference over foreign goods, and he would be one of the exclusive suppliers to the Court of Louis XVIII. This concept caught the fancy of the Duchess and, after a few years, Bauson received her official sanction. Although consoled, he never seemed fully content. The Government insisted all along that Dumas and Descombes, as well as Bellanger and Ternaux, had all made imitation shawls before Bauson.

Bauson's work was finally exhibited in the National Exposition of French Industrial Products, 1819, where he received a silver medal for 'having imagined fabricating shawls, with an *easy and prompt process,* executed by children under the guidance of an experienced worker'. The Central Jury also said that 'the shawls made by Bauson are in every respect similar to the real shawls of Kashmir and can be delivered to the market at a lower price.'[13]

Bauson, however, was outraged at not having received a gold medal, and he wrote a letter a few months later expressing his disgust and disappointment with the government's attitude (or rather the attitude of the Central Jury) and boldly demanded a passport and permit to take his looms out of France into another country where he would be appreciated![14]

Bauson's anger was finally appeased by receiving a gold medal in the Exposition of 1823. The government, to reward his years of labour, also offered him a stipend of 300,000 francs.[15] His reputation had grown internationally and the King of the Netherlands, it seems, took a great interest in his shawls and offered to put a large establishment for the fabrication of Kashmir shawls under Bauson's direction.

---

10 National Archives Paris F12-2414, letter from Héricart de Thury.
11 ibid., letter dated 18 Jan., 1816.
12 The daughter of Louis XVI.
13 Expo. 1819, Rapport du Jury Central.
14 National Archives, Paris, F12-2414, letter of 22 Oct., 1819.
15 ibid., letter of 27 April, 1822.

A popular motif used by Bauson in his early shawls was the 'arlequiné' — a design very much enjoyed by Parisians (see Plate 64), first produced in great quantities in Srinagar. The arlequiné shawl consisted of a palla in which each boteh repeat was compartmentalised by a separate ground colour. He claimed to have achieved, through his own dye experiments, tonal nuances which imitated exactly and with 'absolute harmony those of India'.[16]

The loom techniques employed by this scrupulous shawl-maker were very similar to those of Kashmir, except of course for the fact that he engaged young orphan girls as weavers. An experienced worker sat in the centre and carefully directed two apprentices to his left and right. A shawl was woven at the rate of one and a half centimetres per twelve-hour day. Bauson's hand-woven shawl was the result of a long, tedious process; eighteen months were required for the completion of a long shawl. However, H. de Thury remarked, 'In spite of their cost, Bauson's shawls were selling daily as Indian ones *without* any suspicion they were made in France.'[17]

If Bauson was never completely satisfied in his relations with the government, he was probably even less happy in his relationship with a former associate, Girard, who also solicited government help. Girard established an atelier in 1819 using the knowledge of weaving techniques acquired from Bauson when they were close friends.

A case was submitted to the consultative committee of the Arts and Manufactures disputing whether Girard or Bauson had contributed most to the 'progress and perfection of industry'. Bauson had woven a long, white, superfine shawl to be presented to the committee as proof of his ability and technique. It had large, rich palms, borders and counter borders along with corner palmettes, and the complete shawl had been conceived *without any lost stitches or seams*. He was well aware that Girard's weaving methods were questionable: it was very easy to fabricate a shawl 'en bridant', by floating the wefts on the underside of the shawl in such a way that the weaving would be accomplished with one hundred espoulins instead of the three hundred ordinarily required. The brocading of the wefts in certain areas of the motif was much simpler and quicker than the interlocking technique. Bauson, a meticulous craftsman, greatly resented this sort of trickery.

The outcome of this long dispute is unclear, because neither man left complete accounts. Girard's company however, did successfully establish itself in Sèvres, with twelve looms and fifty workers, all abandoned girls. Like Bauson, Girard had found a patron, Madame La Duchesse de Berry, and received a silver medal for his fine espouliné shawls in the 1827 Exposition.[18]

The Jacquard Loom

France's strong inertia to modernization was reflected by the long delay in her industrial revolution, and it was due to the influence of a few Englishmen that industrialisation finally occurred within the wool and cotton industry. Macloud had first introduced the carry-barry or flying shuttle to France in 1778, but its use remained very limited until 1815 when, due to Napoleon's encouragement, the cotton industry began slowly to adopt it. Undoubtedly the greatest impetus came from Douglas, an important muslin manufacturer from Manchester, who offered his knowledge and mechanical-engineering experience to the French nation.

As early as 1788 he had proposed the construction of new machines for spinning

---

16 National Archives, Paris, F12-2414, letter of 10 August, 1821.
17 Expo. 1823, p.94.
18 Expo. 1827, p.55. It is interesting to note that the Duchesse de Berry and the Duchesse d'Angoulême detested each other.

Plate 47. The original Jacquard weaving loom, 1804, surmounted by Jacquard's mechanical invention. The mechanism is composed of hooked needles and spring-loaded pins which enmeshed with each of the successive pre-programmed punched cards to form the fabric's pattern.

wool and preparing cloth, but here again resistance was encountered and his ideas were not adopted until 1802. Finally, a brilliant English engineer by the name of Cockerill, under the patronage of Ternaux, devised ways and techniques to improve the French wool industry.[19]

While French industry was busy taking advantage of English technology in Paris, Jacquard was perfecting his new invention in Lyon. In order to arrive at a final prototype, however, Joseph Marie Jacquard studied the eighteenth century inventions of Falcon and Vaucanson which had been stored away for years in Paris. The study was performed under the sponsorship of the government which finally recognised his ingenuity.

The invention of the Jacquard loom had an important effect on the history of the Kashmir shawl in France. Jacquard's popularity began with the public exhibition in 1801 of an eight-pedal loom for which he received the Bronze medal. In 1803 the Société d'Encouragement pour l'Industrie Nationale offered a prize for any one who could come up with a rapid method of weaving fishing nets. Jacquard was invited to demonstrate his new loom. The members of the investigating jury were impressed, and he was awarded a patent on the 18th December, 1805.[20]

During the same year the Society again offered a prize of 3,000 francs for a proper loom to fabricate all kinds of figured and brocaded cloth. Jacquard's creativity again prevailed and in 1807 the Comité des Arts Mecanique announced that he had found the solution to the problem and the 'usage is now generally adopted in Lyon'.[21]

19 Lomüller, pp.63, 95, 155.
20 Prat, p.xv.
21 ibid., p.xvii.

Until that time, we find absolutely no mention of its application to the manufacture of shawls. But the time was ripe and it appeared that at least a few far-sighted individuals began considering this new possibility. Jacquard was now a government employee fulfilling his contractual obligations. He received an annual stipend but asked a mere fifty francs per loom. For each group of machines that were completed and placed into service, he dispatched an itemized account in a letter to the Chamber of Commerce requesting his due payment or 'prime' payable under an imperial decree of 1806. Fifteen looms were put into service during the period 21st–29th April, 1806, but only sixteen were completed during the first three months of the year 1811. All told, fifty-seven looms were made during the years 1806-11.[22]

Like many an innovator before him, Jacquard met with the traditional resistance to change, and to uncertainties of income. The authorities of Lyon, his home town, had stopped payments to which he was entitled. Rumours spread that Jacquard was in Paris seen talking with foreigners, and the Chief Commissioner of Lyon wrote to the authorities in Paris asking that Jacquard should be ordered back to Lyon 'before he sells his invention to the English'.[23]

It seems unlikely that Jacquard would have betrayed his country however. When James Watt was commissioned by the English Government to buy his invention, Jacquard replied, 'I regard it a sacred duty to leave to my native town a discovery which could furnish a foreign nation with a way to ruin our industry.'[24]

A critic at the 1834 exhibition observed that the Jacquard loom was introduced in Paris in 1816, 'not without difficulty', by Fournier Aîné and Co. (Fournier was most probably a shawl manufacturer.) This was the first time Jacquard's name was mentioned by an exhibition critic. The arrival of the Jacquard loom in Paris, in 1816, brought a relief from the difficulties inherent in the drawloom.

Jacquard's underlying intention was not so much to increase the speed of weaving and eliminate the drawboy, but rather the more humane desire to alleviate the excruciating forced child-labour prevalent throughout the industry where boys as young as ten were used to working the existing drawlooms. A boy would raise each of the warp threads through a system of cords. At each throw of the shuttle he was obliged to pull on these stretched ropes which were counter-balanced by heavy lead weights. Furthermore, he was required to call out the necessary weft colour as read from the design in order that the master-weaver could choose the right shuttle. This was an extremely arduous task for children to perform.

The operator of the drawloom had to depend on the drawboy to see that the warps were raised to the right height. If they weren't, the shuttle would often break some of the warps due to the lack of space between them. Another inconvenience of the drawloom was the time required for the boy to choose and pull the cord, not an automatic movement but one which demanded thoughtful hesitation.

The early use of the loom, however, brought new problems which could scarcely be overcome except by substantial modifications. Apart from the actual weaving itself, a whole new group of people had to be trained to use the loom and this of course accounted for a big delay in its initial operation. Before the drawloom could be abandoned it was necessary to reduce the immense quantities of expensive cards indispensable for each design on the Jacquard loom. This is why the loom was limited to small motifs in the beginning.

Just where the first Jacquard shawl was woven is not known, but it is very likely that the Parisians were the first to use the Jacquard loom for this purpose. One enterprising manufacturer proposed to the government, at the early date of 1817,

---

22 National Archives, Paris, F12-2199, letter dated 2 May, 1811.
23 ibid., letter dated 10 Nov., 1814.
24 Grandsard, pp.108-109.

the establishment of a 'new shawl industry using the Jacquard loom, in which three to four hundred workers would be occupied'.[25]

The early Jacquard loom ruined many of the businesses which used it; even after almost twelve years use, employees still lacked motivation and showed resistance towards the machines. Nevertheless, larger companies were able to furnish themselves with more elaborate technology and with the perfection in the spinning of pure kashmir wool, the obstacles which formerly impeded the use of the Jacquard loom were overcome.

By 1822 at least eighty Jacquard looms were being used in Paris to weave shawls of pure kashmir wool. This left a total of 3,190 drawlooms operating in Picardy and Paris together, of which 2,340 were being used to weave shawls.[26] The largest quantity of shawls sold in Paris were woven in Picardy, in such places as Fresnoy-le-Grand and Bohain.

How many Jacquard looms were operating in Lyon is not known but the exhibition of 1823 tells us that both Nîmes and Lyon were represented by twelve manufacturers who certainly employed some Jacquard looms. Once again, the rejection of the loom within the weaving community is manifested by the fact that it was not mentioned at all in either of the two preceding exhibitions in spite of the fact that eighty were in full operation in Paris.

Later on in England the Jacquard loom was employed extensively in shawl making but remained rather unsophisticated up until the mid-nineteenth century. An important French manufacturer, commenting during the exhibition of 1851, ascertained that most of the British looms were lacking the most necessary technical improvements.[27]

The Jacquard operation

The Jacquard loom operates on the principle of punched cards which, when pressed against spring-loaded metal pins, control the raising of the warps. Those pins which align with the holes are pushed through the card, forcing their corresponding crochet needles — or hooks as they are sometimes called — to be raised by vertically moving blades upon which the hooks become caught. Those pins which do not encounter a punched hole are pushed back, horizontally, moving the hooks out of the way so that the moving blades do not lift them.

The figure shown on page 122 is a cut-a-way profile view of an early Jacquard which exposes the pins and hooks in order to give us a clear view of the inner mechanism. This represents a very elementary version of a Jacquard, connected to a comber board which is threaded to weave a cone shawl. This is a very simplified drawing. Here each of the four cones would actually need 400 warps to make up the complete width of the shawl. It is, however, impossible to make a drawing rendering all 1,600 warps.

One can, however, imagine the same mechanism showing 400 hooks and warps instead of the five shown, to perform this weaving. As hook number one rises, it pulls with it four warps, one from each cone. The shuttle (not shown) is then thrown, using the appropriate colour, and the motif begins to form. As the blades descend releasing and picking up new hooks, according to the instructions read from each succeeding card, the next set of four warps is raised and the operation repeats itself. This action is done by the weaver who pulls a cord causing the card-carrying device to rock back and forth.

---

25 National Archives, Paris, F12-2414, letter dated 22 Oct., 1817.
26 Chambre de Commerce, Registre de Commerce T4, Rapport de Ternaux et de Bellanger sur l'Industrie Parisienne de Châles et de Gazes, Séance de Juillet, 1822.
27 Gaussen, 1851 exhibition, vol.4, p.7.

Colour Plate 10. Long shawl, Paris, First Empire. The design is attributed to Isabey, and woven by Ternaux, it is a very rare example of French espouliné weaving with silk warps and cotton wefts. 48 threads per cm. 12 colours. 134cm x 264cm.

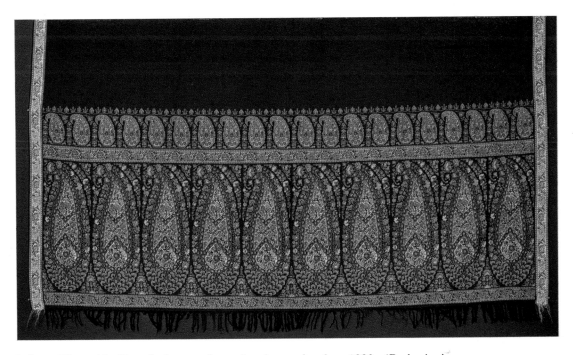

Colour Plate 11. French Jacquard or drawloom shawl, c.1820. 'Pashmina' woollen weft. The long borders are sewn on. 141cm x 298cm.

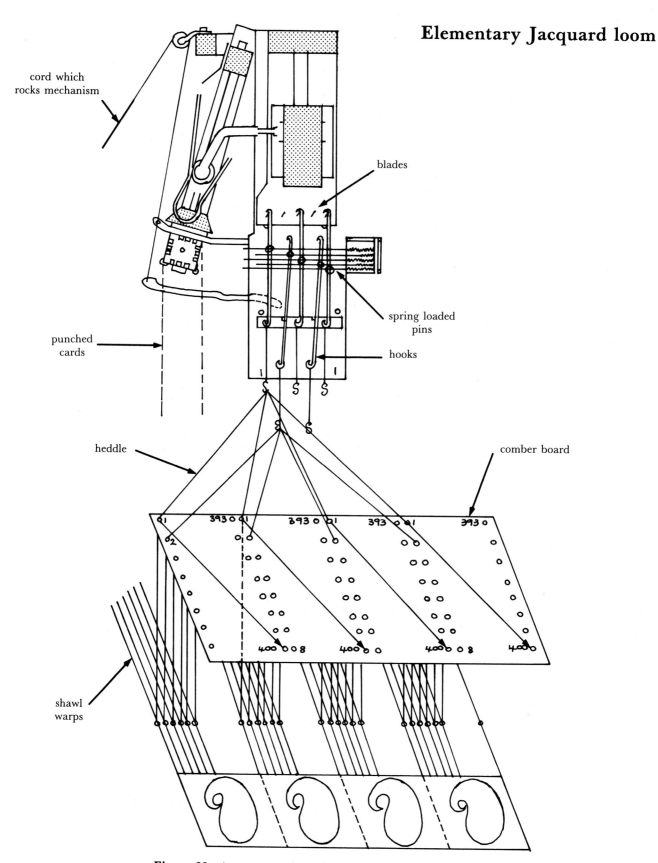

Elementary Jacquard loom

cord which rocks mechanism

blades

punched cards

spring loaded pins

hooks

heddle

comber board

shawl warps

Figure 29. A cut-away view of an elementary Jacquard loom.

122

If the number of cones is increased to eight, four more cords would have to be tied to each hook. Therefore, it can be said that the number of times a motif is repeated is equal to the number of cords tied to each hook. Of course, as the repetition is increased, the array of cords from the Jacquard to the comber board becomes more complicated. As a matter of fact, a Jacquard loom set up to weave a shawl appears to be an absolute nightmare of threads spraying off in all directions.

As the cone (boteh) grew larger and more sophisticated in design, a larger number of Jacquard cards were required. On the other hand, the smaller the motif, the fewer the cards required. It is impossible to enlarge a cone motif without increasing the number of hooks. Figure 29 also does not show the 100 or more additional hooks needed for the weaving of the end borders so necessary for the embellishment of a shawl. The early looms did not have these hooks; because of this we find that the borders were made separately for the early shawls, and then sewn on (Colour Plate 11, page 121), once the shawl was removed from the loom.

Until Deneirouse (see below) and a few others paid serious attention to the improvement of the Jacquard loom, the designs were first limited to small repeats not larger than 15cm wide and a few years later to about 20cm with looms utilizing 600 needles. There was still a limitation to the number of needles which could be put into the mechanism without incurring enormous expense. Furthermore, the early Jacquard cards were large and bulky, and designs employing many colours increased their number. Storage was also a problem since they took up a large space.

The early Jacquard loom was thus unable to imitate the contemporary large Indian designs; the machine was originally made for the weaving of silk, and design effects were produced without the use of heddles. Its repeats were small compared with the large size of the Indian boteh which at this time measured about 50cm in height. In order to weave larger patterns it was often necessary to return to the drawloom but here again it was impossible to enlarge the pattern beyond 12 to 15cm.

Jacquard who had spent so many years developing his loom, abandoned making innovations entirely around 1812, and just supervised loom production. it was not until the end of the first quarter of the nineteenth century that something was done to alter the destiny of this revolutionary loom.

Deneirouse — shawl maker and inventor

Deneirouse, like Jacquard, is one of the great names of the French shawl industry, a shawl manufacturer and innovator who in 1851 published a treatise on shawl weaving in France, a work which had taken him ten years to write. The Treatise had a twofold purpose. Firstly at a time when France was going through an economic slump, and when shawl makers were feeling the pinch, Deneirouse suggested a whole new industry which would alleviate unemployment, gain national approval and at the same time help the depressed shawl weaving centres of France, in Paris, Lyon and Nîmes.[28] Secondly, and of less importance, he wanted to defend his development of the 'papier briqueté', which had been wrongly attributed to another prominent shawl maker, F. Herbert, in the report of the 1839 Exhibition.[29]

At the Exhibition of 1823 two shawls had received attention for the remarkable colour effects and 'the beautiful execution of the palms and borders'. They were the work of Ysot and Eck, using new espouliné techniques. In the treatise Deneirouse paid tribute to them and wrote: 'None of the ''espouliné'' shawls exhibited by any of us [Deneirouse also was an exhibitor in 1823] approached [them] either in design

---

28 Gaussen, 1851 exhibition, vol. 4, p.61.
29 ibid., pp.18-22.

Colour Plate 12. French Jacquard shawl, c.1860. Pashmina woollen weft. 141cm x 365cm.

richness, beauty of the weave, colour vivacity or purity of design in perfect harmony with the fabric.'[30]

When the Ysot and Eck company was dissolved and their espouliné looms, designs and accessories were put up for sale, Deneirouse became aware of Eck's special 'encartage', where each 'duite' or combination of weft colours was painted separately on a card in a 'most complicated fashion'. Deneirouse commented:

> 'I was so taken back by the admirable harmony in their shawls, absolutely similar to those of India, that I resolved to apply this system to the French shawl [drawloom or Jacquard] of which the manufacture seemed to me much more important than using the Indian method.'[31]

This system was the papier briqueté, which Deneirouse simplified first applying it to the drawloom, and above all the Jacquard loom. Within a few years of his discovery, practically all shawl makers were using it.

The Indian designs, once woven, lost the curvilinearity they displayed formerly on paper to re-emerge with outline shapes in broken and jagged lines. Deneirouse's mise-en-carte took advantage of this fact. The mise-en-carte is the technique by which a pattern is transferred from sketch to special cross-hatch paper, which provides the loom with warp/weft instructions. Each coloured square of the paper represented the weft crossing over or under a warp. On the papier briqueté (a type of cross-hatch paper, see Plate 49) the artist was able to draw freely and in total liberty without regard to the printed lines on the paper. Each square, or brick as it was called, represented four warp threads which could be raised by one hook of the Jacquard.

Deneirouse realised also that within the Indian technique there were two weft passes, one exactly the same as the other. The same Jacquard card had only to be repeated in order to imitate the 'caillouté' or rocky style. This had the effect of building up the flower in a step-like fashion, and imitating very closely the Indian shawls. This idea reduced the number of cards required by fifty per cent.

New techniques in shawl manufacturing were kept as closely guarded secrets and

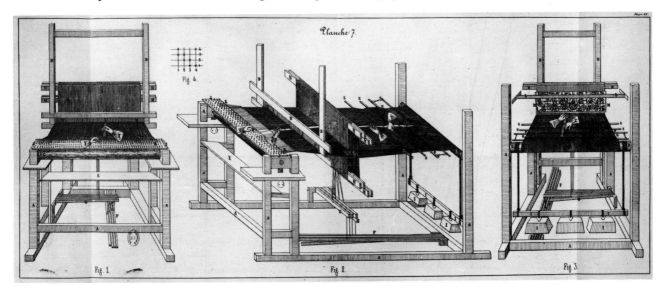

Plate 48. Three views of Deneirouse's efficient espouliné loom without mechanism. The papier briqueté was not required and a separate reader at the opposite end of the loom counted and raised the warps.

---

30 Deneirouse, *Traité...*, p.19.
31 ibid.

because of this Deneirouse worked in tight secrecy in his home town of Corbeil, without the knowledge of his colleagues, between 1824 and 1827. The repeating of the Jacquard cards, along with the papier briqueté, reduced the cost of reading the designs by ninety per cent, and at the same time it was possible to make larger patterns.

Deneirouse's treatise explains the fundamental weaving technique of espoulinage, which involves a choice between two different looms, one of which was a stripped down version of the Jacquard loom. The other loom was fairly similar to that used by Bauson.

The first method consists of a unit very similar to the Jacquard mechanism but simpler (see Plate 49). Instead of the quantities of punched cards which formerly contained the design information, here we have drawstrings directly attached to the Jacquard pins themselves. The other ends of the strings drop vertically alongside the loom, falling across rollers containing the coloured-in design drawn on the papier briqueté. Each 'brique', or grid, represents a minute fraction of the design which is translated to the cloth by a drawboy reader who pulls on the thin string (thin enough to hide the grid). At the same time the weaver passes his espoulin (bobbin) through the warp threads with one hand and with the other he hooks or crochets the succeeding bobbin around the first one, thus interlocking the wefts. This is done

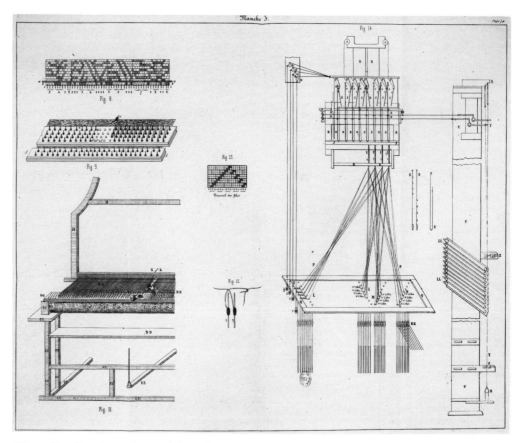

Plate 49. Deneirouse's special mechanical loom based on a stripped-down version of the Jacquard machine. In Figure 14, the reader, in pulling on the heddle cards (YY), raises the hooks which ride up on the blades of the 'griffes' (C). The weaver then steps on the pedal (EE, figure 11) raising the warps (KK) and brocades with his espoulins (HH). Figure 8 shows the papier briqueté across which the heddle cords fall, shown by the numbers. Just below is shown the punched-hole board which organises the espoulins. Figure 15 shows how adjacent weft colours were interlocked with the espoulins (tojis).

until the complete width of the fabric is crossed once in both directions and the twill weave is completed.

Deneirouse pointed out that the advantages of using this method are twofold: firstly, whereas before it was necessary to employ a mechanism in complete harmony with the motif, it was now possible with the design mise-en-carte, a double-core loom, and a one hundred-needle maechine, to execute the most complicated designs using the total width and length of the shawl. Secondly, a shawl made with only one repeat required only three workers: one to read the design and two to brocade.

The second method was much simpler than the first, in that no mechanism was employed. The only prerequisite was that the repeated motif did not exceed 40 centimetres. This loom differed from that employed in Kashmir in that the Indian worker was obliged to count the warps himself and then brocade them, while Deneirouse's system allowed a separate reader to count them *while* the weaver manipulated his bobbins. Thus the weaver, who was formerly occupied with counting warps and then brocading, had only to pay careful attention to the brocade itself (see Plate 48).

It does not seem that the first method was very successful. Deneirouse wrote that he 'would have continued to make shawls by this process if [he] had been able to do the designs of all the widths which were asked of [him]'. One of the main advantages common to both methods, however, is Deneirouse's unique idea of a board, punched with holes, in which the bobbins are held in place while waiting to be used. If we imagine a weaver confronted with hundreds of espoulins in a confused pile and then having to choose the right one, this new method of bobbin allocation can be highly appreciated. Deneirouse argued that although the Indian weaver was extremely adept in counting the warps and choosing the tojis, whatever the dexterity of the worker, a certain lapse of time could not be avoided. The Deneirouse techniques saved time.

Rous, Comet and Co., a creative weaving concern from Lyon, went so far as to make shawls simultaneously using the Jacquard and espouliné methods, thereby imitating the Indian shawls that did not require being shaved on the underside.[32]

Girard continued this technique, and received a gold medal in 1839, despite the pervasive influences of industrial mechanisation, for his '...perfectly successful, Indian-shawl imitation'.[33]

Further developments of the Jacquard Loom

In the late 1820s Bosche, a shawl maker associated with Deneirouse, brought another innovation to the Jacquard loom. This was called the 'double griffe' or 'mécanique brisée', meaning 'split mechanism' or 'split Jacquard'. This technique placed an additional set of blades within the Jacquard. Two hooks were now attached to each of the spring-loaded pins. When the blades rose they took the hooks with them. Those which normally remain at rest would work because of the new set of blades. Thus while one set of blades is rising the other is descending.[34]

The Jacquard loom had now undergone a complete metamorphosis. The double griffe made two Jacquard mechanisms out of one without increasing the size of the unit. It was now an easy matter to place two of these Jacquard machines on one loom which could be put into action with the weaver's foot. Designs of 175cm in width could now result from the manipulation of 6,400 warps. The drawloom, even with the addition of more pulleys, was limited to designs of only 15cm at the most.

32 Expo. 1834, Le Baron Charles Dupin, p.93.
33 Expo. 1839. vol.1.
34 Prat, p.96.

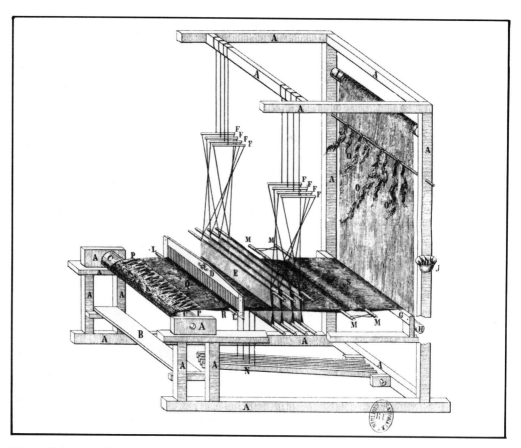

Plate 50. According to Deneirouse this illustrates the Indian loom 'in all its simplicity'.

By 1839 the main centres of shawl manufacturing, Paris, Lyon and Nîmes, each manufactued a different kind of shawl. Paris was the leading fashion centre and generally manufactured the finest shawls.

In Paris three types of shawl were woven: firstly, the 'cachemire pur', woven entirely with the goat fleece of Kashmir. This rarely had less than eight colours, usually ten to eleven, and sometimes as many as fourteen or fifteen. Secondly, the 'châle indou cachemire' which had a warp of silk 'fantasie' and a weft of pure cashmere but fewer colours were employed. Thirdly, the 'châle indou laine' which had a warp of silk 'fantasie' and a weft of fine wool with three to six colours.

In Lyon the 'châle tibet', with a mixture of wool and 'bourre de soie', woven in a square or a rectangle 3 x 1.5 metres, and the 'châle en bourre de soie', with a warp and weft of silk, were woven, though by 1839 it was almost entirely the 'châle tibet'. The 'châle indou', with a warp and weft of inexpensive wool, was woven in Nîmes.

By 1857, Paris and its outskirts contained a total of 729 Jacquards, of which 253 were inactive due to unemployment. Of those remaining in service, about 95 were working to supply furniture fabric. The following is the record of an independent worker using three Jacquard looms, and shows his production during the years 1853-56:[35]

> 1853: 50 long shawls at 94frs each, 33 square shawls at 50frs each
> 1854: 24 long shawls at 94frs each
> 1855: 14 long shawls at 94frs each, 32 square shawls at 76 frs each
> 1856: 24 long shawls at 94 frs each

---

35 *Ouvriers de Deux Mondes,* p.301. Without doubt these were low quality shawls.

Mass Production of the Kashmir Shawl in France

During the Exposition of 1827, Rey exhibited an espouliné loom, but by the Exhibition of 1834, nobody was talking about espouliné shawls any more, most probably because of the tremendous advancements in the Jacquard loom. This method, however, was not forgotten, for the French considered its lack of speed just another problem to be overcome by rapid mechanisation. Such mechanisation was not long in coming.

The 1844 Exhibition cites a certain M. Richard, who designed a machine called a 'battant brocher' to weave shawls by a type of brocading using the espoulinage technique. Although it had not as yet been perfected, the invention received praise for its ability to insert a weft crossing of twelve colours (douze lais). This was seven colours more than any previous machine and, therefore, represented a substantial advancement.

In 1862, Fabard, a shawl maker, invented a machine called the 'battant espoulineur', which seemed to solve many of the problems involved in espoulinage. Unfortunately, the national exhibition archives leave us with very little information regarding the shawls made with this technique, saying only that they displayed the 'same aspect, same rich colours and the same relief, . . . imitating fairly completely those of India'.[36]

The Exhibition review of 1867 contains two references to the mechanization of 'les façonnés brochés'. 'The substitution of the motor for handwork in order to activate the shuttle of the battant brocheur' and 'the set-up of the simultaneous action of the battant lanceur and battant brocheur results in the complete elimination of the brides or weft floats'.[37] This is the first time that reference is made to automation in the shawl industry but in fact since the references concern the perfection of a technique one may assume that some looms had been operated automatically by the (steam) motor for possibly quite some time before 1867. The long shawl in Colour Plate 9, page 95, and Plate 53 is the only known example which illustrates the battant brocheur technique.

The importance attached to this developing industry should not be under-estimated. Since four million francs worth of Kashmir shawls per year were being imported into France,[38] French manufacturers were anxious for new innovations, and Fabard's was an exciting one. In only twenty days and using twenty looms, a complete 'Kashmir' shawl could be woven. In 1862 orders were arriving from all over France with Paris as the centre of activity.[39] Fabard was adamant in asking the French government to prevent a wealthy English company from buying up this new industry. The British offer, of course, was not without several exacting conditions: the shawl maker *and* the looms were to be exported to England. Although information leading to the conclusion of this affair is not complete we can assume that the deal was not consummated because five years later, in the 1867 Exposition, Lecoq and Gruyer were recognised for having made these shawls in France.

By this time, the shawl was on its way out of fashion. This 'counterfeit' sector of France's Kashmir shawl industry was mentioned by critics in the 1862 World Fair in London. A Monsieur Herbert, it was noted, had succeeded in applying an entirely new process of espoulinage and had been able to deliver to the trade, in a short period of time, about two thousand shawls for a total of 400,000 francs.[40]

---

36 Expo 1867, Rapport du Jury, vol.4, p.226.
37 ibid., vol.9, p.209.
38 Expo. 1851, p.9.
39 National Archives, Paris, carton F12-2414, Personal letter to the Comte de Persigny, 20 Nov., 1872.
40 Universal Exhibition of 1862, London, official catalogue.

Counterfeit or Kashmir

Serious study into the fashion, design and weave technique of the French Kashmir shawl has only begun in the last few years. Setting the stage for the first major shawl exhibition was the Musée du Costume, Paris, in 1982, followed by the Musée de l'Impression sur Etoffes, Mulhouse, and most recently the Musée Historique des Tissus, Lyon. All three provided a starting point from which to uncover the many mysteries surrounding the prolific shawl industry of the nineteenth century.

This burgeoning interest has brought to light the problem of recognising the difference between a European Kashmir and a real Kashmir shawl. At present there is no extant exact imitation shawl which can be said with certainty to be of French origin. Unfortunately research in this field is lacking and only a chemical analysis of dyes and wool could provide us with positive proof. However, in spite of the lack of scientific information there are from time to time 'Kashmir' shawls appearing on the market which have an irrefutable wrong feel and look to them. The following brief discussion therefore attempts to show how a counterfeit may be recognised.

If we were working with hand and machine-made carpets, our task would be greatly simplified. This is because we would be dealing with large scale designs woven with heavy wool. The stiff patterns of the mechanical rugs would be immediately detectable. With the Kashmir shawl, however, one is dealing with finely woven 'miniatures' whose designs must be closely inspected, often through a magnifying glass. This would be even more the case if shawls woven with Deneirouse's mechanical espouliné method are ever found.

To begin with it should be assumed that all shawls made in the Orient used the twill tapestry technique of interlocked wefts. These shawls will show on their reverse side many dangling loose threads, some ending in hand tied knots and others jumping from one colour area to another. But most important of all is the visible ridge formed by the interlocking threads between the large areas of colour.

One of the easiest shawls to copy was the moon shawl — possibly because of its small dimensions. During the second quarter of the nineteenth century many of them came from the Punjab. They were made of rough quality wool and their crude designs were so abstract that flowers simply became geometric areas of colour. Recently, a chandar or moon shawl with warps of red silk and interlocked wefts of thick merino wool, was found in a private collection (Colour Plate 13, page 133). It was woven in one piece, which is rare for a shawl of average quality made for a commercial market. And because there are no central joins we find that the botehs run across the entire field all in the same direction. In view of these characteristics and the European-type colour dyes employed, it was most probably made in France.

The French had expressed their disenchantment early in the nineteenth century over the poor quality of shawls arriving from the Orient. Many shawls were made of different pieces which were often poorly sewn together or were badly woven and in need of instant repair. France's 'exact' imitation industry intended to counteract this problem by offering to the public a shawl entirely woven in one piece. A strong sense of pride was involved, as evidenced in the letter sent by General Allard from Kashmir in 1837 (see page 35). One criterion, therefore, for determining whether a shawl is an imitation is whether it is woven all in one piece. Very few Kashmir shawls were, even before the great period of patchwork shawls, and those which were, are usually of exceptional quality and design which suggests that they were from court ateliers. A good example of a possible 'exact' imitation is found in the Textile Museum of Washington, D.C. It is a classic dochalla of few colours and although weft interlocking is completely absent, the shawl represents a very rare example of what the French called 'cachemire français'. Its weaving technique,

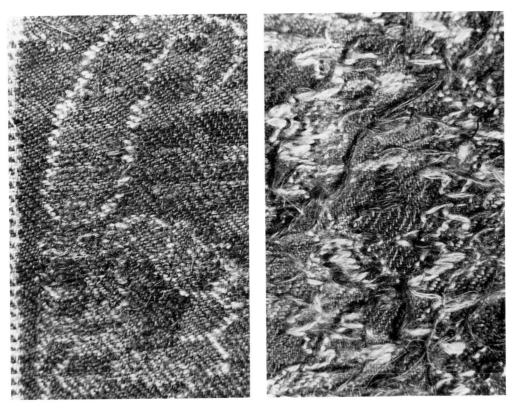

Plate 51 Magnified detail of the front and back of a coarsely woven kani shawl in merino wool.

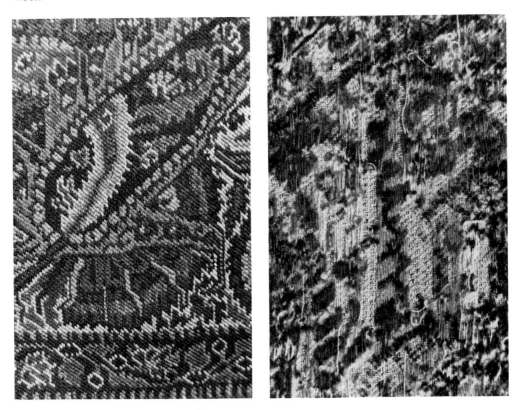

Plate 52. Magnified detail of the front and back of a finely woven French Jacquard shawl.

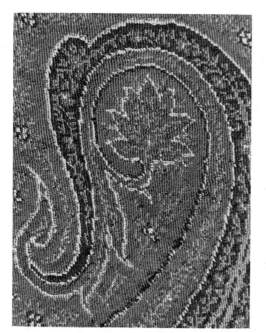

Plate 53. Magnified detail of the front and back of an extremely rare shawl known as 'battant brocheur' a weave which closely imitates the kani weave (see Colour Plate 9, p.95).

called 'broché' or brocaded, was similar to the Indian technique, in its use of the 'espoulins'. These were tiny thin sticks around which the thread was wrapped and which were used to insert the precious imported goat yarn with the same care used in the methods of brocading precious metals, like gold and silver.

Shawls woven on the Jacquard loom are not called exact imitations because of the obvious differences apparent even to the unsophisticated eye. Examining the reverse side of a Jacquard shawl one will find that the weft threads create thin coloured lines which dash across the shawl with a mechanical linearity. All loose and floating weft threads have been razor clipped with fine regularity. Running the hand over the reverse side, there is a touch sensation of rough flannel or of the low cut pile of a soft carpet. The Jacquard shawl has embroidery only on very rare occasions: on the fringes of very fine French shawls. The finer ones frequently have fringe gates which are interlocked using the 'espouliné' technique something the English fringes lack.

There is no difference in an early shawl woven on a drawloom from one woven on a Jacquard loom. According to Gabriel Vial,[41] France's well-known authority on early weaving technology, 'it will be practically impossible to distinguish patterned cloth woven on a drawloom from that woven on a loom equipped with a Jacquard mechanism'.

The first silk employed in imitation Kashmir shawls was called grenadine. It was composed of two silk yarns slightly twisted, but given a high torsion when combined together. Grenadine, supposedly, simulated very well the grain existing in the real Kashmir cloths. French shawls prior to 1813 were almost always made with a silk warp since the imported Indian goat fleece was too difficult for the contemporary French 'fileur' to spin. Consequently, imitations made entirely of pure Kashmir wool would most probably not have appeared until at least that time. The first yarn of pure Kashmir wool was spun mechanically in 1813 by Hindenlang, one of France's important shawl manufacturers.

---

41 Currently Sécretaire Général Technique du Centre de Documentation d'Etude et de Textile Ancien, Lyon. See Bibliography.

Colour Plate 13. French moon shawl, c.1835. 158cm x 158cm. This is a possible example of the espouliné kani weaving technique with woollen weft and silk warps.

Dye colours also play an important role when distinguishing real Kashmir shawls from their French imitations. The French were more able than the English to approximate closely the Kashmir colours, but variety was limited. The Kashmiri possessed an extraordinary sense of colour based on centuries of weaving experience. Shawls coming from the Punjab were heavier and bulkier with a predominating deep red colour. Jacquemont observed that the most popular colour in the Punjab and in India was scarlet, followed perhaps by white.[42] Amritsar was famous for making the best shawls of the Punjab and its dyes came close to those of Kashmir but the wool was limited to that from the local plains sheep and imported Kermani goat fleece.

The next criterion for determining the authenticity of a Kashmir shawl is the technique with which the centre field was joined. This was obviously a great point of interest for Moorcroft who was in Srinagar in 1821. The discrepancies he observed in the woven field are particularly interesting in light of this discussion:

> 'The cloth [matan] thus made is frequently irregular, the threads of some parts of the wool being driven up tightly, and in others left open, from which results a succession of bands, sufficiently distinguishable whilst without colour, but still more obvious when dyed. The open texture is, in a degree, remediable by the introduction of fresh threads; but there is no sufficient cure for that which had been much compacted. One might be led to suspect that there existed some radical defectiveness in the principle of this mode of weaving, not readily mastered, were not pieces of cloth found occasionally of an almost perfect regularity of texture. But the greatest irregularity is discoverable in those shawls which have the deepest and heaviest borders... Such indeed, in some instances, is the degradation of the cloth in the field, as to induce some foreign merchant to cause it to be removed, and another piece to be engrafted within the edge of the border.'

It is odd that Moorcroft does not discuss the weaving competence of the Kashmiri rather than the 'principle of this mode of weaving'. He continues:

> 'But in this case there is no other remedy than a judicious selection of a sheet of the same breadth and fineness; for although two breadths of the narrow cloth might fit the vacant space, yet these must be joined by the rafugar in the middle; and although this can be so done that the bands differ *not in thickness* from the rest of the cloth, yet the join is discernible when held between the eye and the light, from the threads in the joined breadth being *not continuous in the same line*; whereas any irregularity of this nature is drowned in the edge of the border. The best practice to insure a good field seems to consist in weaving the border, in every case separately, and inserting the field by the rafugar.'[43]

Moorcroft does not mention that even when the matan was woven *with* the shawl, it rarely spanned the whole centre as *one* woven piece. Most fine Kashmir shawls contained at least one and often two seams in the matan where the border was *woven* with the field. These seams can be more easily detected, however, by locating the discontinuity in the hashia caused by the difficulty in aligning the design at the end of the pieces. Nevertheless, the hashia was so well joined that an observer might have trouble identifying the matan's seam, even if he held the piece up to the light. Occasionally, the enmeshed warp-ends protrude above the surface of the field; in this case, the seam is easily found.

Legoux de Flaix described how the Kashmiri employed a special darning needle, very long and supple, capable of meshing the warp threads together. Along with other highly specialised techniques, unique to the ancient craft, this has now been lost. If the matan has been entirely replaced, it would have either been sewn or spliced in but in both cases the Kashmiri was clever enough to conceal the front seam with delicate, floral embroidery.

---

42 Jacquemont, vol.3, p.287.
43 Wilson, vol.1, pp.181-183.

Chapter Seven
The French School of Shawl Design

When the Kashmir shawl's boteh was introduced in the West at the end of the eighteenth century, people were immediately intrigued by its meaning and form. The boteh excited interest more by its colour and shape than by its composition, which was rather confused and the French were inspired to adapt uniquely French designs. In Europe, except for clothing made of colourful printed cottons, most ornamentation had been added by the laborious process of rich embroidery. People must have been quite astonished when they first came into contact with these polychromed woollen fabrics, for clothing made by tapestry weaving was unprecedented.

Christopher-Philippe Oberkampf (1738-1815)

Christopher-Philippe Oberkampf was a leader in textile fashion who set up a cotton printing factory in Jouy-en-Josas. The brilliantly coloured motifs for which his establishment became famous acquired the popular name of 'toiles de Jouy'. Inspired by Indian and Oriental designs, these glowing fabrics were envied by all Europe.

Oberkampf began to copy the various boteh patterns found on the shawls brought back by the officers of Napoleon's Egyptian Army. A notice on the frontispiece of an important design album (Plate 55) found among the vast collection he left following the 1840 demise of his factory, reads: 'Most were copied from the first shawls and scarves which were introduced in France at the beginning of this century [1800] by the officers of the Egyptian Army.'

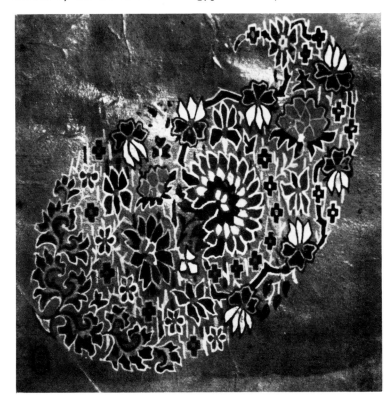

Plate 54. Boteh tracing from Oberkampf's early album, c.1800.

Plates 55a and b. Shawl tracings from Oberkampf's early album, c.1800.

Figure 30. Patterns for printed cloth, Oberkampf, 1808.

Plates 56a and b. Fantasy patterns for printed cloth, Favre Petitpierre, c.1800.

Oberkampf was not a shawl manufacturer, but the boteh patterns he collected represented a significant addition to his design repertoire. He miniaturised them into tiny, repeat motifs for his printed cotton production. Small repeats were very popular at this time and were regularly employed on early printed imitation shawls of cotton and silk.

This miniaturisation is illustrated in one of Oberkampf's albums entitled 'Étoffes Imprimées' or printed cloths. The album is important because it shows the various design changes which occurred between the years 1804 and 1811. We find that he did not actually incorporate the boteh into his printed goods until 1808. Oberkampf employed mainly the outline, or form, of the boteh and avoided the confused floral 'filling' which would have encumbered the overall design. His style shows a cubist-like reduction of the Indian idea into geometric pieces, much as the French created a mélange of African and cubist art one hundred years later (Figure 30).

Petitpierre, Fay and Brulé

Another textile manufacturer, Favre Petitpierre, further illustrates the early development in France of the boteh, or cone, as it was frequently called. A contemporary of Oberkampf, he too elaborated upon the Indian cone in the designs of his cloth-printing productions in Nantes. One of his albums shows exquisite hand-painted motifs in handkerchiefs and neckerchiefs. Here we begin to see the boteh in its full Western form: a kind of zoomorphic convolution with definitely elongated and bent-over tip. There were also other changes; instead of a compact shape filled with irregular and uncommon flowers, we see a simplified design, which resulted in a composite abstraction more suited to European taste (see Plate 56).

These fantastic conceptions foreshadowed future generations of boteh patterns. As a matter of fact they might have been one of the moving forces which engendered the boteh revolution. Already the bent tip of the cone had a rococo element, with one drooping tip as a ribbon which suggested a series of repeated end-to-end parallelograms (see Plate 56b).

The French, with their innate artistic sense and curiosity, were naturally intrigued; not only did they desire to understand these strange Oriental images but they also wanted to transform them into something more suited to their own textile industry. A remark by a reviewer of the 1844 exhibition of French industrial products provides insight into how they viewed the boteh: foreign patterns were '...confused and condensed motifs which end in points...bizarre fruits and crawling branches which wrap around adjacent objects, a confused mass where the eye hardly recognizes either the form or the object...'[1] This remark was typical of those heard earlier in the century as well.

That the Orient represented an exotic mélange of mysticism, religion and customs is demonstrated, perhaps, by the alien paintings exhibited by the 'Orientalists'. The French attached a religious meaning to the boteh symbol, while in reality, as we have seen, it was the result of various floral and vase designs evolving over many years.

In addition to the boteh, floral patterns were also a fashionable design motif on shawls, scarves, and dresses at the beginning of the nineteenth century. The Empress Josephine again serves as an example. She ran into debt just to be able to appear for a single evening in an astounding sheath gown to which fresh rose petals had been carefully sewn. The gown was also profusely embellished with the rarest of exotic feathers and brilliant, dangling pearls.

Two Parisian designers, Fay and Brulé, also demonstrate the importance of floral fashion (see Figure 31, overleaf). They maintained artist ateliers during the periods 1809 to 1824 and 1810 to 1815, respectively. Fay's creations of botehs (palms) and embroideries of 'cashemire' were displayed at the 1823 national exhibition.[2] A contemporary album at the Musée des Arts Décoratifs contains dated drawings of both artists.[3] We see that shawl patterns of a floral nature were not only employed but were also very popular, years before Isabey's famous sketches (see below).

Ternaux and Isabey

The exhibition of 1806 had already shown evidence of industrial progress; most enterprising gauze manufacturers turned towards shawl-making since gauze was not suited to the shawl. In addition, the imitation shawl was having certain problems in the French market. A few years later the well-known industrialist, Ternaux, wrote to the Minister of Interior, Montalivet, of a plan to remedy this situation:

---

1 Expo. 1844, Musée Challamel, vol. 1, p.39.
2 Expo. 1823, Rapport du Jury, L.H. de Thury, p.78.
3 See album No. BB31 Musée des Arts Décoratifs.

1814. *Costume Parisien.* (1446)

Turban de Mousseline, pardessus de Cachemire.

Plate 57 (left). French Kashmir coat illustrating floral fashions, 1814.

Plate 58 (below). Empire shawl, possibly from Fay's atelier, c.1815.

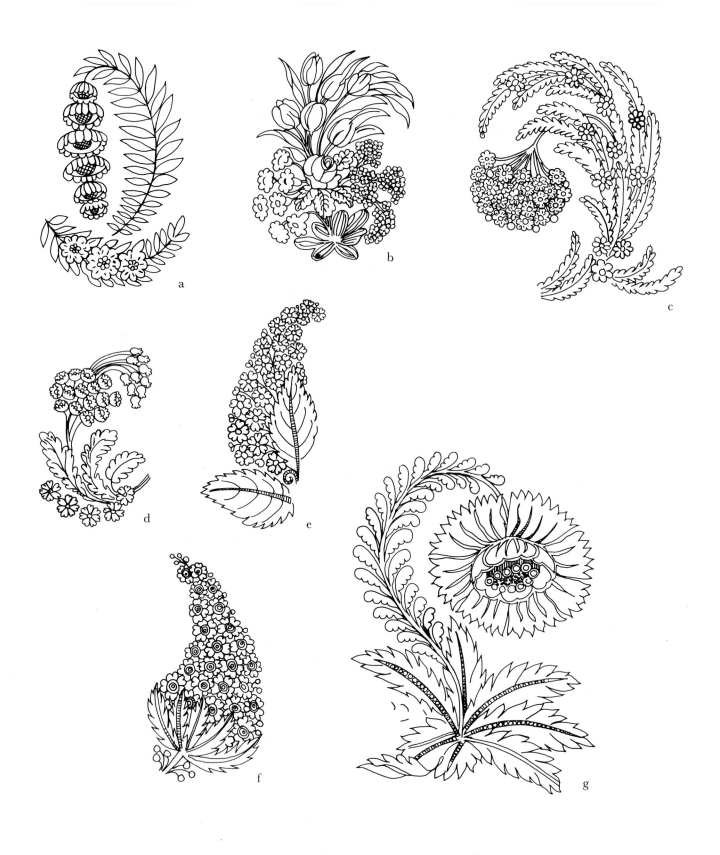

Figures 31a-31g. Seven 'Cachemire' designs for embroidery. a) Fay, 1811. b) Fay, 1811, for the baptismal robe of the King of Rome, born March 20, 1811. c) Fay. d) Fay, January 25, 1817. e) Brulé, July 17, 1812. f) Brulé. g) Brulé, December 18, 1810.

'You know, Monseigneur, with what fury luxury seeks the Kashmir shawl; what quantity of revenue this import takes away, and how much one scorns everything which calls itself imitation. The prejudice concerning this is carried so far that women, agreeing that a ''cashemire françois'' of 600 francs is as good and as beautiful as that which comes from India at a cost of 1,800 and often 3,000 francs, reject the first just because it is ''imitation''.'

The imitation shawl was, after all, only an imitation. Ternaux, a penetrating observer of fashion's caprices, saw that the moment had come to modify its design, not only for his benefit, but also for that of the industry. He continued. 'One is beginning to get tired of these palms [cones] from India without getting weary of the fabric.'

Ternaux asked Napoleon to order twelve shawl designs from the well-known miniaturist and colourist J.B. Isabey. On December 31, 1812, twelve shawls were handed over to the Emperor. Napoleon offered them in turn to his new wife Marie Louise. Although her influence upon fashion was not nearly as dramatic as that of her predecessor, the inspiration of the first lady was always of great importance, and Marie Louise thus played her part in setting the fashion for the 'châle français'. She gave several shawls to her ladies-in-waiting, and also wore them to promote this latest trend. The new style was a triumph. On February 1, 1813, just a month later, the *Moniteur Universel* announced,

'the shawls of MM. Ternaux are a perfect product and the weave has the necessary solidity. The designs are the work of our best artists, and far from the bizarre and confused designs that one sees on foreign shawls. The palms [cones] are replaced by bouquets and garlands imitating the most beautiful European flowers whose clear colours and fine nuances have something of the appearance of painting.'[4]

Parisian society followed Ternaux and Isabey's example; people sought out the 'châles ternaux' which became the latest word in fashion. The flower shawl became popular as Ternaux began to divert women's attention away from the Kashmir shawl of India towards the new French one.

Unfortunately no trace of Isabey's shawl sketches has been found, nor has any shawl yet been found which may be attributed with absolute certainty to Isabey's winter collection. However, the Musée de la Mode et du Costume of Paris in their recent exhibition devoted to the French Kashmir shawl, uncovered three interesting shawl specimens which may very well represent part of the missing collection.

Two of them were lent to the exhibtion by actual descendents of the Ternaux family who had preserved them as heirlooms and considered that they were originally woven by Guillaume Ternaux. The first one is a white shawl measuring 274cm by 146cm, with a 11.5cm border composed of a natural flower meander, having nothing in common with Oriental botany. The second, exhibiting similar attributes of draftsmanship and dyes, is a long cream coloured shawl measuring 264cm by 134cm with palla ends patterned with botehs in the form of naturalistically drawn bouquets of European flowers. The stems of the bouquets are secured to the right of the boteh's base by a graceful snake-like vine which forms the remainder of the bulbous shape. The bouquets culminate at the top in the form of an arching raceme imparting a final delicate touch to a design of extreme elegance. The third shawl, conserved by the Musée des Arts Décoratif of Paris, is identical to the second one (see Colour Plate 10, page 121).

All three shawls were woven in the espouliné technique and display incredible craftsmanship comparable to the fine shah tus shawls of the Mughal period. This is all the more bewildering when we consider that the twill interlock weave was

4 Lomüller, p.179.

Plate 59. Square shawl. Couder, c.1839. This 'renaissance' shawl is obviously a simplified rendition of a cross between the 'Ispahan' (Colour Plate 14, p.144) and the 'Nou-Rouz' (Colour Plate 18, p.154).

virtually unknown in France a little more than a decade earlier![5] A report given to the Société d'Encouragement pour l'Industrie Nationale described the shawls as '...beautifully executed and of fine and tight weave differing from those of India only by the *economy of manufacture which accelerates the work*' (author's italics).[6] This implies that there must have been an efficient loom weaving system which predated Deneirouse's by at least twenty years. From the provenance of these pieces, their superior weave, and the similarity of their design to that described in 1813, we can say that at least part of the Isabey collection has been found.

French designs earlier in the century were stagnant at times but not because talent was lacking. In turn-of-the-century Paris classical Greek and Roman designs were all the rage and a Parisian woman just was not up-to-date unless she was dressed in sheer white muslin, with a high waist and low neckline, and draped in a genuine Kashmir shawl. Not until the 1823 exhibition did the floral motif attain large scale commercial popularity. Its success appears to have lasted throughout the 1820s but it waned by the time of the 1834 exhibition. Perhaps the French public grew tired of the floral motif. Nobody can deny, however, that it provided the groundwork for the first major school of French design.

---

5 It is well known that Ternaux was acquainted with the espouliné technique because of his close association with Bellanger.
6 Alcan, 1847, p.269.

Plate 60. Corner detail of a square shawl by Couder, c.1839. Manufactured by Gaussen. 11 colours. 190cm x 194cm. No mention of this spectacular Jacquard-woven piece has yet been found in French literature. The cartouche repeat of the border recalls the contemporary patterns of the Savonnerie carpet factory.

We have seen how early imitations borrowed traditional ideas from the Orient, as well as depending heavily upon floral designs, the fashion craze which swept Paris early in the century. The discovery of the Jacquard loom, however, not only revolutionised the production of textiles but also opened doors to new areas of design creativity.

With the advent of the imitation shawl there was a sudden need for talented designers. In 1826 shawls valued at 32,000,000 francs were manufactured of which over a quarter were exported.[7] In 1820 and 1822 laws had been passed which prohibited the importing of 'cachemires et les soies de l'Inde',[8] and France relied heavily on purchases made in London from the East India Company. Shawl manufacturers engaged in a desperate search for new motifs.[9] By the Paris exhibition of 1834, however, the ban on wool imports was abolished and Kashmir shawls were freely entering the country on payment of customs duties.[10]

Jean Baptiste Amédée Couder (1797-1865)

Jean Baptiste Amédée Couder, well-known industrial designer, writer, and brother of the painter Louis-Charles Auguste Couder, was the first artist to distinguish himself in the field of shawl design. He opened an 'atelier de dessin' in Paris in 1820,[11] in which work was not limited to shawls, but included many original designs for tapestry, embroidery, rugs and furniture. He is most famous for his series of shawls known in France as the 'renaissance' shawls.[12]

7 Expo. 1827, vol. 2, p.66.
8 See, Henri *Esquisse de l'Evolution Industrielle de la France de 1815 à 1848,* Paris, 1923. These regulations were demanded at the insistence of the French manufacturers who felt undercut by the increasing amount of contraband.
9 Fichel, p.6.
10 In 1796 a law prohibited the importation of 'étoffes tissées' or woven cloth mixed with silk and animal fleece, Lomüller p.180. Rey claims that Parisian shops openly sold Kashmir shawls which had been smuggled into France.
11 Expo. 1855, vol. 3, p.1,223.
12 The best known of these shawls are the 'Nou-Rouz', the 'Odalisque' and the 'Ispahan'.

Colour Plate 14 (two views). The Ispahan shawl, French.
11 colours. 184cm x 184cm. This mandala-like shawl of which
only one known example survives, is of paramount importance in the history of European Kashmir shawls. Queen
Marie-Amélie, impressed by a painting of the shawl exhibited
at the National Exposition of 1834, ordered a woven copy of
it. Amédée Couder, its designer, combined the then newly
advanced and highly complex Jacquard-loom technology with
the severe requirements of the shawl's sophisticated design
in colour contrasts and high warp-weft resolution. Persian inscriptions are found in the centre and under the trio of
minarets in the shawl's corner. They read respectively:
'Couder and Gaussen 1834'. 'Ispahan' and 'Exhibited at the
Exposition of French manufactured products 1834'. See exhibition catalogues, Lévis-Strauss, 1983, pp.56, 64, 65, and
1982, p.82. See also Ames, 1982, p.59.

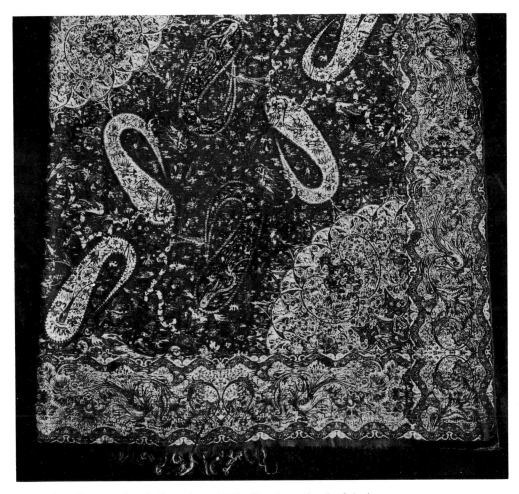

Plate 61. Square shawl, French, c.1835. Couder school of design.

Couder travelled to India several times; his long and perilous voyages served to sharpen his innate talents and offered him the opportunity of combining two rich cultures. He was a man of intense human understanding and, far from being preoccupied with his own self-interest, he devoted a great deal of his time to teaching industrial artists. Still, as much as he influenced the French shawl, many of his ideas often ran counter to the general mood and taste of shawl fashion, perhaps because his designs, based upon strong architectural concepts and luxurious if not baroque ornamentation, often carried over too much the now dated Empire style.

Couder was well liked and admired by his colleagues. In 1835 the Central Jury of the Exhibition of French National Products awarded him the title of France's most outstanding industrial designer. In 1850 a petition was signed by the most distiguished shawl designers of Paris requesting his nomination to the Legion of Honour.[13]

Couder's interests in industrial design were extremely varied, and he later devoted much time to architectural endeavours. In 1840 he proposed a full plan and description of a 'Palais des Arts de l'Industrie', the only known copy of which exists at the library of the Victoria and Albert Musem.[14] The curious thing about this work is that the frontispiece is dedicated to a Monsieur Willson, possibly a reference

13 National Archives, F12-5115, letter dated January 3, 1850.
14 A. Couder, *L'Architecture et l'Industrie comme moyen de perfection sociale*, Paris, 1842.

Colour Plate 15. Square shawl attributed to Couder, French, c.1835. 189cm x 186cm.

Colour Plate 16. Square shawl detail attributed to Couder, French, c.1835. 186cm x 188cm. The endless Chinese knot is seen within the painted cupolas.

Plate 62. Scarf desgined by Couder, Paris, 1834. 3m x 77cm. It has the same inscription as the 'Ispahan' shawl (Colour Plate 14, p.144).

to Stephan Wilson, the person who first introduced the Jacquard loom into the British Isles.[15]

A painting of Couder's first known shawl is on view at the Conservatoire National des Arts et Métiers, Paris. The shawl was first exhibited at the 1823 Exhibition of French Industrial Products, at the Louvre. Although little is known about immediate public reaction it is clear that several of its unique features were to have a profound influence on future shawl designs.

In the painting shown in Plate 64 we can see repeated mihrabs or arches lining the middle field or 'dhoor', of the shawl, an important pattern which was soon afterwards transferred to the end fringe. This fringe pattern was very popular on succeeding generations of shawls.

Couder used the fringe pattern again on his 1834 Ispahan shawl (Colour Plate 14, page 144). It was used by the firm of Chambellan and Duché for their 'Hindus shawl', exhibited in 1839. Berrus made liberal use of this pattern in his shawl designs prepared for the Great Exhibition of 1851 in London. At the same time, the fringe pattern reached Kashmir where it was adopted as a convention for practically all shawls destined for European export.

We can also see in Plate 64 Couder's unique placement of the boteh within the framework of the mihrab. He believed the boteh to be a religious symbol, and it is not unlikely that his interpretation was drawn from early Persian prayer rugs of the sixteenth and seventeenth centuries. This idea was to have a lasting effect on shawl design.

15 Rothstein.

Plate 63. Square shawl attributed to Couder, Paris, c.1823. 138cm x 138cm.

Couder was the first to employ the total surface area of the shawl fabric as his design medium, drawing his inspiration probably from the well-known medallion carpets of Persia or from the square moon shawl whose matan was always decorated. Prior to this, the Jacquard long-shawl's matan was never used for decoration. In Plate 64 we can see that Couder dismissed the convention of repeating the same boteh design and offered instead five variants repeated to make a total of ten. He also used variegated coloured ends, an idea adopted from Kashmir shawls typical of the 1820s in which often the end warps had been dyed to produce this effect. This was called the 'harlequin' shawl.

The quality of the real Kashmir shawl was rapidly deteriorating, and new design techniques had to be developed. Up until this time France's shawl industry had

Plate 64. Long shawl painting by Couder shown at the 1823 Exposition, Paris. Five different botehs decorate the 'harlequin' palla.

received its design inspiration from India. This was no longer true. Srinagar had been reduced to a ghost town by the famine of 1834 and the few shawls which reached Europe were rough and cheap imitations from the surrounding cities and countries such as Persia, Afghanistan and the Punjab.

Rey, in his 'Study', severely criticized the Kashmir shawl:

'One can say there is such a shawl composed literally of pieces and fragments; the cones from one end of a long shawl do not resemble each other nor those of the other end. If they do look alike in form, they differ in colour tint. The corner motifs of a châle à rosace [moon shawl] are not the same as the centre, or they might be embroidered when the centre is brocaded. The rosace itself might be composed of two unmatched halves. But above all, the imperfections abound in the châles à fond plein, [i.e. shawls of which the 'matan' or centre field has been worked with a pattern]. It is not rare to find them streaked by a variety of four or five designs...'[16]

The economist Jérome-Adolphe Blanqui, acting as head of the Conservatoire des Arts et Métiers also criticised the shawl. He wrote in 1836:

'...the narrow borders [the shawl's hashia] had given way to large ones, the cones had become very large and the liveley colours had disappeared. Almost always, the Indian shawl, that our women were proud to put on their shoulders, were already worn and the colours faded; in this case they were revived and repainted by colourists without the women's knowledge. Still better, not only were the shawls old, dirty and threadbare but they were even patched-up.'[17]

Couder was convinced that the smooth contours of Oriental designs could be achieved through a careful mise-en-carte which would avoid the 'cassures' or jagged edges that appear in Kashmiri weaving.[18] He also took advantage of the recent improvements of the Jacquard loom especially the papier briqueté invented by Deneirouse, and the 'double griffe' which allowed a pattern repeat of 1 ¾ x 3 ½ metres (see Chapter Six).

The French seemed to have tried everything to divert attention from Kashmir shawls, and after the 'natural flower' period and the commercial failure[19] of Couder's 'renaissance' shawls new tactics had to be found. No wonder, therefore, that Couder and other artists paid serious attention to the new cones from Kashmir, and began to incorporate them into their own creations. That the scope of the design was virtually unlimited appeared a perfect way for testing the versatility of the Jacquard innovations. Thus, with the advent of the 1844 Exhibition of French National Products, a new turning point in the history of shawl design seemed to be approaching.[20]

Of Couder's designs, at the exhibition, one observer wrote,

'...a large shawl inspired from India where one finds charming details; instead of these heavy palms [cones] rounded-off at the lower ends, leaves are seen ending in the form of a lance ['feuilles lancéolées'] which attach themselves to their light stem with rare elegance...'[21]

The shawls in the 1844 exhibition represented a transition from the bizarre Indian designs to those typifying the smooth contours later to be called Art Nouveau. Who can say whether Hector Guimard (1867-1942) was not influenced by these swirling, sinuous lines of woven fabric? Or, for that matter, Alphonse Mucha (1860-1939), the artist best remembered for his posters and who immortalised Sarah Bernhardt?

16 Rey, p.143.
17 Blanqui, 'Conservatoire des Arts etc.', pp.420, 425.
18 Couder, 'Analyse du Dessin etc.', 1834, pp.3, 4.
19 Expo 1844, Challamel, vol. 1, p.39.
20 Expo 1855, Rappot du Jury Mixte, vol. 3, p.122. A royal decree admitted industrial designers to compete in the national exibitions only from 1834 onwards.
21 Expo 1844, Musée Challamel, vol. 1, p.40.

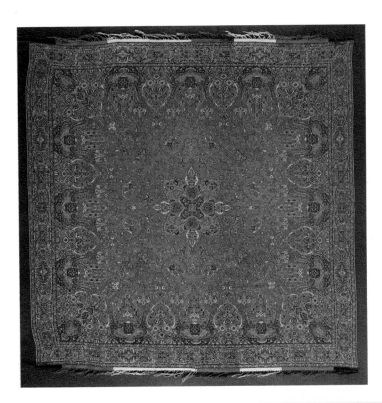

Colour Plate 17 (two views). Square shawl, attributed to Couder, c.1835. 187cm x 190cm. Notice the endless Chinese knot within the pointed cupolas. This is a typical Couder characteristic, also found in the 'Ispahan' (Colour Plate 14, p.144).

Plate 65. Long
shawl painting,
signed Couder,
c.1851.

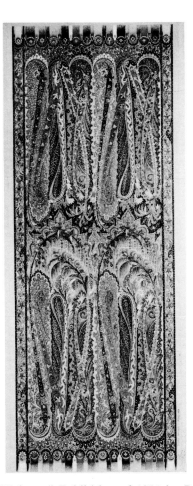

Plate 66. Shawl paintings shown at the Universal Exhibition of 1851 by Berrus.

Anthony Berrus

Another important shawl maker was Anthony Berrus, who founded his atelier in 1840. Berrus was one of the most creative and prolific artists of the nineteenth century. He requires special attention not only for his school of design but also for the enormous influence he exerted both in Europe and in the Orient.[22]

A few of the shawls were influenced by Couder's 'renaissance' style. The repeated mihrab arches found in Couder's early shawls were subsequently employed by Berrus in a chef-d'oeuvre of shawl design. The painting portraying this shawl is now on display at the Conservatoire National des Arts et Métiers, Paris. It was featured at the 1855 Exhibition and shows the boteh as a divine symbol, illuminated by a burning red ground and framed in a tall Gothic arch capped in mihrab style (Plate 70). Berrus' general and most commercially popular style, however, might best be described as fantasy. He employed ideas from the Far East with bizarre forms of fantastic flowers and tropical forests (Plate 66). His famous animal-like botehs and Persian calligraphic-type trellis work produced shawls of such great beauty and originality that his fame spread quickly throughout Europe. The zoomorphic boteh became one of the trade marks of his atelier and was profusely copied, not only by major shawl centres such as Paisley, Vienna and Lyon, but also by the Kashmiri weavers themselves (Plate 68).

---

22 The Musée des Arts Décoratif, Paris, contains the largest collection of Kashmir design albums in the world. 50 alone can be attributed to Berrus.

Colour Plate 18. 'Nou-Rouz' shawl. Designed by Couder for the 1839 exhibition, Paris. 12 colours. 165cm x 389cm. The Spring's equinox is celebrated as the first day of the year among Persians, and called Nou Rouz. It is one of their principal holidays. During the 19th century, cannons and musical instruments were heard the whole day while the Shah received the hommage of dignitaries of his empire, each offering him presents according to his rank. Here, Couder expresses his great affinity with Persian culture combining it with European Gothic art.

The shawl, manufactured by Gaussen, was woven with red warps and displayed a green ground. More than 101,000 Jacquard cards were employed to weave this complex design which in fact only occupies one quarter of the surface of the whole shawl. Running the cards backwards and forwards four times was required in order to achieve this symmetrical section of the full image. This shawl was exhibited in Paris in 1982 and Lyon in 1983.

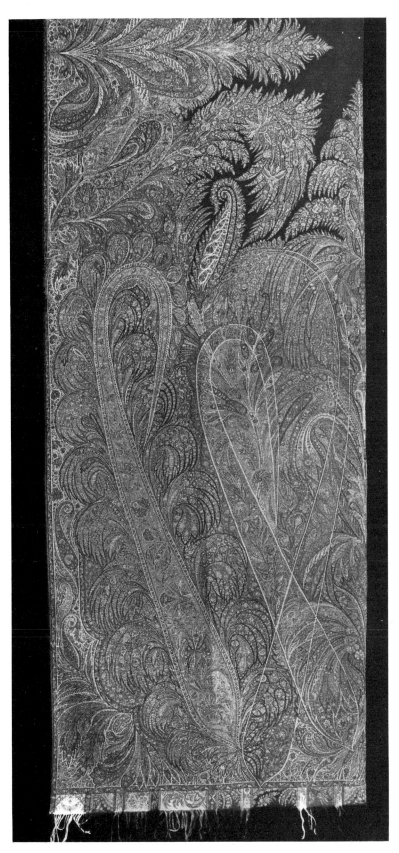

Plate 67. Quarter detail, French Jacquard shawl, possibly by Berrus, c.1850.

Plate 68. A rare masterpiece of French shawl design, probably by Berrus. Woven in Kashmir, c.1850. 157cm x 370cm.

Plate 69 (left). Shawl painting by Berrus shown at the Universal Exhibition of 1855.
Plate 70 (right). Shawl painting by Berrus shown at the Universal Exhibition of 1855. The boteh is enshrined.

Plate 71. French Jacquard shawl, initialled in corner fringe gate 'FM' (Fortier Maillard).

Berrus personally sketched all designs coming from his atelier. He received an honourable mention at the 1844 National Exhibition, just four years after having founded his workshop. The designs he displayed were judged as being in the Indian style where the contours were pure and unbroken. By 1855, Berrus' shop employed over a hundred workers, compared to the thirty working there in 1844. They were engaged in translating designs for the mise-en-carte of the Jacquard loom. Monsieur Delacour, Berrus' right-hand man, was responsible for enlarging his sketches and making samples of all the shawl details, while a Monsieur Gourdet was responsible for colouring and mise-en-carte. At this time his company attained a turnover reaching 250,000 francs.[23]

Berrus was the first to break away and develop his own individual style. In contrast with Couder, who was more of a scientific innovator, Berrus was a pure artist who confined his talents wholly to the shawl's canvas. In essence, he took Couder's theory and put it into practice. The idea was actually simple: to break away from the jagged edges of the declining Kashmir shawl and transfer the smooth contours of the new sweeping botehs on to the Jacquard cards so that a faithful reproduction of the design would appear in the woven fabric. Berrus created an efficient task force to accomplish this feat; the effort involved in manufacturing the cards was still enormous and required unlimited patience. All this was a prerequisite for the weaving of his designs, which, by the time of his arrival in the shawl business, was already far removed from the Oriental image.

Berrus, Parquez,[24] Vichy, Braun, Chebeaux, and of course Couder, were all graduates of what was by then a firmly implanted system of design ateliers

---

23 Expo 1855, Rapport du Jury etc., vol. 3, p.1,223.
24 Parquez, ostensibly, was in possession of the collection of design albums originating from the then defunct Oberkampf factory. He probably purchased these valuable books either just after Oberkampf's death in 1837 or more likely during the auction sale of the company's assets in 1844.

Colour Plate 19 (two views). Moon shawl, possibly Couder school, French, c.1840. 184cm x 184cm. The spectacular central medallion bursts with explosive energy. This effulgent style may derive from a school of shawl design which enjoyed a brief popularity around 1810. The outer border retains the Kashmiri flavour of the 1820s.

Plate 72. Shawl
advertisement,
Paris, 1847.

throughout Paris, Lyon, and Nîmes. They represented the élite of this field, and their talents were greatly admired abroad. Braun sold 50,000 francs worth of shawl designs to the firm Montis, Glasgow, during the 1851 Universal Exhibition.[25] Chebeaux's creations were sold to the firm of John Monteith, James Black and Hamiel, also of Glasgow, and to the firm of Simpson, Young, Buttersworth and Brook of Manchester. The shawl artist was not only compensated by a good salary, his talents brought additional rewards of fame during the 'campaigns' of the national and the international exhibitions. Since 1834, when the industrial artists were first recognised and allowed to present their works, shawl designs along with manufactured articles were often the featured attraction. One critic felt that shawl designers, just as sculptors and engravers who sign their names to their work, should enjoy similar recognition. Indeed, many long Jacquard shawls were initialled, usually on the extreme ends within one of the arches or 'gates' of the fringe (Plate 71).

Mid-nineteenth century shawl design

By the mid-nineteenth century the school of shawl design was divided into three categories: 1) traditional Indian shawls characterized by classic Oriental style, accurately copied right down to the smallest detail; 2) designs subject to the caprices

---

25 Expo 1855, vol. 3, p.1,222.

Plate 73 (left). European loom-woven Kashmir shawl, c.1820. See Plate 176 for similar pattern.
Plate 74 (right). Jacquard shawl fragment, probably French, c.1835. 59cm x 135cm. All the essential Sikh design characteristics appear in this fragment.

of fashion, where the motifs were modified substantially and were fantastical in character; 3) a combination of the first two where the Indian outline was conserved but detail expressed imaginative changes.

Each school served a very definite function, satisfying the special needs of either domestic or foreign markets. The Indian school agreed principally with the demand of French taste while, on the other hand, the whimsical, exotic designs satisfied a particular foreign market. The former catered to the conservative palate of ladies desiring a loyal copy of the Indian product, while the latter suited the avant-garde.

The proprietors of the large establishments which successfully grew up in Paris, Saint-Denis, Puteaux and Essone followed Oberkampf's example. Before long, designers were attached to all branches of the textile industry. Among the most remarkable 'dessinateurs' at the end of the eighteenth century were two Lyonnaise artists, Philippe de la Salle and Bouy.

In 1847, Paris had sixty-six artist-workshops employing 721 people. These workshops catered to industries of many foreign nations and built a reputation for successfully forecasting coming fashion. At the same time representatives of these nations came to Paris looking for artists willing to direct their ateliers.

The superiority of French design had been respected for a long time in Europe. The Austrians, as far back as 1751, had commissioned French artists to instruct their apprentices in the art of velvet weaving. Seven years later an industrial design school was founded with the adoption of French techniques and staffed, also, by French instructors.[26]

British firms frequently sent for Parisian shawl designers, both to renew old styles

26 Geijer, p.163.

and to create new ones. In Paisley, for example, the company Keer, Scott and Kilner often used France's best talent to enrich their knowledge of colouring and mise-en-carte techniques.[27] Soon after, this situation was reversed, and the English found it easier to dispatch their chief artists to Paris, for three or four months of apprenticeship.

One of the most prestigious British companies of the early shawl era was Gibbs and Macdonald. Their high quality products, woven during the period 1804-36 were, for the most part, modelled after the French imitation shawl, especially after the defeat of Napoleon in 1815. At this time Mr. Macdonald made it a habit to visit Paris every year to obtain new designs.[28]

In 1834 there are records of an English shawl artist, Thomas Barker Holdway, who was sent to Paris to study the latest techniques in this field. His visit was due to the fortuitous results of a first prize and forty pounds which he won for his shawl designs.[29]

Throughout this cultural and cooperative exchange of artistic ideas Paris remained the centre of creativity and production. Practically all important foreign production centres had their mise-en-carte performed in Paris. This method made for tremendous reductions in industrial expenses which were simply translated into the purchase and transportation of the pre-programmed Jacquard cards. Therefore, nobody was ever absolutely sure whether the shawl was woven in Paris, Glasgow or Vienna!

Fleury Chavant

In spite of the creation of a school of industrial design, few books of Kashmir patterns were available to aid and provide manufacturers with working guidelines to achieve successful imitation shawls. In 1837, however, Fleury Chavant, an industrial designer turned publisher, produced a periodical entitled *Album du Chachemirien*. Its utility lay in the full scale drawings traced from recent shawls of new designs which were woven in Lahore, Ispahan, Kabul, Kashmir and Chandahar. English shawl makers also procured editions of Chavant's work, and both the Paisley and Norwich museums today contain examples of his album.

Shawl makers everywhere were now well informed of the latest Oriental trends in shawl weaving and designs arriving monthly from the East.

It is higly plausible that the *Cachemirien* was based on the very shawls sent from India by General Allard after his return to Lahore in 1836. Poitevin, the reviewer of the 1867 Exhibition, explained that this large group of Kashmir shawls was exhibited in the boutique of the dealer Gagelin, the same dealer who 'instructed' Allard before his return to India. Poitevin wrote: 'This occasion created such publicity that it set the style for other dealers to follow.'[30]

Before this time Europe was largely unaware that the Kashmir shawl was so widely imitated in the Orient. The *Cachemirien* proved an invaluable guide for those whose sights were aimed at the export market — especially at the Middle East where heavy overland taxes on shawls from Kashmir made them extremely costly. The Kashmir shawl was, for example, often more expensive in Arabia or Turkey because of the heavy overland taxes imposed on the caravans. Industrialised Europe's cheaper shawl competed favourably against those woven by hand in the Orient and satisfied a ready middle-class market.

Chavant's influence on design was thus undoubtedly strong, and although he

27 Expo 1862, Rapport du Jury, p.122.
28 Whyte, p.23.
29 Whyte and Swain, 1962, p.61.
30 Expo 1867, p.173.

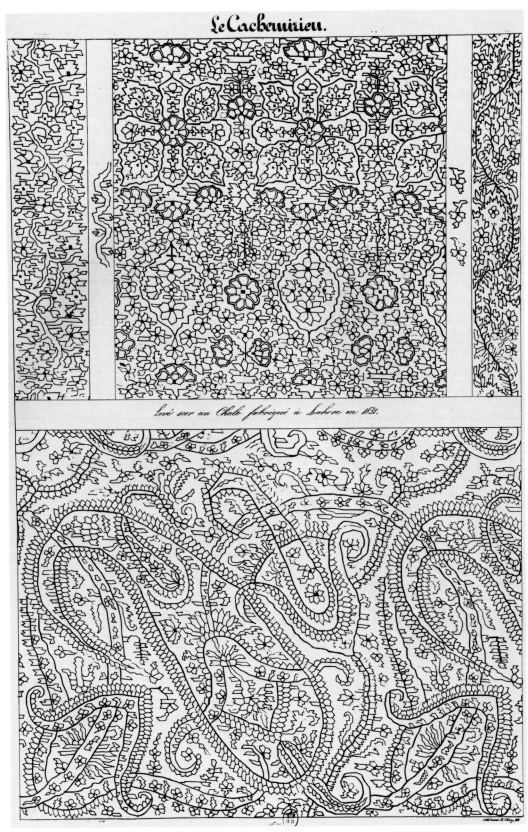

Le Cachemirien.

Levé sur un Chale fabriqué à Lahore en 1831.

Plate 75. Tracing from Chavant's *Le Cachemirien*. Top, c.1800; bottom, shawl woven in Lahore in 1831.

le Cachemirien.

Plate 76. Tracing from Chavant's *Le Cachemirien.* A shawl woven in Teheran.

164

Le Cachemirien.

Plate 77. Tracing from Chavant's *Le Cachemirien*. A shawl woven in Teheran.

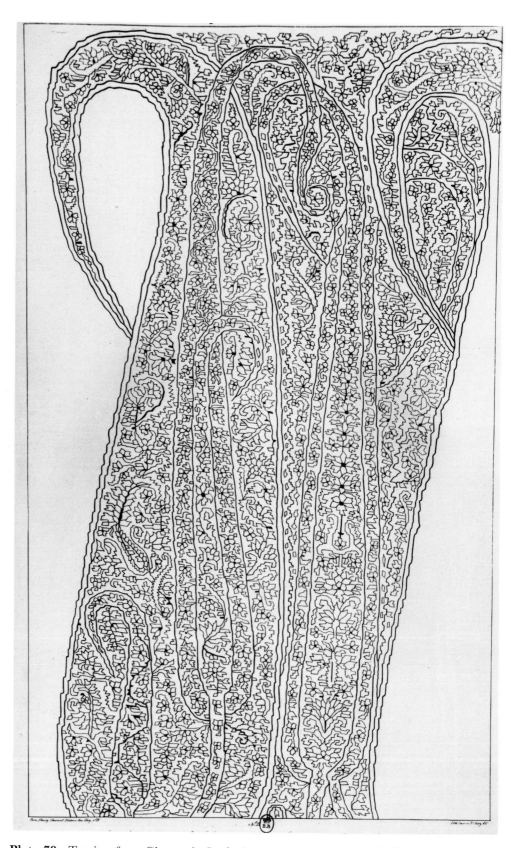

Plate 78. Tracing from Chavant's *Le Cachemirien*. A shawl woven in Kandahar in 1825.

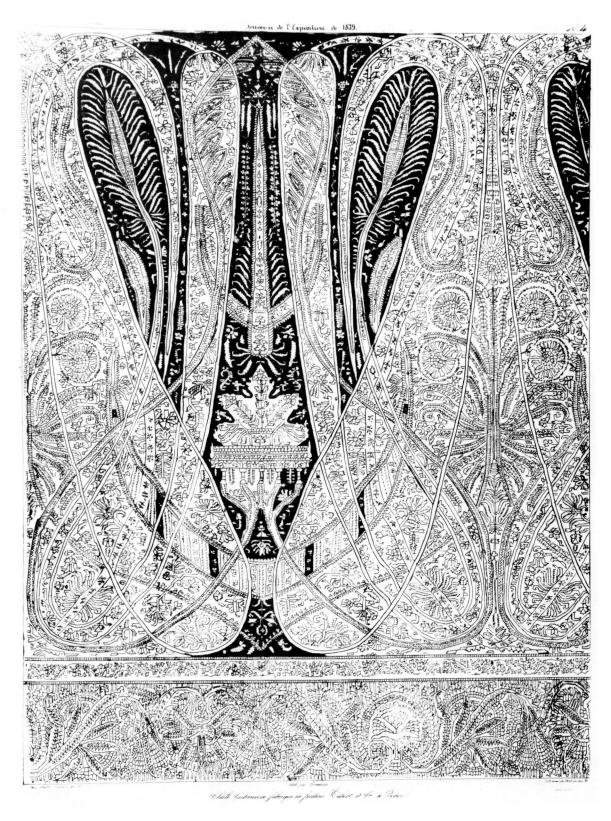

Plate 79. Tracing from Chavant's *Souvenir de l'Exposition de 1839.* A Kashmir shawl manufactured by Frederic Herbert and Co., Paris.

Plate 80 (above). Tracing from Chavant's *Souvenir de l'Exposition de 1839*. A 'Hindu' shawl manufactured by M.M. Chambellan and Duché, Paris.

Plate 81 (opposite). Tracing from Chavant's *Souvenir de l'Exposition de 1839*. Shawl woven with pashmina wool by Bournhonet, Tenaux's successor.

Plate 81

himself did not create any new designs, he wisely engaged the most reputed Parisian artists. They either copied from existing woven designs or produced original ones and their names greatly enhanced the prestige of his publications.

The *Cachemirien* clarifies, in a small way, some of the developments of the 'boteh' in Europe, as Chavant carefully points out earlier motifs which prevailed during the Rey, Ternaux, Bellanger and Lagorce period. The first botehs are described as 'caillouté' (literally tiny stones, but the word 'mosaic' would be more appropriate) which was the style of the 'naissance du cachemire'. Other styles were called the 'Bengale', 'à rubans', 'à palme superposée' and 'à pagode'.

In another of Chavant's albums, entitled *Le Dessinateur de Cachemires*, coloured drawings similar to the drawings in the 'Cachemirien' are shown, but with the additional features of some delicate drawings in chinoiserie style. An occasional pagoda is found. This far Eastern style reappears in a shawl manufactured by Chambellan and Duché at the Paris Exposition of 1839 and is also reproduced in Chavant's *Souvenir de l'Exposition 1839* along with a few 'renaissance' shawls as mentioned above. Chavant published about 25 albums altogether.

Conclusion

In this chapter we have exposed the principal artists and manufacturers whose legacy of accomplishments predominate the annals of nineteenth century France. Through Ternaux we sensed the intense drive of a great industrialist to harness the compelling force of fashion. Couder jolted the shawl industry awake with his Indo-Gothic architecture, glittering Oriental figures, and caparisoned elephants and camels. Berrus mesmerized the public by the sheer force of his 'inner-sanctum' designs, in which the boteh was enshrined, and temples camouflaged by fantastical jungle foliage, evoking 'A Thousand and One Nights'. In the field of invention and loom technology it was not so much genious that counted but hard work and determination to satisfy an urgent need. Jacquard, Bauson, Deneirouse, and Fabard and doubtless many others played a crucial role in elaborating on the loom's sophistication. The French Kashmir shawl exemplifies a fusion of art and industry. Together with its Indian progenitor, the kani shawl of Kashmir, they represent two inseparable textile art forms of the nineteenth century.

Plate 82. Long shawl called 'the Procession'. 162cm x 357cm. Jacquard woven and designed by M. Pin. Shown at the 1867 Exposition.

An Illustrated Guide showing the chronological development of Kashmir Shawl Patterns

from the 17th to the 19th century

Plate 83. Shoulder mantle. Mughal, 17th century.

In this exquisite shawl in the collection of the Textile Museum, Washington, a very narrow palla is decorated by freely spaced leaning tree shrubs on a rich salmon ground. The bases of the trees rise from 'barred-cross' roots and support a slightly sinuous branch axis of angular leaf clusters and flowers in faded rose-violet and pale green. In the unique hashia, also freely-spaced, tear-drop flower buds alternate with small angular blossoms along a trapezoidal meander (see Figure 16a, p.72)

Colour Plate 20.

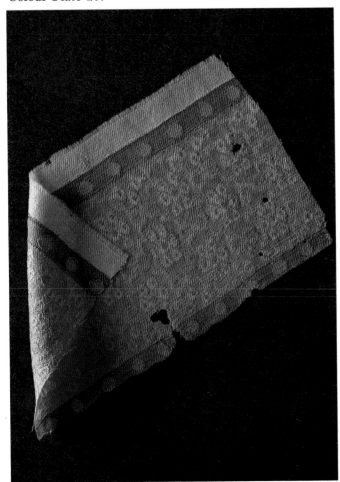

Colour Plate 21.

Colour Plate 20. Waistband (hashia fragment). Mughal, early 17th century. 17cm x 5cm.
Colour Plate 21. Waistband (hashia fragment). Mughal, early 17th century. 6cm x 9cm.

Two incredible specimens of the finest known kani weaving in the world. Their texture is like silk to the touch and one would believe that they were actually woven from pure shah tus. Obviously, by the width of their borders, they are pieces from a patka or waistband. Indeed Colour Plate 21 is surely from the fabulous palla fragment now conserved in the new Kuwait Museum (see *Islamic Art in the Kuwait National Museum,* p.155) and although it is not shown here, it is still worth commenting on. It is without doubt a very rare specimen of floral design in shawls. There is a queer aesthetic quality about it which tends to repudiate the classic Mughal school of floral representation where so often we find gracefully outstretched leaves and branches. The Kuwaiti piece seems to be devoid of this cliché-type elegance: the leaves are stiff, sharp and pointed, the flowers appealing and the bizarre leaf-securing stem catches us completely by surprise with its unnaturalness.

A tracing of Colour Plate 20's angular meander can be seen in Figure 16b, p.72.

Plate 84. Shoulder mantle (fragments). Mughal, c.1700. Top, 10cm x 7cm; bottom, 18cm x 21cm.

The bottom fragment is part of a collection of kani fragments found in a jacket belonging to the Sultan of Mysore, Tipu Sahib. In contrast to the previous piece the difference here between leaves and flowers is more distinct. The needles on the branches imply a rose bush. The Chinese cloud hashia may appear slightly incongruous with the botehs' style. A charming aspect is provided by the turned-over flowers. Notice also the indeogram root-securing device which coincidentally means earth in Chinese. See Plate 99 for an almost identical hashia pattern. The top fragment is probably part of the vertical hashia of the palla fragment.

Plate 85. Waistband. Mughal, c.1700. 68cm x 410cm.

Probably one of the oldest forms of the kani shawl is the patka. Archetypal patterns are often found in the kani patka which may have been popular during the Sultanate period of pre-Mughal India. The chevron pattern on this 'garden shawl' (see Plate 108) is often depicted in Mughal decoration and it frequently suggests the idea of running water. The thin trapezoidal meander decorating the zig-zag lines relates closely to the hashias in Plates 86 and 87. Because of the similar colour tones of burnt orange, white and pale green, Plates 85 and 86 may be contemporary pieces.

Plate 86. Waistband (fragment). Mughal, 17th century.

From the motifs on the hashia of this tiny fragment we may speculate on the design of the lost palla. The sharply angular meander is composed of a claw-like cluster on arunning and unusually thick vine, which alternates around a group of three 'star' flowers. It is possible to reconstruct a full cycle of the meander's repeat with the design information found in the fragment (see Figure 20, p.77). In the guard borders we again find a trapezoidal pattern which has a certain Coptic look to it. This same pattern can be also found in Plates 85 and 87.

175

Colour Plate 22. Waistband. Mughal, 17th century. 70cm x 460cm.
Also shown as Plate 100 where full details are given

Colour Plate 23. Waistband. Mughal, early 17th century

This is one of the most beautiful and perfect patka specimens in the world, part of the Bharat Kala Bawan's magnificent collection. Although the boteh's base, in the form of a Chinese ideogram, appears heavy compared to the rest of the plant's principal stems, its style embodies the very quintessence of early 17th century Mughal shawl artistry. An archetypal shawl pattern is implied when the palla's hashias and boteh share common botanical elements and a fine balanced symmetry is elegantly attained.

The boteh's overall beauty is cleverly enhanced through the effects of pale yellow outlining. The resulting chromatic aspect is surprising and suggests a bush of flowers glistening with rain drops in the sun. Illuminating the centre of each of the pale blue flowers are the bright yellow and vermillion specks which also provide a warm, uncanny illusion of flickering lights. The shawl's rare wool and the incredibly soft touch sensation offered by its diaphanous folds is derived from the finest shah tus which after more than 300 years of excellent conservation still emits a shimmering golden lustre.

Plate 87. Shoulder mantle (fragment). Mughal, 17th century. 51cm x 136cm.

Decorating the light saffron ground are botehs composed of dark blue flower blossoms outlined in white and tomato red. The stems, emanating from a vase-like object, are arranged in a parallel fashion. The green leaves at the boteh's base are tinged with dark yellow to expose their undersides. The whole of the boteh is balanced carefully by a single stem resting on the ideogram root. All that remains of the vertical hashia is the guard border which relates exactly to the trapezoidal meander of Plates 85 and 86.

Plate 88. Shoulder mantle (fragment). Mughal, early 17th century. 18cm x 69cm.

This superb piece is an unparalleled example of Mughal court weaving. Set like cut diamonds in a bracelet, freely spaced multifaceted flowerbuds reflect the finely detailed hashias of the shawl fragment's palla. Expressed through the vertical stem's triple flexion, a smoothly rising undulation draws the observer's eye to the large flower cluster at the boteh's top. Again we find the roots secured by a strange device in the form of an ideogram. Colours: pink, crimson red, light and deep bluish green.

Plate 89. Shoulder mantle (fragment). Mughal, early 17th century. 18cm x 56cm.

This charming pattern in its pure simplicity again demonstrates the direct link of the kani-shawl industry to the Mughal court workshops. The opening rose bud counterbalances the large tilted rose of madder red, pale yellow and indigo blue. The bud is incorporated into the hashia's meander which highlights the palla's overall effect. However the intentional use of red on the leaves just above the ideogram root appears to lose its effect of leaf folding. The boteh's windblown leaves are of faded greyish green outlined in pale blue.

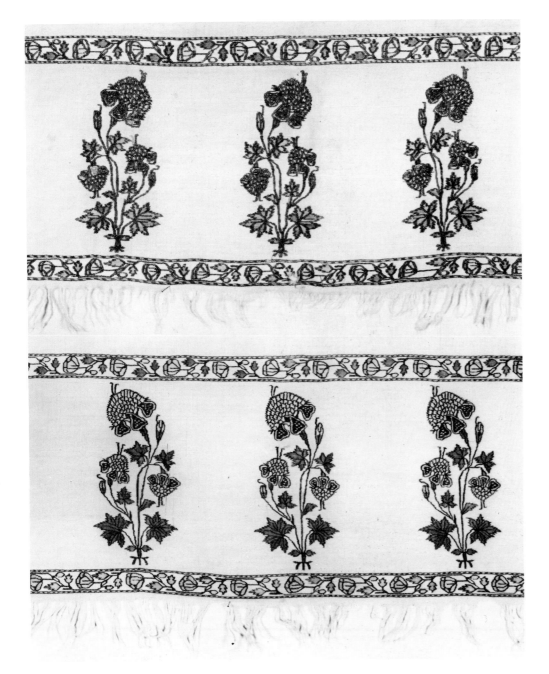

Plate 90. Shoulder mantle. Mughal, early 17th century. 126cm x 237cm.

Another masterpiece of Mughal court weaving relating in extreme rarity to Plate 88. The hashia's unidirectional flower meander follows a rather rigid geometrical draftsmanship. However, its meticulous detail is beautifully completed by the running rhomboidal specks of the guard borders. Oddly enough the boteh's flowers with their hanging petals appear waning despite the appearance of new buds. The veining of the large opposing leaves at the bottom is unique. A striking thing about this elegant kani piece is the way the stems are secured. It is the only known piece in which the root securing device actually approaches the curving strokes found in Chinese ideograms. Similar design characteristics may be found in a piece conserved at the Association for the Study and Documentation of Asian Textiles, Paris (accession number 1276). The latter's whimsical design suggest hovering butterflies.

Plate 91 ▲ ▼ Plate 92

Plate 91 (opposite above). Waistband. Mughal, early 17th century. 68cm x 484cm.
Plate 92 (opposite below). Waistband. Mughal, early 17th century.

Forming the main theme of these rare and exquisite patkas (waistbands) are of course the Chinese clouds (see Plate 32). The botehs' blossoms are rather bizarre. They look like 'bent-tip' strawberries or they may be a kind of rose abstraction. The accumulation of cloud wisps at the botehs' base, in the form of leaves, suggests a drifting or floating sensation. In Plate 92, the colour combination is unusual: white outlined, dark blue blossoms and yellow outlined, pale green, leaves contrast against a rich cochineal ground. (See Figure 18, p.76 for detail of the vertical hashia.)

Plate 93. Waistband. Mughal, early 17th century.

In this illustration the shawl has been folded over to reveal the meticulously fine weaving of the underside. From a distince it would be very difficult to guess the back from the front side. It is surprising to discover patka hashias on a shoulder mantle. The boteh which patterns this light brown shawl consists of pale-red roses and faded blue leaves outlined in blue. Supporting the stems is an anvil-like Chinese ideogram. See Figure 21, p.78, for a line drawing of the hashias.

Plate 94. Waistband. Mughal, c.1700. 63cm x 341cm.

This piece from the Bharat Kala Bhawan, Benares, embodies the fine characteristics by which Mughal shawls are known. On a soft salmon-pink ground, white sprigs form four regular rows across the shawl's palla. The butis' laterally pointed leaves, inspired from the rank shawl idea, may indicate a possible early 18th century date of manufacture. The hashia design is unusual, with rows of disconnected sprigs rather than a meandering vine.

Plate 95. Shoulder mantle (fragment). Mughal, 17th century. 133cm x 280cm.

This palla of poppy plants is a fragment of a long shawl. The vertical hashia differs from the horizontal which is why it is sewn on, rather than woven with the original palla. Nevertheless, it contains a very fine meander of angular stems and leaves unlike the sinuous stem of the horizontal hashia. The large leaves of the boteh tend to dominate the design, thus lessening the grace of the simplified poppy blossoms and their irregular curving stems. The red dye which shows signs of running and the unusually coarse wool employed in the weave would tend to indicate a product not woven within the auspices of the Mughal court. It may have been woven in Lahore where the Mughals made an earnest attempt to weave fine Kashmir shawls.

Plate 96. Waistband. Mughal, c.1700.

In this magnificent patka conserved by the Calico Museum, Ahmedabad, we find beauty and grace in a rose boteh pattern. Rising sinuously within the boteh's centre is a branch which instils an inner movement to the flower clusters. Below, one of the four racemes terminates with a curious device resembling an insect. The racemes are winged onto a bespeckled and irregular mound containing four queer protrusions. See Plates, 102, 113 and 119. These protrusions may indicate cloud whiffs. Again in the hashia we see this bold trapezoidal meander which may relate to that in Colour Plate 21, p.173.

Plate 97. Waistband. Mughal, 17th century.

According to 17th and 18th century literature, pure white shah tus was reserved strictly for kings and dignitaries of high rank.

In view of the elegant artistry of the exquisite white patka in Plate 97 it may be attributed to a Mughal court workshop. A curious addition to this rose boteh is the line just above the Chinese ideogram root which supports the two leaf branches. The branches, apart from the main stem do not follow a similar style to earlier specimens. Often in 17th century kani botehs and especially in Mughal carpets, branches are arranged in a stiff vertical fashion, almost parallel to each other (see Plates 87 and 91). The large vertical hashias mimic the botehs' floral elements by a bold meander of identically repeated rose blossoms, rose buds and leaves. In the horizontal hashia the guard border's rhomboidal flecks and slanting lines of the angular meander give vibrancy to an otherwise compressed design.

Plate 98. Waistband. Mughal, 17th century.
70cm x 420cm.

In Plate 98 of the Calico Museum, although less finely drawn, we find a similar boteh style. A further rendition of the ideogram root is seen here.

Plate 99. Waistband. Mughal, 17th century.

The designation 'rank' shawl is applied to this type of shawl. Rank or military grade may be implied by the stacked array of stiff leaves. However, their development into this abstract form was by no means immediate. It is felt that they evolved slowly through an ever increasing abstraction of the 'chinese cloud' shawls. Evidence of this theory is seen in Plate 98, from the collection of the Textile Museum, Washington. The flat leaves separating the full blown roses are actually still connected to their vestigial 'clouds'. Compare Plate 99 with Plates 91 and 92, also with Plate 84 for lateral hashias. The vertical hashias in Plate 99 are of 19th century origin (see Figure 19, p.77, for line drawing study of vertical hashia).

Plate 100. Waistband. Mughal, 17th century. 70cm x 460cm.

The white king's-wool shawl of Plate 100 is from the fabulous shawl collection of the Bharat Kala Bhawan, Benares. Its bright saffron yellow flowers, in the form of 'pin-wheels' are also utilised for its hashia pattern. The pin-wheel and bent-tip strawberry flowers were employed together to become a common hashia pattern in the early to mid-18th century (see Plates 134 and 135). The claw-like leaf cluster of the root relates somewhat to that of Plate 98. Also shown as Colour Plate 22, p.176.

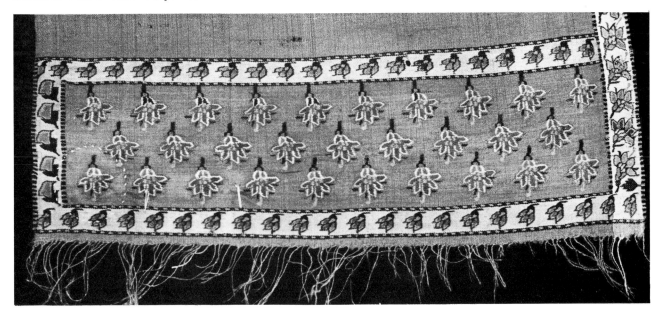

Plate 101. Turban. Mughal, c.1700. 25cm x 327cm.

This uncommon orange-saffron kani piece is characterised by its disparate collection of hashia patterns. The disconnected floral repeat is similar to Plate 94 and Plate 101 may be its contemporary. However the twisted fringes are something usually seen on 18th century shawls, especially on patkas.

Plate 102. Waistband. Mughal, 17th century.

Botehs containing a mélange of flowers are rare indeed. In this impressive patka conserved by the National Museum, Delhi, a perfect floral balance within the bouquet is achieved. The pivotal point for this balance is provided by the lower rose which is hung upside down like a pendulum. The cog-wheel flower and the mound with its curious protrusions should be compared with similar features found in the Mughal carpet, Plate 221. Also compare the isolated leaf, located between the top two flowers, with the regimented leaves of Plate 119.

Plate 103. Shoulder mantle (fragment). Mughal, early 18th century. 74cm x 127cm.

This charming little mughal fragment of black outlined tree shrubs provides a nice addition to our knowledge of early 18th century shawl patterns. The hashia, with its freely spaced trifoliate meander and arching stroke is from the same fine artistic hand as the main pattern. This is not always the case, but when it is, one can infer that the shawl in question may have been woven in a court atelier.

Plate 104. Shoulder mantle. Mughal, c.1700. 141cm x 312cm.

Besides the 'bent-tip' strawberries at the boteh's base, the colour scheme of rose red on a green ground is unusual. The small 'leaf-flags' attached to the frail stems and the claw-type root are important design elements associated with shawl pieces of this period. An identical shawl to this piece is conserved by the Calico Museum, Ahmedabad.

Plate 105. Shoulder mantle (fragment). Mughal, early 18th century. 129cm x 168cm.

A shawl pattern of distinction is offered by the fine harmony of red roses on saffron ground and their perfectly symmetrical butis.

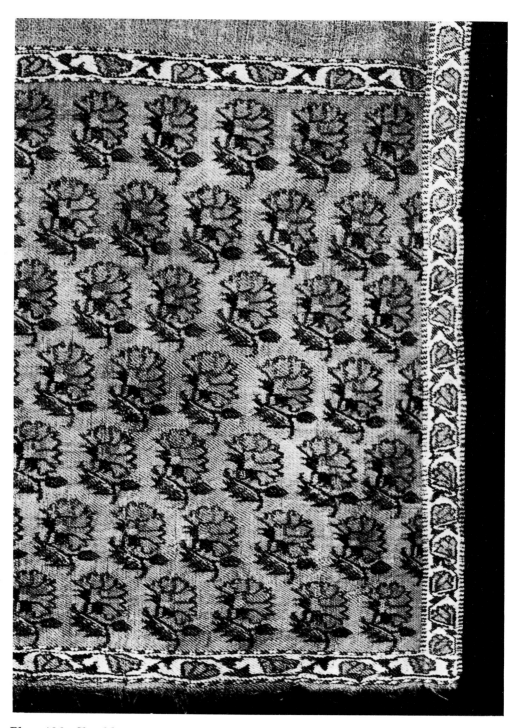

Plate 106. Shoulder mantle. Mughal, early 18th century. 133cm x 320cm.

In Persian and European literature the rose is the flower of love and poetry. In miniature paintings of the 17th and 18th centuries Mughals are often seen posing while holding up a rose blossom in one hand or while extending it to their favourite concubine. Shawls of this type may have been offered as sentimental gifts.

Contrasted by a pale green ground the 'winged-leaf' buti's tilted-rose blossom is outlined in dark red. the winged leaf indicates the 'fold-shading' by a yellow tinge on its up-turned surface. The long sweeping branches and crocus flowers of the hashia are of a style popular during this period.

Plate 107. Shoulder mantle (fragment). Mughal, early 18th century. 68cm x 21cm.

Rose blossom butis are finely illustrated by this kani piece which has a similar but more constrained hashia pattern to Plate 107. The tips of the serrated leaves, rising from the 'Chinese' root are well drawn to support the two opposing tilted rose blossoms.

Plate 108. Shoulder mantle. Mughal, 18th century. 135cm x 306cm.

The chevron was a popular Mughal ornament, often used to suggest running water. Variations of this theme can be seen in the well-known 'garden' carpets of Persia in which the troughs that distribute the fountain's water are indicated traditionally by a chevron pattern. Thus 'garden shawl' would have been an appropriate soubriquet. Colours: blue and off-white.

Plate 109 (above). Shoulder mantle.
Mughal, mid-18th century. 324cm x 142cm.

We find here a novel respite in design style which breaks away from conventionality. The idea of these unusually large round flower blossoms borders on the absurd; yet the bold spherical effect, subdued by the angularity of the frail stems has a surprising charm.

Plate 110 (left). Shoulder mantle (fragment).
Mughal, early 18th century. 19cm x 13cm.

The assemblage of four rose pots is unusual for this period. They provide a device for elevating the tinged red and blue perfoliate leaves which, opening in a kind of cornucopia fashion, pour forth large oval shaped flowers. Flower blossoms which predominated in various boteh styles of the mid-18th century became exposed to the popular fashion of circular floral shapes such as those seen in Plate 111.

The use of flower pots and the leaves place this piece around the middle of the 18th century. However, the group of small serrated base leaves, secured by an anvil-like device, and the delicate hashia possibly suggest an earlier date.

This piece offers a glimpse into the little known transitional styles immediately preceding the Afghan period.

Plate 111 (above). Shoulder mantle. Mughal, mid-18th century. 315cm x 135cm.
Plate 112 (opposite above). Shoulder mantle (fragment). Mughal, mid-18th century.
21cm x 104cm.

Apart from the boteh's two-tone base fronds, the distinguishing aspect of these two pieces consists of a style which may be viewed as a 'technique of characterisation'. The continuing popularity of a large, if not exaggerated tilted blossom at the boteh's top is seen in Plates 111 and 112 and in Colour Plates 24 and 25, pp.199, 201, as a major theme of their overall composition. Plate 111 is a stunningly beautiful Mughal court example of this technique. At its base is a jagged blue mound with red dots possibly representing swimming fish. Distorted perspectives are often found in Mughal miniature painting allowing the artist to show both interior and exterior views simultaneously. This boteh style suggested by the large circular flattened flowers, represents undoubtedly the precursor of the radial flower technique — a technique which became popular during the third quarter of the 18th century. The symmetrical leaf displacement at the boteh's base in Plate 112 shows a similarity to the rank shawls in Plates 99 and 100.

Plate 113 (opposite below). Shoulder mantle. Mughal, mid-18th century. 137cm x 320cm.

This pairs well with the cog-wheel boteh of Plate 111 especially with its drooping serrated leaf, although its weaving execution does not come even close to the latter.

Plate 112

Plate 113

197

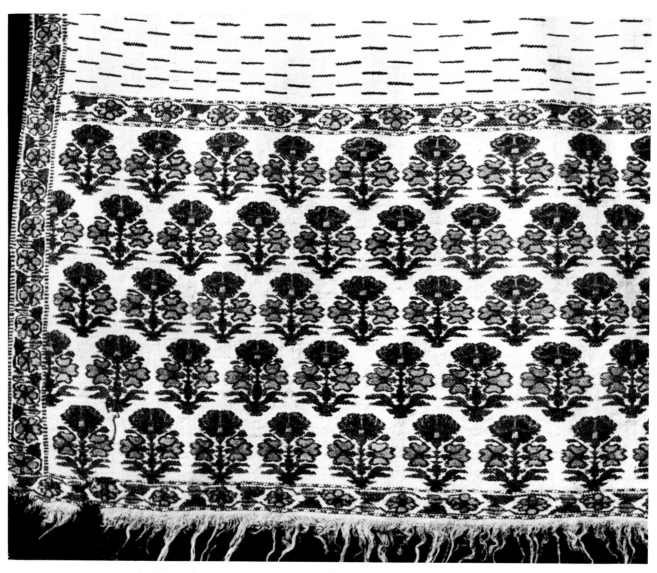

Plate 114. Shoulder mantle. Afghan period, Mughal style, late 18th century. 125cm x 300cm.

Rose-tulip buti on an 'anvil-like' dish line the palla. The staggered rows of short lines in the matan blend harmoniously with the sharply pointed leaves of the buti. Only two other known pieces have such a decorated matan. One is at the Association for the Study and Documentation of Asian Textiles, Paris, accession number 1691. The other is conserved by the National Museum, Delhi, accession number 56-153/1.

Colour Plate 24. Waistband (two views). Mughal, mid-18th century. 127cm x 220cm.

The luminescent peach ground, the rather bulbous botehs with their full-blown tilted roses (as the cock of a hat), and the expansive strokes of the draftsman's hand, have indeed created a special charm in this patka. As in Plates 96, 99 and 111, there is a stepped-mound with curious dots inside it. The lateral hashias and the field's butis relate somewhat in style to the moon shawl in Plate 152. Despite the restraining curvilinearity of the boteh's exterior and the orderly arrangement of flowers, the artist has made an earnest attempt to space the floral elements freely.

Plate 115. Shoulder mantle. Mughal, mid-18th century. 139cm x 330cm.

One of the most beautiful shawls of the 18th century. The exterior wrap of red roses is supported by a curved stem which forms the boteh's interior cone. The stem rises from tall fern branches which flank a central raceme. The latter extends upward from a vase-like object. The vase is secured in place laterally by two Chinese clouds which enhance the narrow base of this otherwise very elegant boteh. The distinct flower in the boteh's centre is a blue iris, outlined in yellow and red. The hashia is composed of a contemporary pattern of tiny oval-flower buds set in a kind of hexagonal opening formed by the angularity of the foliate meander.

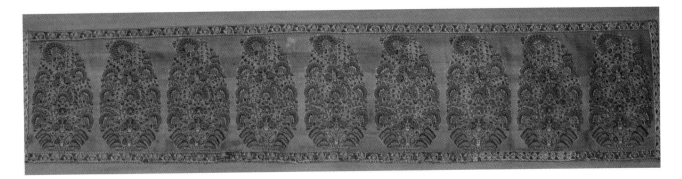

Colour Plate 25. Shoulder mantle (fragment) (two views). Mughal, 18th century. 26cm x 123cm.

The idea of the rank shawl is suggested by the vase's flanking rows of serrated leaves. The vase itself is decorated by a floral cross which became the convention until the end of the 19th century. Note the other small vase just above the central rose. The boteh is constructed around the symmetrical play of large roses. What sets this particular pattern apart stylistically are the thick rose stems. See Plates 102 and 144 for similar treatments. Compare the contemporary two-tone hashias of Plates 111 and 112 and Colour Plate 24. This colour designation comes from the hashia's rosettes which appear divided in half by the distinct outlining of blue on the bottom and red on the top.

Plate 116. Shoulder mantle. Mughal, mid-18th century. 138cm x 318cm.

A mughal hunting shawl, with people and animals portrayed in a splendid array of bright crisp colours on a rich salmon ground. In the shawl's top left corner two attendants are warming themselves around an open fire. In contrast to the rest of the palla's salmon ground, the top row of animals appear on a green ground. Many objects are unrecognisable, for example underneath the white horse appears a thick blue line resting on three yellow 'wheels'. Four vertical grey stacks rise curiously from this line. On the other hand, blue is used to colour the caparisoned elephant upon which sit a stout Mughal and an elephant boy. A hunter, with raised spear in hand, mounted on a white horse, is seen attacking a leopard.

Another leopard is shown in the process of devouring a fallen white deer. Behind the horse stands the hunter's retainer. In the lower left corner stands a chimerical figure outlined in bright red, and wearing a large yellow turban or hat. The remaining colours are pale yellow, saffron, reddish salmon, black and beige.

Plate 117. Shoulder mantle. Mughal, mid-18th century. 132cm x 320cm.

Another Mughal hunting shawl contemporary with Plate 116, and in a similar style. Although more finely drawn than Plate 116, the scene is nevertheless much less dramatic as no actual combat is depicted except for a leopard in the lower left corner, chased by a retainer brandishing a sword and shield. In the upper left corner an important Mughal personnage appears enthroned, waited upon by two attendants while a third is waving a large banner. A Mughal on horseback admires a bouquet of flowers while in front a caparisoned elephant carries another Mughal and his two attendants. Colours: chrome and mustard yellow, orange, pink, fawn, crimson red, grey, bluish green, blue and indigo blue and black on a white ground.

Plate 118. Shoulder mantle. Afghan period, c.1770. 190cm x 133cm.

This buti-palla was supposedly brought from India in about 1770 by Thomas Coulson. The hashia, similar to that in Plate 115, offers a small but interesting transitional link in shawl iconography due to the shawl's known purchase date. These particular hashia patterns were then quite popular but disappeared almost compeltely by the end of the 18th century.

Plate 119. Waistband. Mughal, mid-18th century. 466cm x 72cm.

A truly stately effect has been ingeniously created by the use of racemes arranged in stiff rising columns of regimented rectilinear flower buds. The blue and yellow flowers are outlined in black as are the mound's diverging racemes.

Plate 120. Shoulder mantle. Mughal, mid-18th century. 113cm x 137cm.

The similarities illustrated by this piece and that in Colour Plate 26 demonstrate how a particular style was perpetuated although in a minor role. The cartoon-like cogwheel flowers of Plate 120 reappear in the butis of Colour Plate 26 at the base of the raceme. They also feature there in the hashia pattern in which they develop an unusually fine and unique meander.

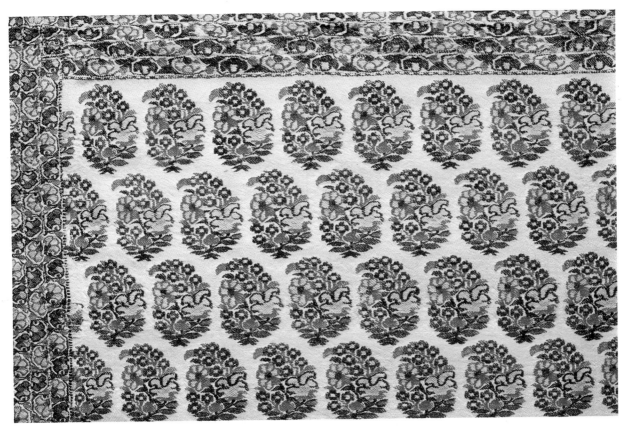

Colour Plate 26. Shoulder mantle (fragment). Mughal, mid-18th century. 48cm x 88cm.

Note the flowers used in the border of Plate 120 reappear in the butis of this shoulder mantle. They also feature as the hashia pattern. The style here, especially in the lower leaves and root recall the undulating style in Plate 144.

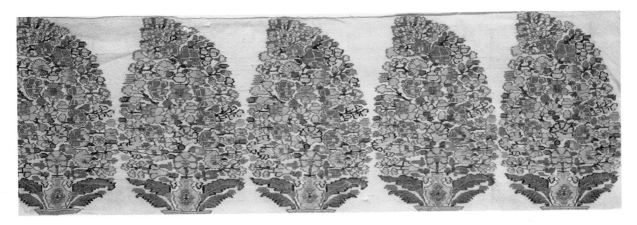

Colour Plate 27. Shoulder mantle. Afghan, c.1770. 20cm x 93cm.

Very little elbow room is provided for the regiment of botehs in this example, something which may tend to confuse the shawl's chronological sequence. Perhaps if the hashias were not missing, we would be able to decipher more clues. The two pairs of 'wings' and the incongruous vase are pleasing as are the lower saw-tooth leafy fronds which represent drooping leaves almost folded in half. Compare the vase with Plates 135 and 136. The morphology of the boteh and its cluttered floral content is similar to that in Plate 123.

Plate 121 (above). Shoulder mantle. Mughal, mid-18th century. 142cm x 316cm.
Plate 122 (opposite above). Shoulder mantle (fragment). Mughal, mid-18th century.

Despite the heavily charged multi-floral bouquet, an overriding Mughal impression persists in Plates 121 and 122. The former is far from a masterpiece of weaving. Nevertheless, its style is quite out of the ordinary and worth appraising. The mound displays those queer protrusions we find on Plate 102; as a matter of fact the mound is rather 'busy' with many kinds of botanical devices. Up at the boteh's top we see that the large rose is flanked by small flower clusters in the form of crosses. This same phenomenon can be seen again in Plates 125 and Colour Plate 28, p.210. The hashias are simply lovely, and they may be much earlier than the botehs. They exhibit a rare shawl flower species which is something like that in Plates 120 and Colour Plate 26, p.207. Their draftsmanship is much finer than the botehs.

Plate 122 ▲

Plate 123. Shoulder mantle. Afghan, 18th century. 137cm x 321cm

This piece falls in well with the preceding two shawl pieces. The floral content is somewhat cluttered and the boteh has a stubby appearance similar to that in Colour Plate 27, p.207. The unusual amount of white thread highlighting, popular around 1800, is atypical here.

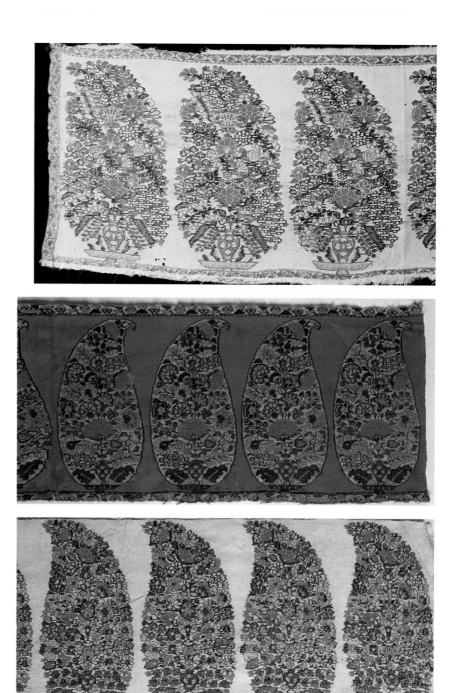

Colour Plate 28 (top). Shoulder mantle (fragment). Afghan, c.1770. 136cm x 21cm.
Colour Plate 29 (centre). Shoulder mantle (fragment). Afghan, c.1770. 22cm x 87cm.
Colour Plate 30 (bottom). Shoulder mantle (fragment). Afghan, c.1770. 19cm x 115cm.

These three examples display the 'Qajar' boteh, with its Persian and Afghanistan affinities, also seen in Plates 124 and 125. In Colour Plate 28 may be seen the star-leaf clusters and large saw-tooth fronds also seen in Plate 125. Colour Plate 30 displays a large rose, around which flower buds radiate, similar to that in Plates 124 and 125. Colour Plate 29 is the most intriguing; the botanical naturalness of and free-spacing among the boteh's flowers recall a definite Mughal elegance, uncommon among the other pieces in this group. But why did the artist enclose this fine bouquet in a sharp curvilinear cone and surround it in an aggressive red ground colour? Perhaps the artist, reared in the Mughal school, perfunctorily succumbed to the new wave in fashion that demanded the cone form.

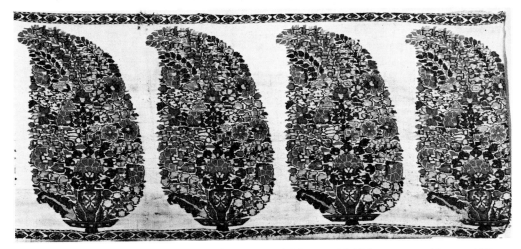

Plate 124 (above). Shoulder mantle (fragment). Afghan, mid-18th century. 19cm x 106cm.
Plate 125 (below). Shoulder mantle. Afghan, c.1770. 279cm x 117cm.

The name 'Qajar' has been given to the type of boteh in these two pieces. The appellation derives from their similarities in form to those found on the patterned trousers of a girl in an early Qajar dynasty painting, hitherto the only known 18th century Oriental painting in which a Kashmir shawl boteh is positively identifiable (see Falk, *Qajar Painting,* 1972). They are transitional pieces providing an important link between earlier types as in plates 121, 122 and 123 and later pieces as in Plates 162, 164 and 166 and Colour Plate 39, p.256. Plates 124 and 125 share obviously distinct design elements. In each is a large rose around which flower buds appear to orbit, radiating like spokes of a wheel (see also Colour Plate 30). Racemes sprout at the cone's vertex as if bent by the wind. Compare the two-tone hashia in Plate 125 with those in Plates 111 and Colour Plate 24, p.199. Also note the small feathered-edge cone to the right of the radial flower in Plate 125, and the star-leaf clusters and large saw-tooth fronds (see also Colour Plate 28).

   Going back over two hundred years, the style of this unique group of shawls (see also Colour Plates 28, 29 and 30) may have been closely identified with the contemporary fashion of Persia and Afghanistan whose cultures were strongly intermixed. Indian taste preferred rather more naturalistic botehs as in Plates 134, 135 and 136.

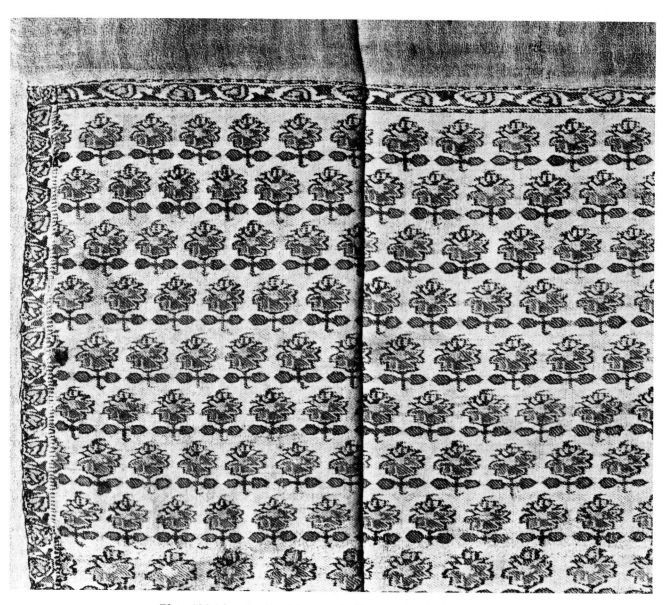

**Plate 126 (above). Shoulder mantle (fragment). Mughal, early 18th century. 30cm x 26cm.
Plate 127 (opposite). Shoulder mantle (fragment). Mughal, early 18th century.**

Although the crocus flower is seen only in the hashia of plate 126, the hashia of both
fragments contain the long arching meander which matches in style to Plates 106 and 107.
The bow-tie sprigs with umbrella handles in Plate 126 create a visually satisfying floral-
linear pattern.

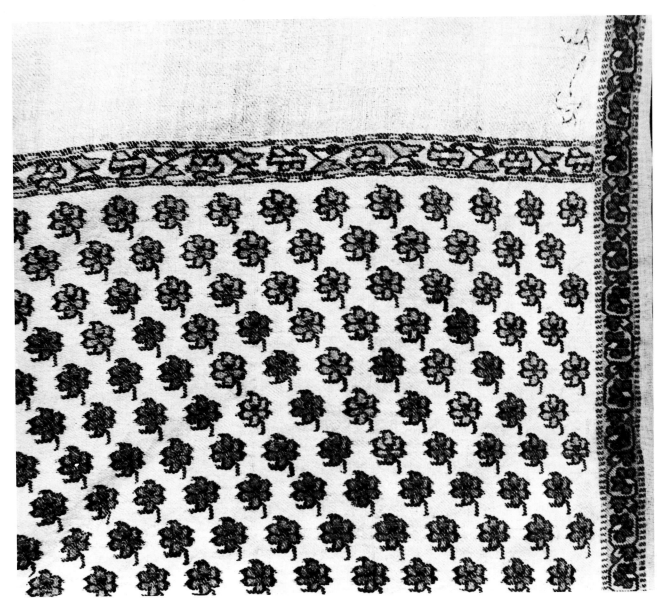

Plate 127

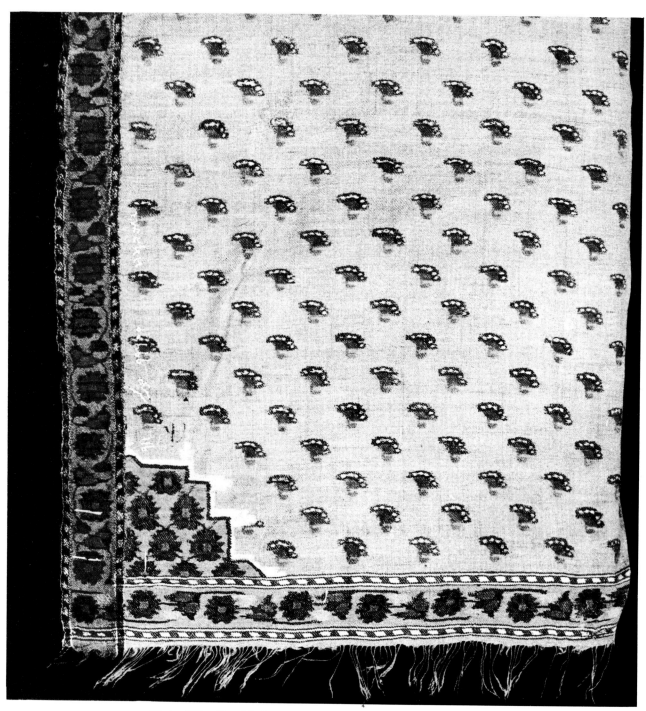

Plate 128. Kerchief or 'moon' shawl. Mughal, mid-18th century. 113cm x 114cm.

This is probably the earliest known moon shawl. The white stripes of the hashias' guard borders flanking the unusual white rhomboidal specks indicates an archetypal pattern and a distinct departure from the standard patka patterns normally employed. A unique beige-rose coloured ground illuminates the diapered field of jewel-like flower buds whose stems terminate in an umbrella-handle shape. Red roses and dark green leaves outlined in black form the matching vine meander of both hashias. The small size of the central and quarter medallions provides further clues to a very early fashion of decorating the fields of head cloths.

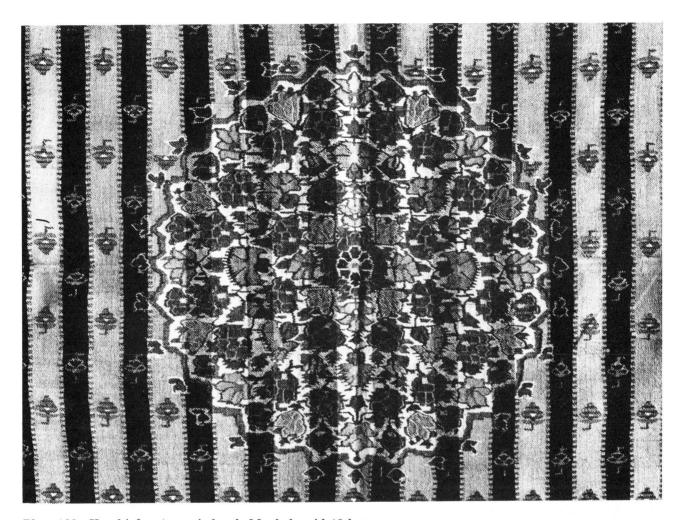

Plate 129. Kerchief or 'moon' shawl. Mughal, mid-18th century.

Chanders of the 18th century drawn in a naturalistic or even semi-naturalistic style are rare indeed. The floral inspiration of this extra-fine tus kerchief is, for the main part, Mughal. This is evident from the crocus and pin-wheel type flower of the three-flower repeat which describes the outer circumference of the central medallion. The crocus disappeared in Kashmir patterns after the last quarter of the 18th century. See the hashias of Plates 106 and 107. The pin-wheel type flower can be seen to predominate in the boteh of Plate 100, probably at a time when it was very popular. However in later patterns we find it was relegated to a minor floral detail, such as here, or in hashia designs up to the first quarter of the 19th century.

Colour Plate 31. Waistband. Afghan, late 18th century. 69cm x 640cm.

Also shown as Plate 135 where full details are given.

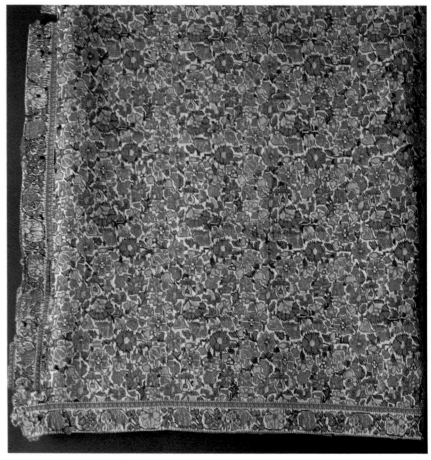

Colour Plate 32. Patterned 'kani' fabric. Afghan, late 18th century. 90cm x 126cm.

This type of fabric was woven to be cut up for garments such as trousers, vests, socks and hats. It is similar to that shown in Plates 142 and 143. The motifs in this fabric included a large single red rose stuck in a pale yellow vase mounted on a raised dish.

Plate 130. Shoulder mantle. Afghan, mid-18th century. 127cm x 300cm.

The pagoda-like sprigs on a rich salmon ground are distinguished by the angularity of their green flower petals, stacked in three levels. The well-designed hashias, which retain the pagoda theme, blend harmoniously with the palla's elegant pattern.

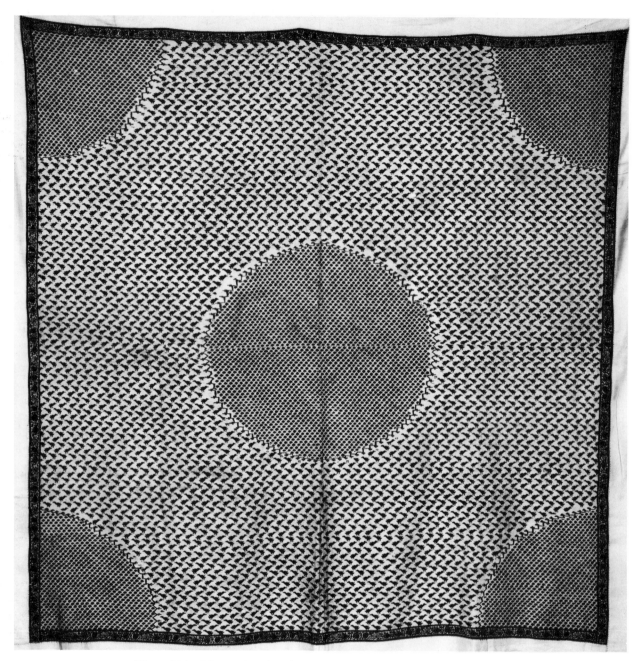

Plate 131. Moon shawl. Afghan, early 19th century. 80cm x 80cm.

Close inspection of the chandar or moon shawl reveals a unique field pattern of small ducks facing the same direction in alternating rows. The zig-zag arches of the quarter medallions have been 'pricked in' with a pale-green dye. Enclosed inside the medallions is another pattern of pagoda-like sprigs similar to that of Plate 130. The cloud-band hashia (sewn on) of 'bent tip strawberries', roses and 'pin-wheel' flowers is beautifully executed with a rare fineness. The horizontal line across the centre reveals where the two separate halves of the shawl were joined. The irregular spacing where the ducks approach the medallions circumference indicates that a proper pattern weave solution was not achieved — something extremely difficult with a pattern of this nature. The large size of the medallions tend to preclude the dating of this piece before 1815.

Plate 132. Shoulder mantle. Mughal, mid-18th century. 219cm x 135cm.

Pale salmon-coloured marigolds appear joined in horizontal rows by their pointed blue leaves on a white ground. The normally monotone hashia of hexagonally enclosed flower buds is here enlivened with red, blue and yellow.

Plate 133. Shoulder mantle. Mughal, mid-18th century.

This is another variation of the same theme as in Plate 132 although here the pointed base leaves are drawn in less delicately with a supporting raised dish on a mound. The tricoloured tulips of yellow, green and red, resembling a chain of tiny clochettes, form a novel pattern on a ground of luminescent salmon pashmina, a colour for which the Mughals retained a predilection.

Plate 134. Waistband. Afghan, late 18th century. 385cm x 135cm.

Although the delicately woven flowers are reminiscent of an earlier Mughal style, the large vase, dish and racemes would tend to date this patka boteh well into the Afghan period. Other design devices which advance this argument are the two palmettes in the boteh's centre and of course the separate vase of roses between the botehs. Compared to the large serrated drooping pistil in Plate 111 the one in this example assumes the more noble shape of a crown.

Plate 135 (above). Waistband. Afghan, late 18th century. 69cm x 640cm.
Plate 136 (opposite). Waistband. Afghan, late 18th century. 636cm x 67.5cm.

These two pieces are variants of Plate 134 and are grouped here because of their unusual vase similarities and chromatic range. In Plate 135 (also shown as Colour Plate 31, p.216) the white-outlined flowers of pale blue, grey, green and various shades of red are all artistically highlighted by the patka's exotic ground colour of rosy peach. A burnt orange ground is employed in Plate 136 although the same colour scheme as in Plate 135 is retained to enliven the otherwise less finely drawn flowers. Compare these vases to that in Colour Plate 27, p.207. The hashias in Plates 134, 135 and 136 show a particularly well-defined and freely spaced meander and they retain, along with the cloud band motif, the fine Mughal touch of the 17th century patkas.

Plate 136

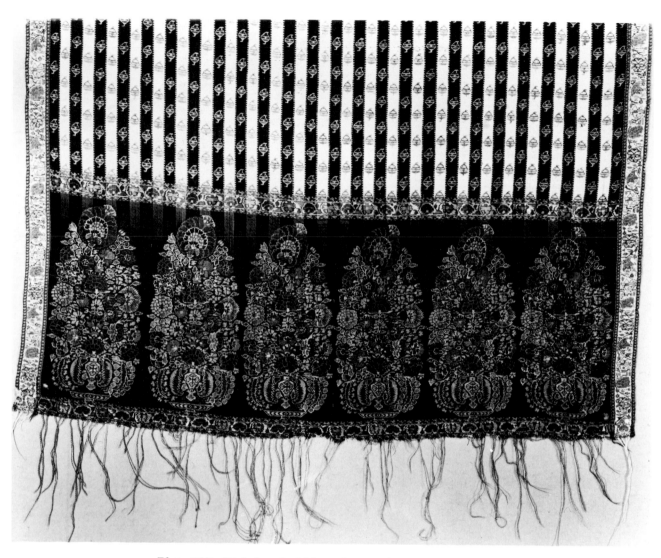

Plate 137. Waistband. Afghan, late 18th century.

The magnificent stately botehs which pattern this waistband represent the finest woven specimens of their genre. At the base is a large raised dish which supports a curious bell-shaped object surmounted by a tall vase. The vase is enclosed on either side by two hanging arched and serrated fronds the undersides of which are illuminated by tinges of yellow to illustrate leaf-folding. Serrated leafy fronds of this type were closely associated with Ottoman court embroideries. Flanking these fronds and enclosing the boteh's base are two large racemes, one in blue and the other in red.

The novel ikat-dyed warps of the khatraaz field represent an interesting artistic intrusion into the palla. Identical boteh patterns, although less fine, are conserved by the Calico Museum, Ahmedabad, and the Victoria and Albert Museum, London.

Plate 138. Waistband. Afghan, late 18th century. 896cm x 74cm.

Although entirely woven in one piece, the full length of this unusually long patka is divided in half by the red and white matan (not shown here) whose colours extend into the palla. Representing the initial developments of the 'coif' boteh technique are the detached flower branches alongside the boteh's top. At the bottom, touching the hashia are separate botehs which represent variants of the 'bow-tie' style (see also Plates 105 and 126). The lower half of the boteh is distinguished by three 'radial' floral arrangements the centres of which are dominated by roses and vases.

Plate 139

Plate 139 (opposite). Moon shawl. Afghan, c.1800. 148cm x 149cm.
Plate 140 (above). Patterned kani fabric. Afghan, c.1800. 75cm x 295cm.

Although in terribly poor condition the checkerboard moon shawl shown in Plate 139, from the Boston Museum of Fine Arts, is nevertheless the only surviving example of its type. It is interesting to point out the large difference in weaving precision between the central (only a quarter of which is visible in this illustration) and quarter medallions and the winged buti flowers of the shawl's field. The latter are more finely drawn. Also it can be seen that a proper weaving solution was not arrived at where the checkered field meets the quarter medallions. This indicates that the shawl was probably not woven in a court workshop. However, despite this, we find an unusual design element here, something which is generally reserved only for the botehs of long shawls. This is the combination of vase, dish, leafy fronds and radial flower. Other features help to date this unique piece around 1800. One is the medallion's sawtooth-edged spandrels, a style which falls in well with that of Plate 157. It should also be noted that the checkerboard pattern is rarely seen on shawls before 1800.

Plate 141. Shoulder mantle(?) (fragment). Afghan, late 18th century. 75cm x 54cm.

Whether this small fragment originally represented part of a palla's decoration or an overall field pattern is not certain. A good guess would be that it is a fragment of the latter as this particular design has not yet appeared on any known palla. The compactness of the hashia's floral meander indicates that it was of the vertical type, which had probably extended the full length of the shawl. Note that the lower foliate part of the winged butis relates to that of the checkered moon shawl in Plate 139. The butis are contained in a rhombic trellis pattern of sawtooth leaves. This sawtooth style prevailed at the turn of the century and can be clearly seen in other pieces such as in Plates 123, 156 and 157.

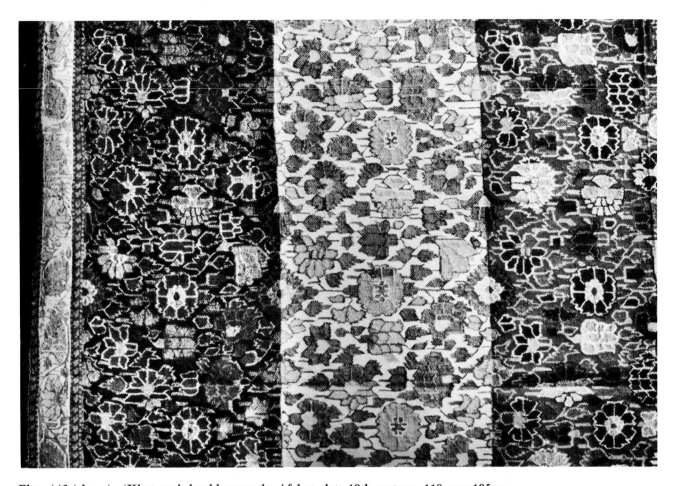

Plate 142 (above). 'Khatraaz' shoulder mantle. Afghan, late 18th century. 110cm x 185cm.
Plate 143 (overleaf). 'Khatraaz' shoulder mantle. Afghan, late 18th century.
106cm x 375cm.

Normally woven in the same dimension as the long shawl, i.e. approximately 1.35m x
3.20m, these intricate 'millefleurs' patterns must have taken at least two years to complete.
See also Colour Plate 32, p.216. This type of tapestry fabric was also used for such clothing
as trousers, vests, socks and hats. Plates 142 and 143 show similar flowers, crocus, marigold
and tulip. The end hashia in Plate 143 is unusual in that it contains the same pattern as
the vertical hashia except for the bent-tip strawberry.

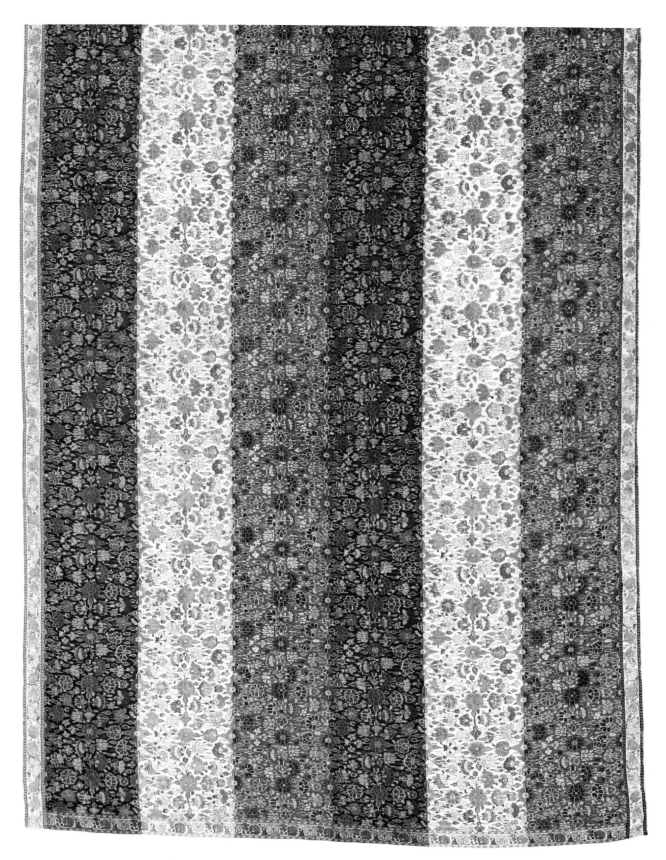

Plate 143. See previous page for caption.

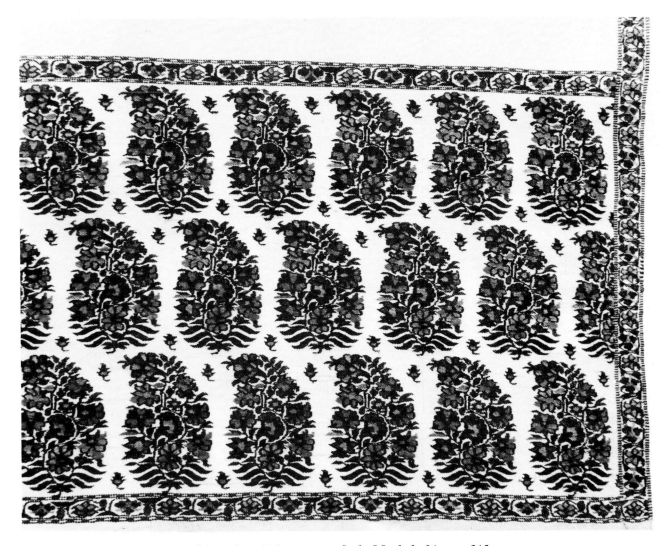

Plate 144. Shoulder mantle. Afghan, late 18th century. Style Mughal. 24cm x 315cm.

This elegant palla from the Jagdish and Kamla Mittall Museum of Indian Art, Hyderabad, contains several transitional features worthy of attention. The tiny solitary flowers foretell the arrival of ever-increasing ground embellishment. At the same time the vertical hashia exhibits an unprecedented trilobed flower which may have formed the prototype for later hashia patterns found in Plate 147 and Colour Plate 35, p.236. The fine movement created by the arching interplay of the two central flowers set on wavy leaves attests to a sophisticated level of Mughal artistry. In one corner of the palla an inscription in Devanagari reads: 38 Narayan 52. Colours (on white ground): mustard yellow, fawn, pink, crimson, red, bluish green, indigo and black.

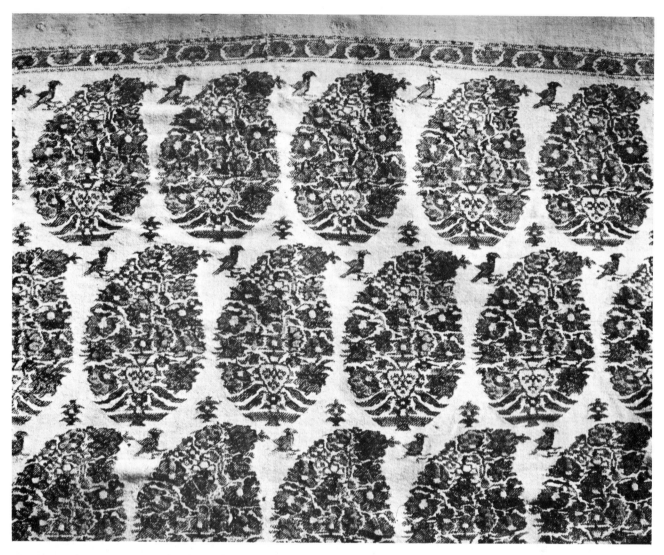

Plate 145 (above). **Shoulder mantle. Afghan, late 18th century. 21cm x 85cm.**
Plate 146 (overleaf top). **Shoulder mantle (fragment). Afghan, late 18th century.**
Style Mughal. 21cm x 97cm.
Plate 147 (overleaf below). **Shoulder mantle. Afghan, late 18th century.**
Style Mughal. 129cm x 308cm.

These three bird shawls and those shown in Colour Plates 33 and 34 (opposite) are from various collections in India and France. The birds illustrated resemble a type of tame minor bird prevalent in Northern India and especially in Srinagar where they are known as 'Hura'. Although the style is not nearly as fine as in Plate 144, Plate 145 does share some common features with it by the trefoil projection at the buti's top and the wavy fronds at the bottom. Plate 146 recalls a 17th century Mughal style. As a matter of fact it may be noted that among the buti shawls in general early classic styles often subsisted. In the coif boteh of Plate 146, the serrated leaf projections above the three roses might appear strange if it was not for the same design device of the earlier pattern in Plate 111.

A heavy symmetry invades the buti in Plate 147 through the exaggerated treatment of the large vase, dish and leafy fronds. The trilobed flower meander of the hashia is particularly unusual and may be compared to that seen in Oberkampf's tracing (Plate 50b).

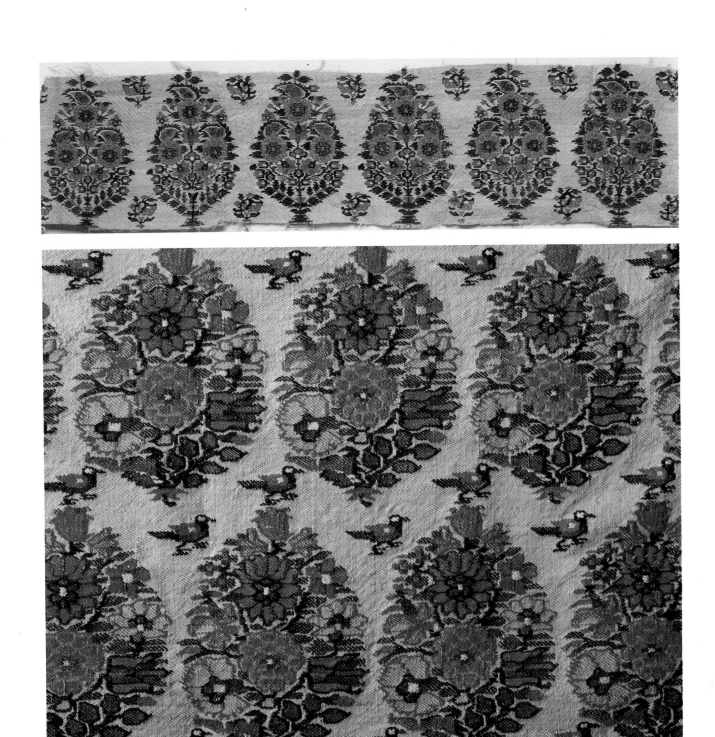

Colour Plate 33 (above). Shoulder mantle (fragment). Afghan, late 18th century. Style Mughal.
Colour Plate 34 (below). Shoulder mantle (fragment). Afghan, late 18th century. Style Mughal. 17cm x 36cm.

These two bird shawls are similar to those in Plates 145, 146 and 147. Their patterns reflect memories of the 17th century Mughal style as did many of the buti shawls of the Afghan period. Particularly well done in Colour Plate 33 is the buti's base of winged leaf and raceme which protrude obliquely from a stylised ideogram and umbrella-handle stem. Both display a charming elegance against a saffron ground.

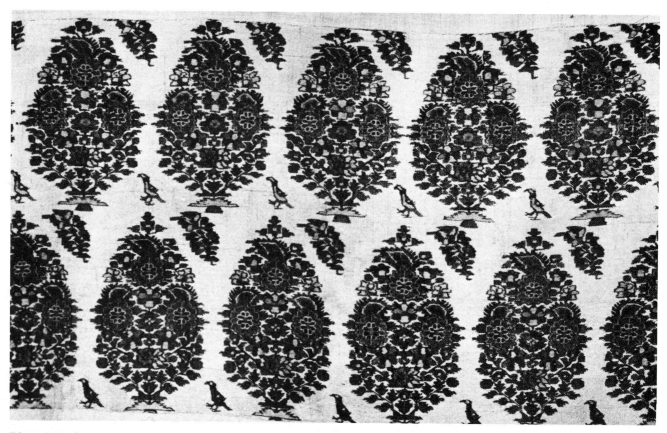

Plate 146. See p.232 for caption.

Plate 147. See p.232 for caption.

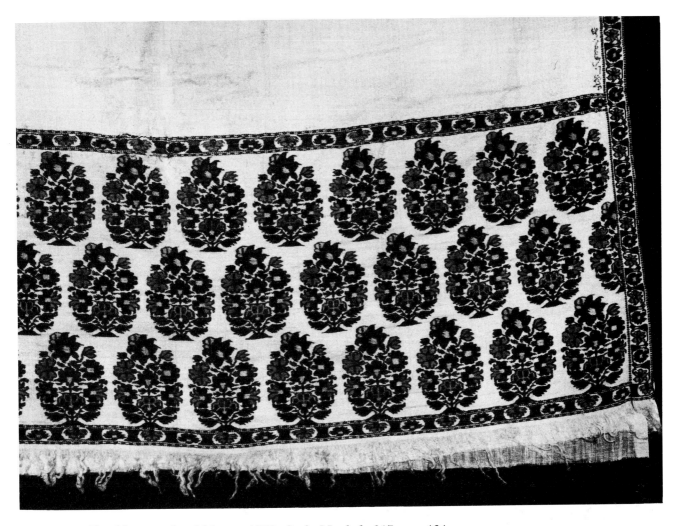

Plate 148. Shoulder mantle. Afghan c.1800. Style Mughal. 317cm x 134cm.

The butis in this example are gracefully woven and coloured in rich earth tones of cochineal, madder red, saffron and an unusual amount of forest green. The winged fronds provide a light touch to a buti pattern in which the flowers are woven with a charming delicacy. It is apparent here as in many other elegant patterns that the shawl artist carefully considered the entire field design as a complete ensemble rather than as a series of isolated elements. In the horizontal hashia the detailed floral meander has degenerated, leaving thick blocks of woven colour to separate what has now become a floral repeat. This is rather strange, for the vertical hashia has nevertheless retained intact its detailed meander (compare with Plate 144).

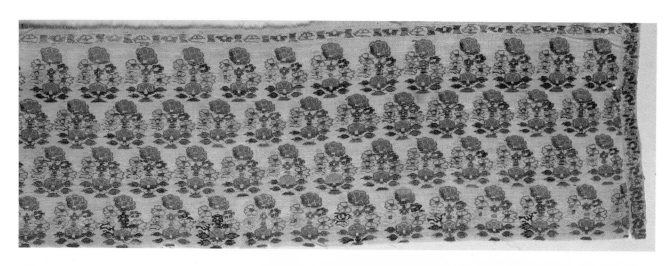

Colour Plate 35 (above). Shoulder mantle (fragment). Afghan, c.1800. Style Mughal. 17cm x 120cm.

Colour Plate 36 (below). Shoulder mantle (fragment). Afghan, c.1800. Style Mughal. 22cm x 120cm.

These shawls display similar buti patterns to that in Plate 148. We can also see examples of degenerated hashias where the meander has been simplified into a heavy floral repeat.

Plate 149 (right). 'Moon' shawl.
Afghan, late 18th century. 122cm x 134cm.
Plate 150 (below). 'Moon' shawl.
Afghan, late 18th century. 123cm x 134cm.
Plate 151 (overleaf). 'Moon' shawl.
Afghan, late 18th century. 127cm x 134cm.

Besides being woven all in one piece these three contemporary moon shawls all share similar attributes in weaving style, pattern and chromatic tones. In Plate 150 we find a winged leaf buti and umbrella stem that bespeckles the sky blue field. Its hashia, identical to that in Plate 151 is composed of a floral repeat of pin-wheel flowers and roses. It is interesting to note that one rarely finds a matching pair of both vertical and horizontal hashia patterns. The corner detail photo of these early chandars is designed to illustrate this incongruity and to show clearly the solution of field/medallion weave integration, one of the most difficult feats in moon-shawl weaving. Twisted fringes were a common finishing touch on patkas and chandars made during the second half of the 18th century.

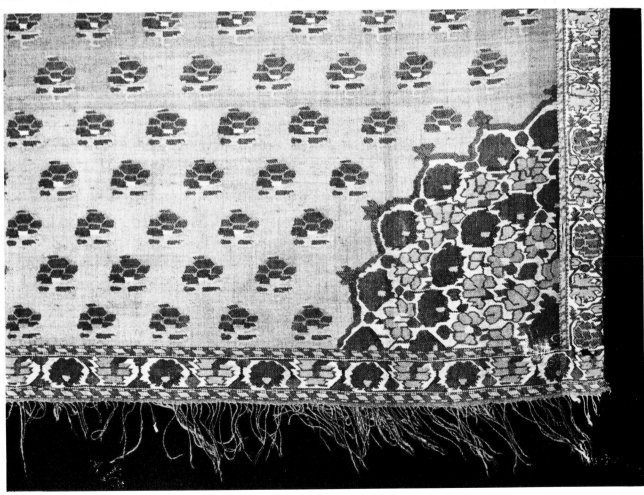

Plate 151. See previous page for caption.

Plate 152. 'Moon' shawl. Afghan, late 18th century. 96cm x 95cm.

A luminescent saffron-yellow field and white-ground medallions patterned with polychrome flora of mustard, pink, madder red, bright sky blue and forest green, all combine to make for a very attractive piece. Through its dazzling display of colours this fine shawl, possibly shah tus, despite its rather crude weave, evokes the exotic spirit of the Orient. Due to the gross variations in weave the corner shown does not distinctly illustrate the small vase and dish which are more readily visible in the other corners.

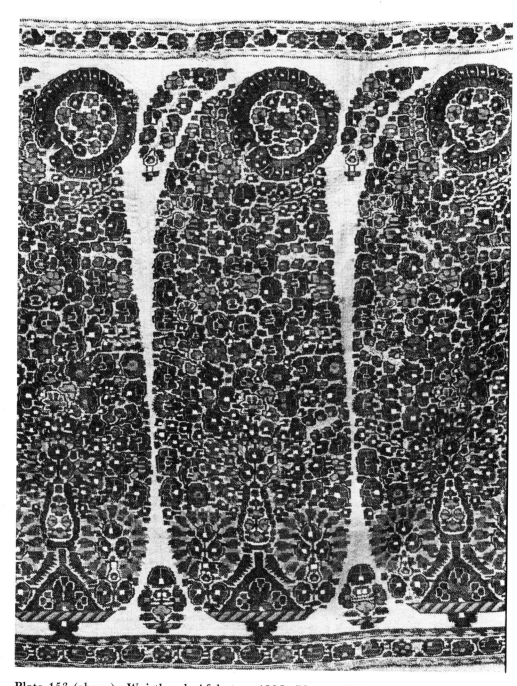

Plate 153 (above). Waistband. Afghan, c.1805. 73cm x 389cm.
Plate 154 (opposite). Waistband. Afghan, c.1805. 75cm x 488cm.
Plate 155 (overleaf). Shoulder mantle (fragment). Afghan, c.1805. 30cm x 135cm.

It seems that the number of boteh styles is endless but when several of the same species can be conveniently grouped together, finding a common denominator in the form of a descriptive appellation can often prove very useful. Therefore, of the three presented here and those in Colour Plate 43, p.263, equally we might say 'mosaic coif boteh with radial top rose'. In Plate 153 we find three radial flowers and vases at the boteh's base similar to Colour Plate 38, p.256, a Mughal style carried over from the Qajar botehs. The radial technique is found among the dense mosaic of Plate 154 supported by scalloped-edge leafy fronds. Later on these kind of rococo leaves evolved to completely surround the boteh from top to bottom. See also Plates 180 and 181.

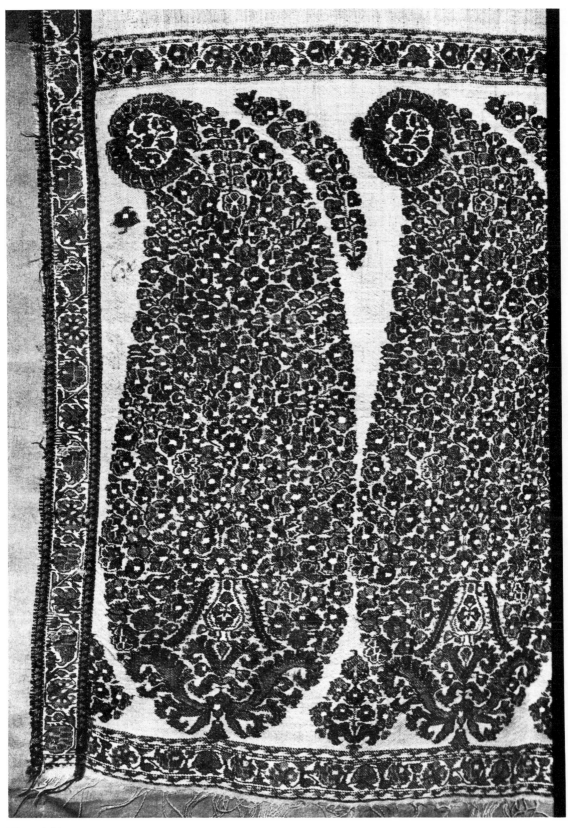

Plate 154

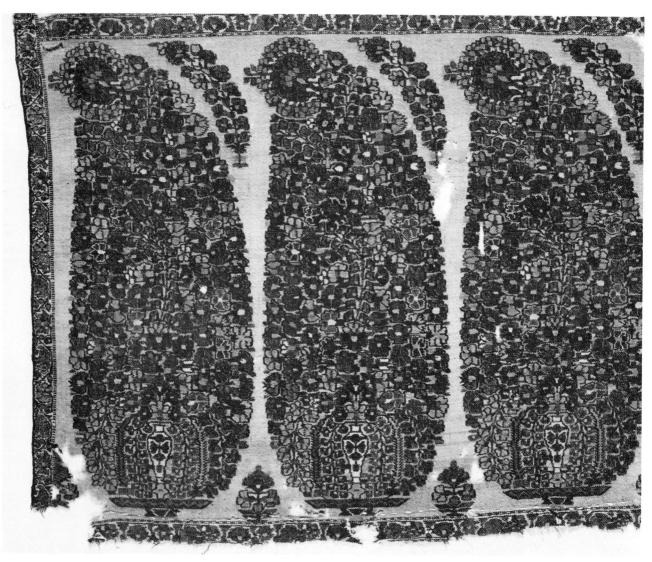

Plate 155. See p.240 for caption.

Plate 156. Shoulder mantle. Afghan, c.1805. 137cm x 304cm.

The boteh's chromatic scheme is distinguished by a profusion of pale green or greyish flowers on a deep indigo blue ground. Featured above the vibrant radial flower is again the design device of a small serrated-edge boteh which belies the strong 18th century aspect of this conservative shawl. The twin branch connection drawn vertically in the top hashia's floral interstices are indeed unusual.

Plate 157. Patterned kani fabric (pieced fragment). Afghan, c.1800. 100cm x 73cm.

This all-over plaid kani fragment and that in Colour Plate 37, both very worn and patched, are the only existing patterns of their type presently known. Although the flowers are better defined in Colour Plate 37, both fragments share a similar dense floral nature and mosaic construction of geometric shapes. These shapes also bear resemblance to the 'whirling' border pattern of the prayer hanging in Plate 161b. What strikes us most in Plate 157 is the unusual amount of leaf outlining in white thread. Also seen are small serrated-edge 'botehs' similar to those in Plate 156. Adopted from patterns such as those found in Plate 111, these 'botehs' crystalised into an independent motif at the turn of the century, a fact which readily dates such patterns to around 1800.

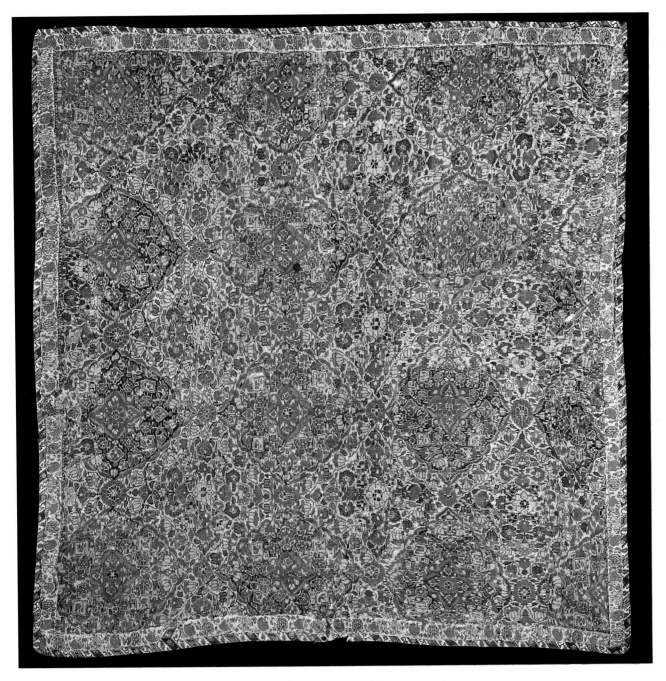

Colour Plate 37. Patterned kani fabric (pieced fragment). Afghan, c.1800. 73cm x 75cm.

Compared with Plate 157 the flowers are better defined in the present example and comparable with those found in the khatraaz pieces of Plates 130 and 132. The focal point is the large star rose contained within a quadrangle of elongated leaves. Surrounding this is a field of various angular flowers further contained within a trellis pattern also lined with serrated leaves. This popular style of serration is found in many kani weaves produced at the turn of the century.

Plate 158. Shoulder mantle. Afghan, c.1815. 136cm x 330cm.

The new innovation of compartmentalised botehs by alternating ground colour appears to have received its initial start from patka pieces such as Plate 138. Again, as in Plates 159 and 160, the small 'serrated-edge' botehs which appear intermingled within the coif botehs' floral collage is the main style characteristic of this piece. Also the matan's checkerboard pattern of 'winged-leaf' buti represents the continued popularity of a century old pattern. At the botehs' base is the floral-cross decoration normally woven on the missing vase. (See also Couders *arlequiné* shawl, Plate 64.)

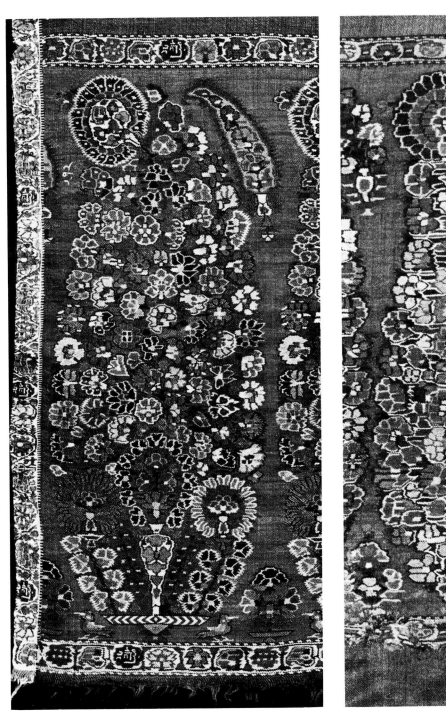
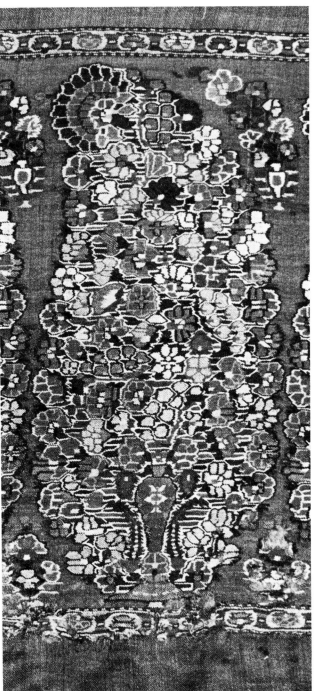

Plate 159 (left). Shoulder mantle. Afghan, c.1800. 135cm. x 382cm.
Plate 160 (right). Shoulder mantle. Afghan, c.1810. 200cm x 98cm.

The prevailing theme of these pieces relies heavily on the play of contrast. This is achieved by the heavy outlining of the flowers against a dark bordeaux ground in white or light yellow. Again the serrated edge boteh in Plates 156 and 157 has been further elaborated and brought into focus in the coif of Plate 159. Its vertical hashia is another miniaturised version of the patka's 'bent-tip strawberry' and 'pin-wheel' flower pattern. Plate 160 is an example of white outlining brought to an extreme to the extent that the design has fallen prey to a mass of white horizontal lines.

Plate 161a. 'Millefleurs' kani weave. Mughal, c.1770.

An extremely rare and exquisite piece illustrating a synthesis of Mughal and Central Asian styles.

Plate 161b. 'Millefleurs' prayer hanging. Afghan, c.1815

This magnificent 'millefleurs' kani piece derives its name from the Oriental carpets in which this rare type of design is found. Under the 'rolled' arch which suggests cloud formation is seen a profusion of flowers, racemes, vase, dish, etc. The 'radial' flower arrangements echo clearly the important shawl style which became popular during the late 18th century. Nevertheless the guard hashias flanking the large outer border demonstrate a compressed variation of the 'bent-tip' strawberry and 'pin-wheel' leaf pattern — a variation which developed about 1800. The top border's pattern is alternated by large palmettes and squares each emitting concave white stripes arranged diagonally. The bottom border eliminates the palmettes and organises the strips in a spiral fashion. In style and chromatic range this piece relates closely with Plates 159 and 160, especially by the profusion of white outlined flowers.

Plate 162 (above). Shoulder mantle. Afghan, c.1810. 135cm x 274cm.
Plate 163 (opposite). Shoulder mantle. Afghan, c.1810. 117cm x 254cm.

If the Renaissance painters Lotto and Holbein have preserved a particular style of Turkish carpet in their work, then certainly France's court painters Girodet, and Ingres may stand equally as a point of stylistic reference for the particular boteh style in Plates 162 and 163. The style may be described as the arching-raceme coif boteh and Plate 162 is probably one of the finest examples of its genre. The yellow vase, with trefoil-cross marking, containing a radial spray of flower buds is exceptionally well drawn. The vase stands on a tripartite flower cluster which reflects a similar one between the botehs. Despite the usual compactness of the boteh a great effort has been made to retain botanical reality. It is interesting to note that rarely do vertical and horizontal hashias share the same style, especially during the end of the 18th century. Plate 162 is no exception to the rule. It can be seen, however, that the flowers are basically the same and in many cases it may be that the vertical hashia is simply a compressed version of the horizontal one. This is due in part to the silk warps of the former and especially to the vertical weaving angle. Among the delightful multi-coloured hues of this piece are the dominating blue and yellow flowers outlined mostly in black which combine to form a pattern of handsome botehs illuminated by a brilliant mauve ground. The hashia pattern in Plate 163, a sinuous chain meander, shows a new development which echoes the Empire style (see Appendix I).

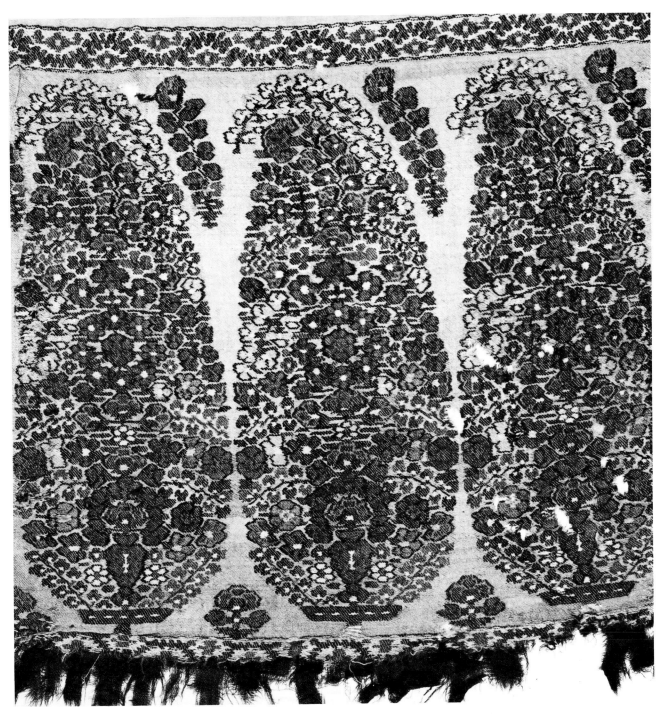

Plate 163

Plate 164. Shoulder mantle. Afghan, c.1800. 129cm x 304cm.

The style of this kashmir shawl is similar to Plate 163 though much less finely woven. The soft pastel colours on a 'burnt' saffron ground, make the shawl very attractive. The thin delicate hashias are representative of the period (see also Plate 165). The vertical hashia is a repeat of three flowers; a yellow 'pinwheel'-type, a small nondescript flower of blue, red and yellow, and a red and yellow rose bud. Note again the serrated-edge boteh in the cone.

Plate 165. Shoulder mantle. Afghan, c.1810. 137cm x 315cm.

This boteh-patterned shawl illustrates a new development in the 'coif boteh' technique. The coif and the boteh have merged to become one. The boteh's base is composed of two 'ram's horn' leafy fronds supported by a mound. The right leaf supports further the boteh's cone of flowers while the left leaf supports the rising arched raceme. Later on the raceme underwent a further development to envelop the boteh completely.

Plate 166. Shoulder mantle. Afghan, c.1810. 135cm. x 318cm.

The double hashia and rare khaki colour suggest a military aspect to this well-drawn, flamboyant piece. The delicately woven, four flower bud repeat in both vertical and horizontal hashias is further enhanced by an excellent choice of rich colours. The vertical hashia pattern relates to Plate 164 by the double separation of buds and the squareness of the angular vine meander. The squareness results from the continued fusing of foliate meander elements which lost their naturalness over time. The artist has taken full advantage of this transmutation, enlivening them with bright alternating red and green thread. Each flower of the hashia stands out sharply and distinctly due to the illuminating effect of carefully detailed outlining. Some of them assume the aspect of cut gems.

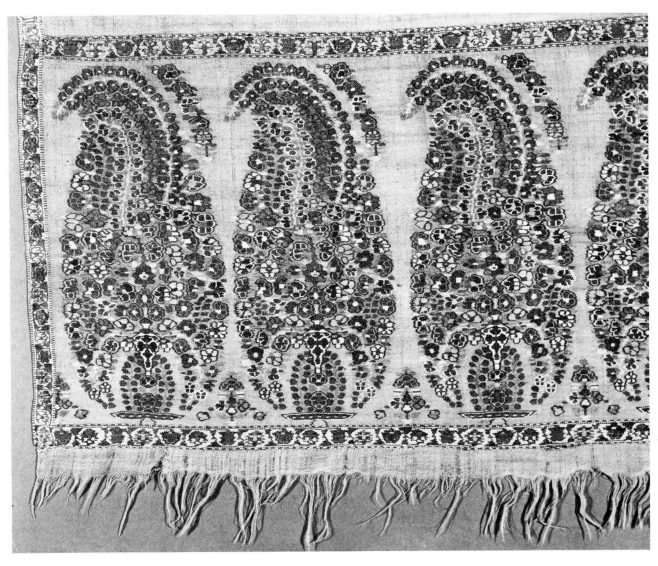

Plate 167. Shoulder mantle. Afghan, c.1805. 270cm x 127cm.

An 'Empire' boteh (also seen in Colour Plate 39, overleaf) woven in graceful style from the Museum of Fine Arts, Boston, Mass. It is distinguished by the horseshoe curve of its base and the added sinuousity of the inner top raceme.

**Colour Plate 38. Sholder mantle (fragment).
Afghan, c.1800. 91cm x 152cm.**

One of the finest kani weaves of the turn of the century.
These exquisite botehs display a stunning *tour-de-force* in
design creativity. Taking advantage of the flexible
morphology of the boteh's base elements, the naqqash
has artfully combined three distinct schools of shawl
draftsmanship. Starting with the mound and its bifur-
cated two-tone fronds we have an interesting revival, as
in Plate 166, of a mid-18th century Mughal theme. See
Plate 111, 112 and 113. The exaggerated curling of these
scalloped-edge fronds signals the beginning of a design
device which later on enveloped the whole boteh. See
Plates 180 and 181. But the exciting nature of this
predominantly Afghan boteh lies in the use of the 'radial-
flower' technique. This dochalla in its original form
probably displayed three horizontal and two vertical
hashia strips. In the second strip of the latter, notice the
trilobed flower within the repeating red roses. This design
blend can also be seen in Plates 157 and undoubtedly had
already become a principal hashia theme as in Plate 147.

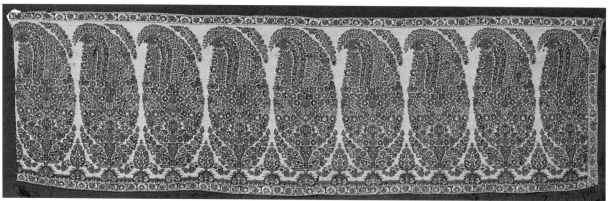

**Colour Plate 39. Shoulder mantle (fragment).
Afghan, c.1810. 29cm x 120cm.**

Balancing the boteh by its bulbous base is a vase posed delicately in the middle of the
encircling arch of the two flower clusters. This multiple curvilinear style, set on a saffron
ground, recalls the contemporary Napoleonic laurel crown. The symbol of the laurel became
popular during the Consulate, extending well into the First Empire. The vertical and
horizontal hashias consist of an uncommonly large floral repeat of eight or seven flower
respectively.

Plate 168. 'Moon' shawl. Afghan, c.1810. 140cm x 154cm.

One of the most finely executed moon shawls, this piece embodies the beautiful qualities of the late Afghan style. Smooth curving arches described by the medallion's spandrels, and detailed polychrome flowers all evenly spaced, are just some of the few characteristics immediately noticeable in this tight detail. A pair of large 'radial' flowers are highlighted under the pointed domes within the quarter medallions. Exceptional care was taken to insure that both hashias were identically woven. The floral draftsmanship should be compared with that in Plate 171 and Colour Plate 41, p.259, also moon shawls.

Colour Plate 40. 'Moon' shawl (two views). Afghan, c.1810. 200cm x 190cm.

This piece with its intense cosmic image with direct appeal, illustrates a fine example of one of the most difficult kani weaves and a moon shawl whose curves are exceptionally smooth and unbroken. The weaver is forced to make many corrections to oppose the warp twist which tends constantly to distort the curvilinear pattern with every weft shot. An exquisite richness of colour and delicacy of design is exhibited by the large and very uncommon khatraaz (stripe) border in this example. It shares similar characteristics in style and colour to the previous moon shawl.

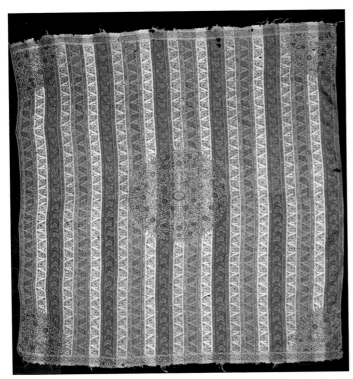

Colour Plate 41. 'Moon' shawl (two views). Afghan, c.1815. 160cm x 160cm.

In the moon shawls of this period we come across another distinct design pattern which enjoyed a large popularity. The central medallion is composed of rosettes in the form of flattened flowers in an orbiting fashion around a large central flower and is similar to that in Plate 170. It is particularly interesting to see how the idea of a 'transparent' central medallion on a colourful khatraaz background creates the illusion of a moon in free suspension. The beautiful colours, the rich rose, dark indigo, and the bright cochineal virtually disappeared after the early Sikh period.

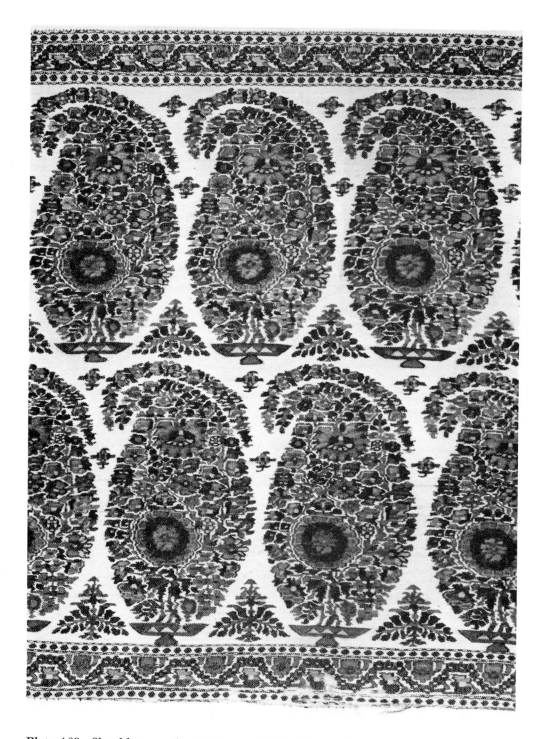

Plate 169. Shoulder mantle. Afghan, c.1815. 270cm x 127cm.

The hashia's 'chain' meander and guard border's hexagonal flecks developed into a popular pattern in early Sikh period shawls. Yet the boteh's floral arrangement remains steeped in late Afghan style. This may be observed in the two large round roses and especially the crooked branch which creeps up from the dish to surround the circular rose invading the rest of the boteh's interior. Many of the coif boteh's colours show signs of having been 'pricked in', notably the mint green and saffron yellow which have left smudge traces.

Plate 170. 'Moon' shawl. Afghan, c.1815.

In the moon shawls of this period we come across another distinct design pattern which enjoyed a large popularity. A central medallion is composed of rosettes in the form of flattened flowers uniformly arranged in pairs and in an orbiting fashion round a large central flower (see also Colour Plate 41, p.259). The medallion's field contains a dense foliage of scattered racemes.

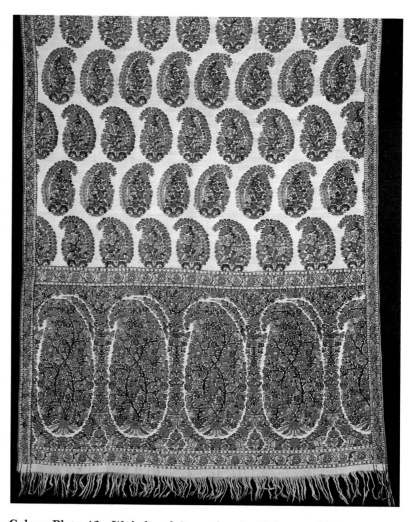

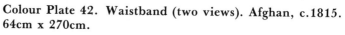

Colour Plate 42. Waistband (two views). Afghan, c.1815. 64cm x 270cm.

The importance of this piece is that it represents one of the earliest developments of full ground ornamentation. As in Plate 169, the creeping branch retains the same style. The matan's 'ram's horn', coif boteh may be compared with Plate 165.

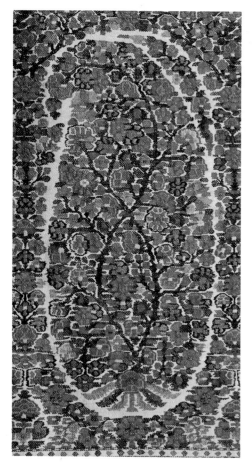

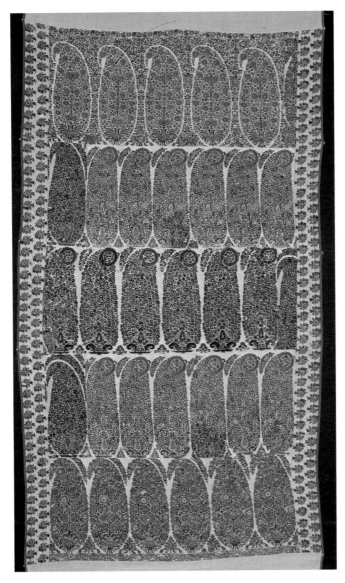

**Colour Plate 43.   Shoulder mantle (pieced collection of palla fragments).
Afghan, c.1800. 92cm x 156cm.**

This piece is a collection of palla fragments joined together to form a modern shoulder
mantle. They illustrate botehs on a saffron ground — a popular colour at the turn of the
18th century. Those of both the bottom and the top rows share the same theme of rosettes
growing from stiff vertical branches. The stiff branches suggest the beginnings of the 'tree'
boteh as in Plate 172. In the second and third rows from the top, the cone botehs are
basically identical except for slight variations in detail. For example, the appearance of the
small serrated-edge boteh is absent in the third row.

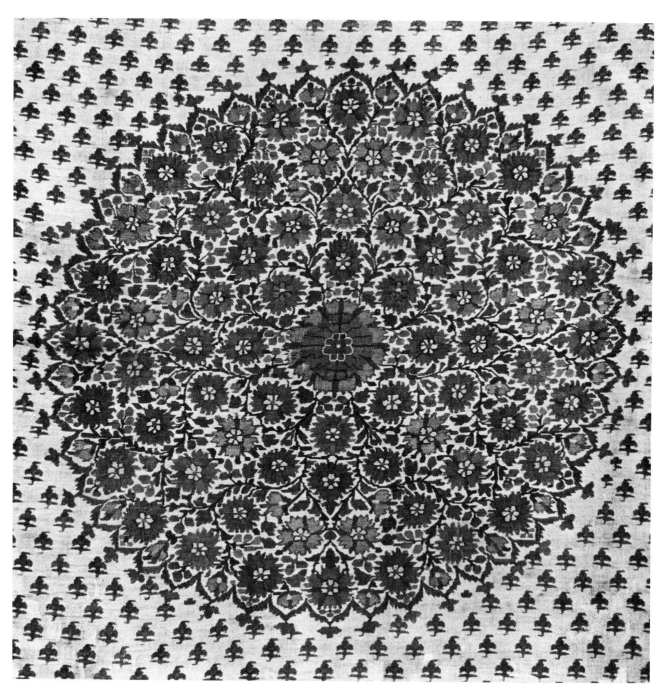

Plate 171a (above) and 171b (opposite). 'Moon' shawl. Afghan, c.1815. 149cm x 140cm.

A distinct transitional style underlies the basic concept of this fine moon shawl. Its style departs from the 'Afghan compression' of compact and minute flower buds, racemes, etc., to create a freedom of botanical movement recalling a style reminiscent of the contemporary Norwich drawloom shawl. The meticulous detail applied to the chandar's scalloped circumference suggests a shawl made by a master weaver.

Plate 171b

Plate 172

Plate 172 (opposite). Shoulder mantle. Afghan, c.1810. 136cm x 316cm.

In this superb pattern, we can see the stamp of the same draftsman's hand throughout the hashia and the boteh as is found in Colour Plate 44, p.273, indicating that we are dealing with an original design. What often happens is that in successive shawl copies the talims contained only the boteh pattern weaving code. As a result boteh patterns became crossbred with the displaced hashia talims. This sample might be placed among the group of Plates 175-178 because of the thick knotty roots at the boteh's base. This ingenious root treatment invariably evokes a queer comic relief to loosen up an otherwise stiff design.

Plate 173 (above). Shoulder mantle. Afghan, c.1810. 130cm x 312cm.

Recently a number of shawls have been found exhibiting the delicate style of fine draftsmanship seen here; woven products of a distinct atelier. The dense diapered field of Plate 173 is framed by a marvellous hashia pattern featuring rectilinear branches, a motif popular during the First Empire. Often the predominant colour is a pale green. See Plate 174. (The AEDTA collection, Paris, conserves three fine examples from this school of draftsmanship.)

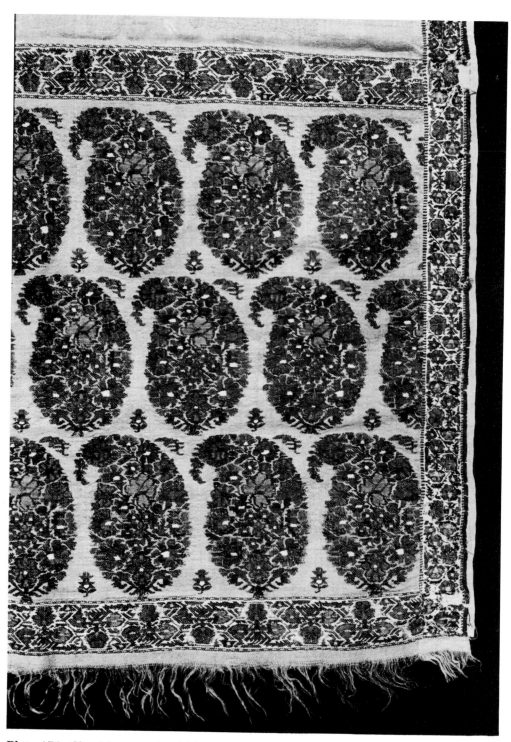

Plate 174. Shoulder mantle. Afghan, c.1815. 129cm x 300cm.

A saffron ground and pastel flowers provide a warm illuminating aspect to this handsome buti shawl. The hashi's green serrated leaves and red, blue and rose coloured flowers follow a similar school of design to the previous piece. The idea of these flowers, set at right angles, may have been taken from the popular vase decoration of flowers set in the form of a cross.

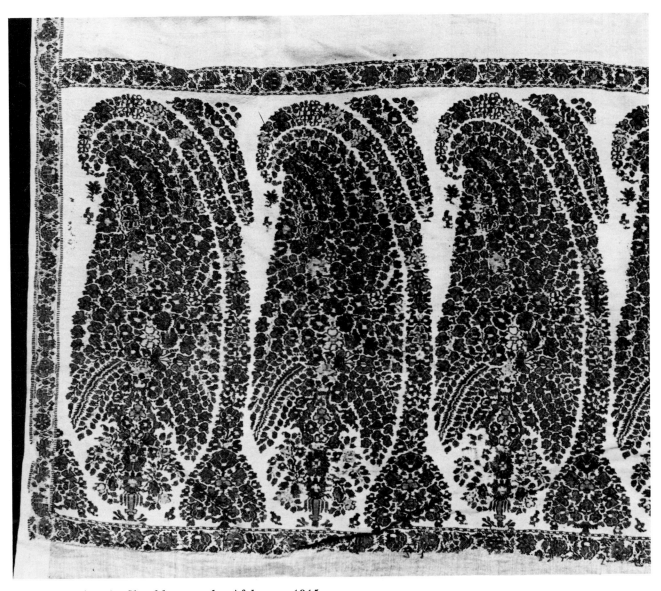

Plate 175 (above). Shoulder mantle. Afghan, c.1815.
Plate 176 (overleaf). Shoulder mantle. Afghan, c.1815. 127cm x 330cm.

Although botanically of an entirely different nature, these two pieces share a similar pattern
by the large encircling coif branch of flowers which rises from between the botehs. Plate 176
from the Victoria and Albert Museum is a masterpiece of kani weaving. The boteh's well-
proportioned style draws much of its influence from the traditional school of the 18th century
shawl artists as shown for example by the radial flower. (See Plate 73 for an almost exact
European imitation of this boteh.) The ponderous branches are probably descendents of the
stiff-branch boteh seen in Colour Plate 42, p.262, which probably provided the initial
impulse for the development of the 'tree' boteh. Notice the identical draftsmanship of Plates
172 and 176, especially in the hashias, also the corner branch ornaments of Plate 187,
although in the former the foliate meander was given exceptional design emphasis. Another
'tree' boteh is conserved in the Bharat Kala Bhawan which indicates that this style may have
enjoyed a considerable popularity.

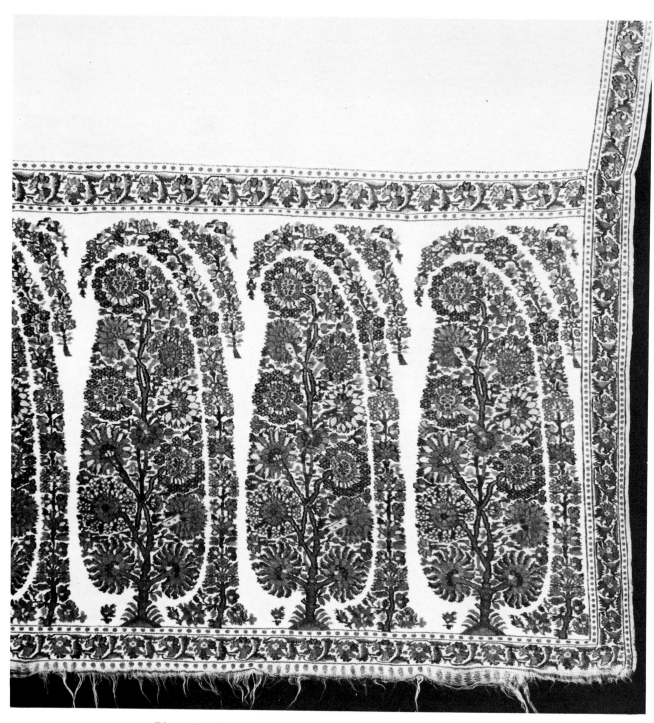

Plate 176. See previous page for caption.

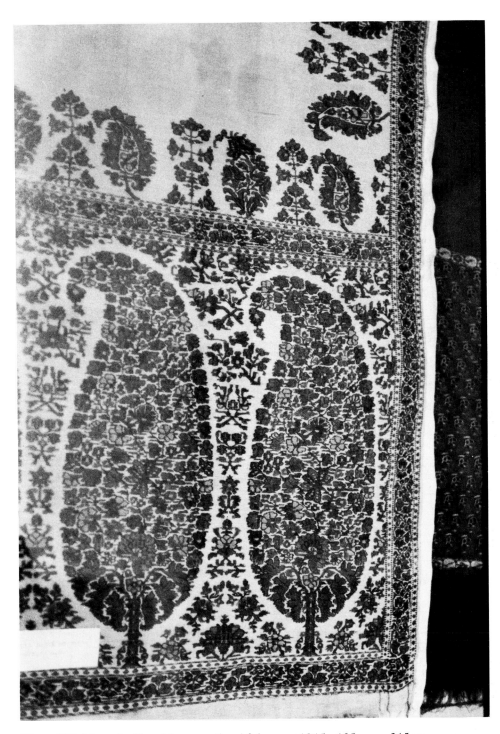

Plate 177 (above). Shoulder mantle. Afghan, c.1815. 135cm x 315cm.
Plate 178 (overleaf). Waistband. Afghan, c.1815. 50cm x 308cm.

These examples are similar to the previous two pieces in the large supporting trunks of the botehs. They remain true to the excellence of late Afghan weaving by their crisp floral detail. It is always interesting to come across two Kashmir shawls which share almost 'word for word' the same weaving pattern. This is the case of the two pallas here except that the boteh outline in Plate 178 shows leaves instead of flowers. Similarities end here; the richly woven hashias of Plate 178 retain some of the most beautiful remnants of earlier Mughal weaving. The matan of this piece is of a later date.

Plate 178. See previous page for caption.

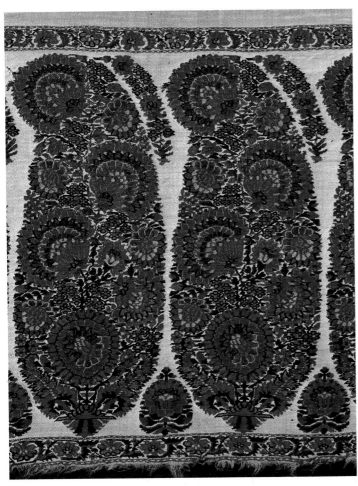

Colour Plate 44. Shoulder mantle.
Afghan, c.1815. 135cm x 304cm.

Every once in a while one encounters a pattern which takes you by surprise and leave you in awe. Here you can see the hand of the same draftsman as that of Plate 172. The novel use of large circular roses in bright reds, yellows and blues endows this exceptionally fine shawl with a wonderful cheerfulness.

Colour Plate 45. Shoulder mantle.
Sikh, c.1820. Style Afghan. 140cm x 290cm.

This type of elaborately worked, long shawl is popularly known as a 'jamawar' or gown piece. The matan's blue patterned field of floral sprays is entirely kani woven. Luxurious weaves of this order required years of labour before being removed from the loom. The treatment of the boteh's flowers and base correlate closely with those of Plate 179.

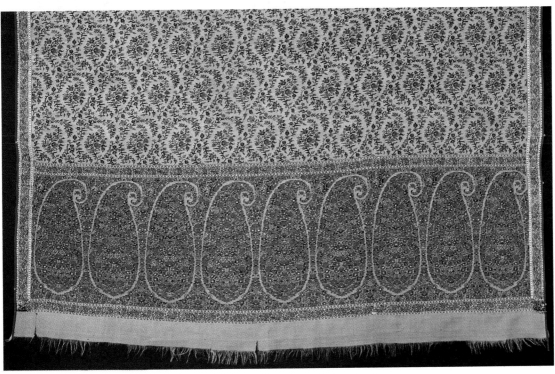

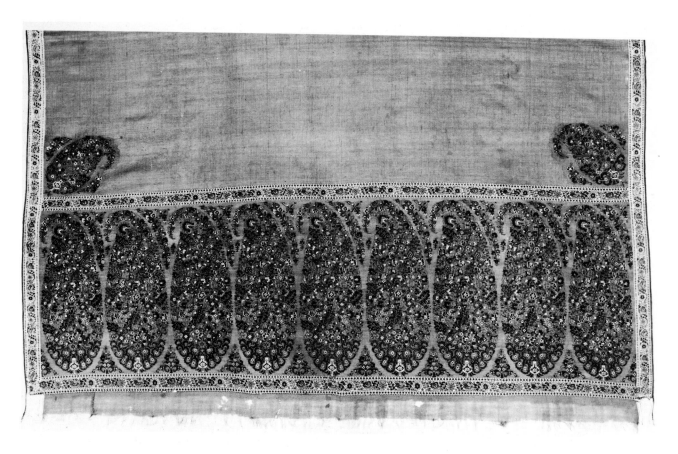

Plate 179 (above). Shoulder mantle. Afghan, c.1815. 322cm x 135cm.
Plate 180 (opposite). Shoulder mantle. Afghan, c.1815. 55cm x 135cm.
Plate 181 (overleaf). Shoulder mantle. Afghan, c.1815. 292cm x 135cm.

Grouping these three Kashmir shawls together is their common particularity: the boteh's scalloped outlining. This develops initially from the boteh's base foliage in the form of stylised leaves as seen in the khaki ground shawl of Plate 179. This design device, by extension, was further elaborated upon and becomes the highlight of Plates 180 and 181. These also relate to each other by their similar style of 'flattened' roses and thick stems. The treatment of their hashias is especially well-finished and thought out.

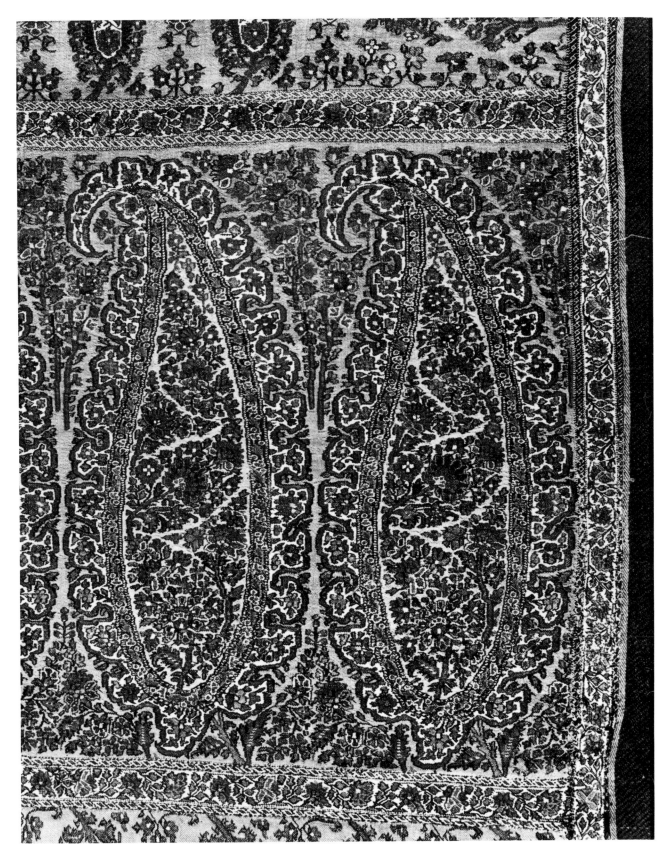

Plate 181

Plate 181. See p.274 for caption.

Plate 182 (above). Shoulder mantle. Afghan, c.1815. 140cm x 388cm.
Plate 183 (overleaf). Shoulder mantle. Afghan, c.1815. 135cm x 294cm.
Plate 184 (overleaf opposite). Shoulder mantle. Afghan, c.1815. 170cm x 135cm.

This group carries over many of the vestiges of the fading Afghan style. Their patterns are constructed by the use of a 'fancy' mound, around the theme of an 'elevated' boteh. The distinct raceme loop at the boteh's base in the form of a ribbon in Plate 184 suggests European influence. The bright, cochineal-red shawls of Plates 182 and 183 share identical hashia patterns of 'radial' rosettes, and their chromatic range relates especially to the kani prayer shawl of Plate 161b.

Plate 183. See previous page for caption.

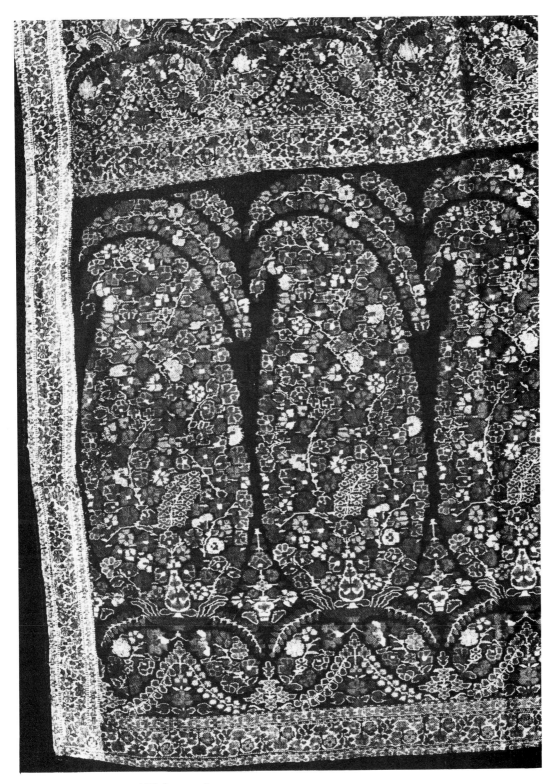

Plate 184. See page 277 for caption.

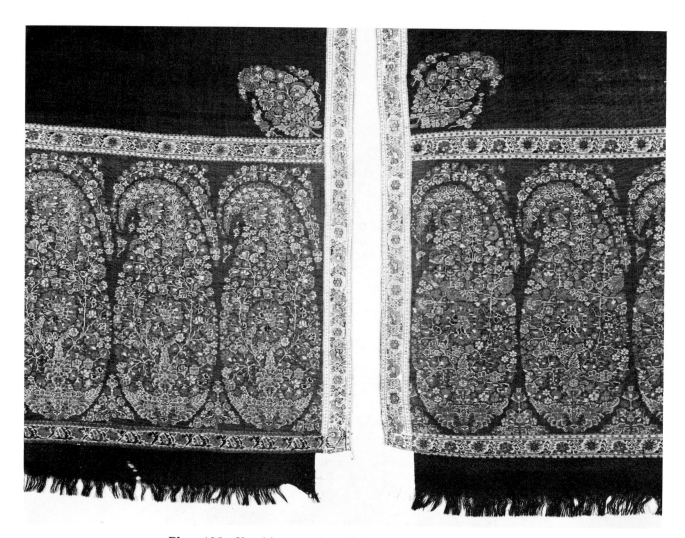

Plate 185. Shoulder mantles. Afghan, c.1815. 309cm x 137cm.

The pallas of this identical pair (dochalla) of indigo blue shawls, conserved by the Boston Museum of Fine Arts, have been placed side by side to illustrate their slight differences in weaving. This is due to the different looms which made them. The boteh's design, which was coded on the talim card, remains the same. However, variations in the weft thread and the beat of the loom's comb are enough to alter significantly the shape of the pattern. For style, compare the large radial flower enveloped by intertwining branches with Plate 169. The complete floral style too, seems to have taken on a slightly new development the succession of which may be seen somewhat in Moorcroft's drawing (Plate 38c) but without the racemes.

Plate 186 (above). Shoulder mantle. Afghan, c.1815. 131cm x 307cm.
Plate 187 (overleaf). Shoulder mantle. Afghan, c.1815. 130cm x 315cm.
Plate 188 (overleaf opposite). Shoulder mantle. Afghan, c.1815.

These patterns illustrate design impulses from a variety of sources. Kashmir's early 19th century exposure to European decorative arts is suggested by the tassle and ribbon theme found in these three pieces — a theme most likely borrowed, in turn, from the Chinese. However, the corner ornament in Plate 187, in the form of a tree with two trunks, pays a Mughal respect to the influence of Persian miniature painting. Maybe this is why, in comparing the uneven ribbons in Plate 187 with the perfect ones in Plate 186, one feels inclined to believe that the hashia border of the former is more of an interpretation than an actual copy. The ribbon, or bow tie theme, is continued in the khatraaz piece of Plate 188. Compare the hashias of Plate 186 with those in Plates 172 and 176. The collection AEDTA, Paris, contains an identical shawl to Plate 186.

Plate 187. See previous page for caption.

Plate 188. See page 281 for caption.

Plate 189. Shoulder mantle. Afghan, c.1815. 133cm x 262cm.

A simple yet dignified tall boteh pattern consisting of green, pale green, light rose, saffron and light blue flowers, enclosed by the boteh's shell of crenellated flowers aligned in three layers. A significant increase in boteh height is apparent here.

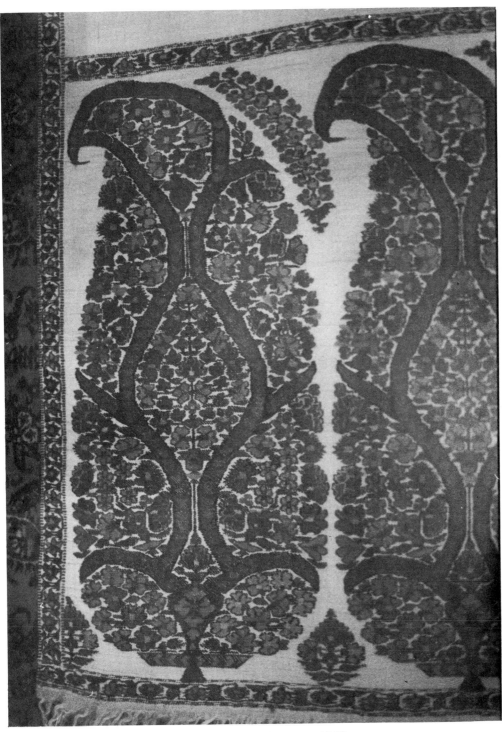

Plate 190 (above). Shoulder mantle. Late Afghan, c.1815.
Plate 191 (overleaf). Shoulder mantle. Afghan, c.1815. 133cm. x 24cm.

Although they are obviously of two distinct schools of design these two shawl pieces illustrate the beginning of the development of the hooked vine. The arrival of the tree trunk and its pointed burls as in Plates 176, 177 and 178 was most likely the stylistic impulse which led to the trellis pattern in the exquisite shawl of Plate 190. The boteh of Plate 191 has also fallen prey to the 'trellis' influence, but on a more subtle level. (See page 90 for further discussion of Plate 190.)

SHAWL BORDER: Pashmina wool, woven.
Kashmir, about 1810.
I.S.70814-83.

Plate 191. See previous page for caption.

Plate 192. Shoulder mantle. Afghan, c.1815. 133cm x 310cm.

This 'feathered-coif' boteh shares, in a way, a very similar style to the tree trunk boteh of Plate 178 except that here the boteh is detached from its foliate shell. The shawl's draftsmanship is excellent, although its foliage defies botanical identification, and the resulting pattern is very smart.

Plate 193 (above). Shoulder mantle. Sikh, c.1825. 133cm x 306cm.
Plate 194 (opposite). Shoulder mantle. Sikh, c.1825. 135cm. x 270cm.
Plate 195 (overleaf). Shoulder mantle. Sikh, c.1825.

A similar boteh style provides the common ground for the grouping together of these three exotic shawl patterns. It has been found that almost all the botehs whose vertices end in curling and in split layers, resemble each other rather closely. The tiny buti which 'pops out' from under the top of the botehs is also a noticeable common factor. In each case the hooked vine plays a strong role.

The hooked vine overlaid with small flower petals in the form of lunar crescents forms a very novel hashia meander in Plate 193. In Plate 194 the inner cone's checkered pattern offers a gay harlequin aspect to the shawl.

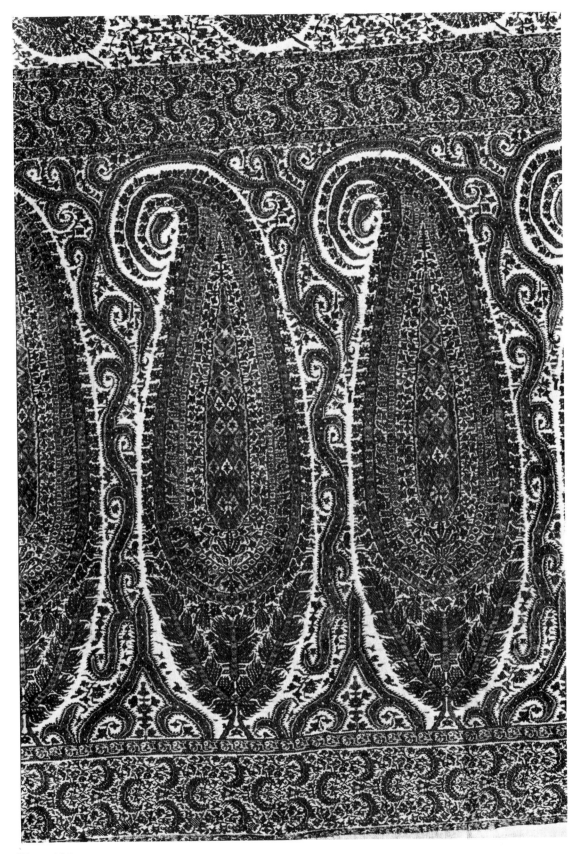

Plate 194

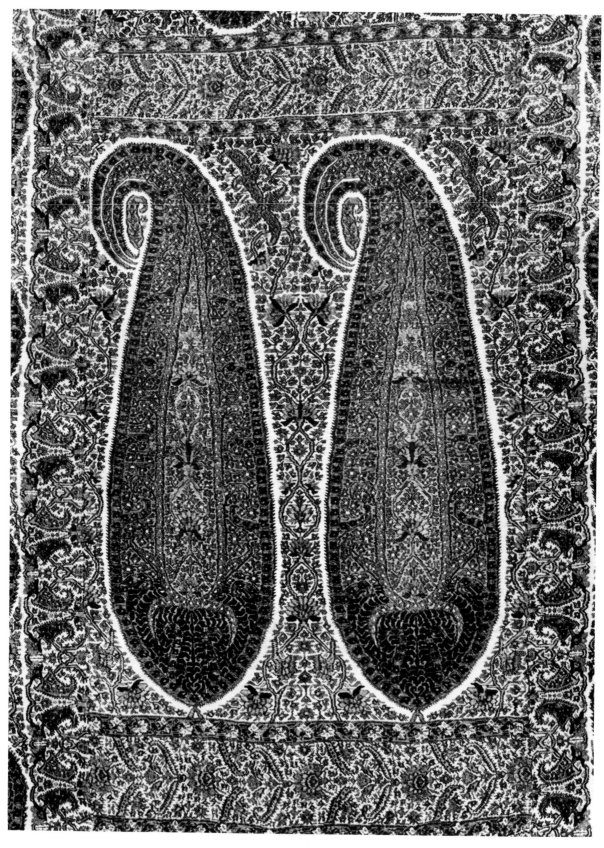

Plate 195. See p.288 for caption.

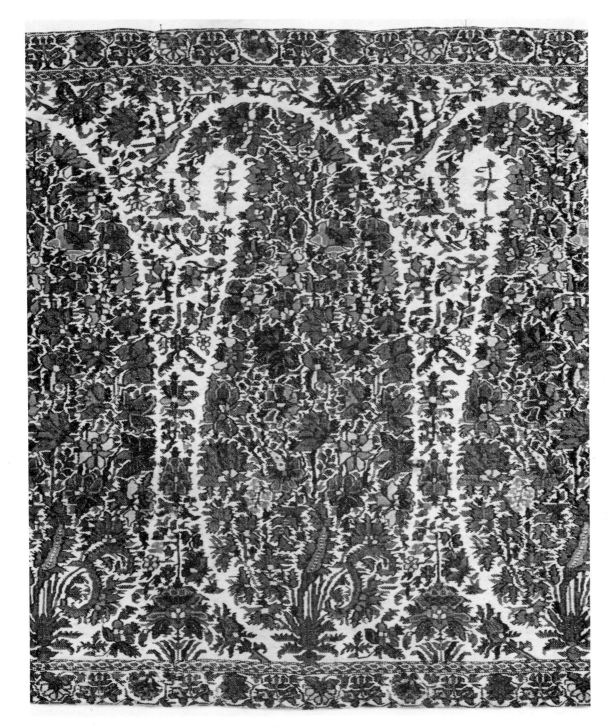

Plate 196. Shoulder mantle (fragment). Sikh, c.1820. 35cm x 130cm.

Kani and European tapestry weaving are very similar. What differentiates them significantly is the lack of shading techniques in the former. This example and Colour Plate 46 (overleaf) are unusual inasmuch as they show a departure from the traditionally flat two dimensional effects exhibited by earlier shawl designs. This is achieved not exactly by shading in the strict sense of the term, but by the subtle use of dark thread outlining as opposed to lighter colours traditionally employed on earlier pieces. Also the naqqash has carefully avoided the flattened flower style by illustrating leaves which overlap.

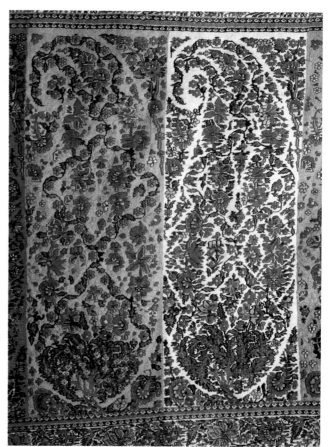

Colour Plate 46. Shoulder mantle (two views). Sikh, c.1820. 314cm x 134cm.

One of the most beautiful Kashmir shawls. The colours are from high quality dyes and they blend harmoniously. The colour of the flowers changes depending on the compartment's ground colour (what the French called 'arlequiné'). Exceptional attention was devoted to highlight the rich cochineal field (matan) with an elegant all-kani woven trellis pattern. Adding a graceful movement to the delicate draftsmanship of the boteh is the ogival pattern formed by the rising meander which falls gracefully at the cones vertex. Within each compartment can be seen the ubiquitous fool's cap, an identifying Sikh period characteristic. The effect of shading is similar to that in Plate 196.

Colour Plate 47 (detail). Khatraaz kani fabric. Sikh, c.1825. 128cm x 129cm.

It is interesting how the Kashmiri artist substituted the ubiquitous arabesque for the hooked vine. In this rich and colourfully patterned jamawar we find a graceful synthesis of Hindu-Islamic elements. Note the lunar crescents which bisect each join of the trellis' ogive pattern. Compare the dyes with those in Colour Plate 43. Two different types of yellow alternate across the shawl's field; mustard and saffron.

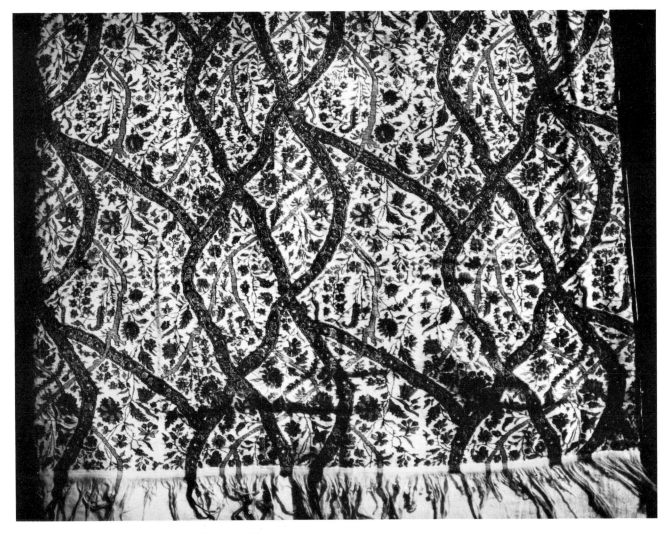

Plate 197. Shoulder mantle. Sikh, c.1820.

A variety of stylistic impulses combine to pattern this rare white jamawar conserved by the Calico Museum, Ahmedabad. The delicate, wandering stems, the subordinate interlacing vine with its truncated branches, and the radial flower of the fool's cap device, all owe their origins to earlier classical Kashmiri and European styles. The subordinate vine relates to that found in Plate 176. This jamawar pattern is identical to the one which decorates the field of an exquisite moon shawl conserved by the Victoria and Albert Museum.

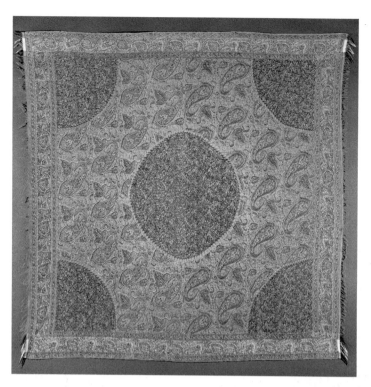

Colour Plate 48.
'Moon' shawl (two views).
Sikh, c.1830. 168cm x 170cm.

The unusually large guard stripes which add width to the hashia tend to suggest a later date for this piece, compared with those in Plates 198, 199 and 200. However, the fine draftsmanship and scrupulous attention given to the symbolic forms, born during the Sikh period, may contradict this claim. The chandar's pale-blue field is comparatively sparse, a fact which highlights the play of richly coloured botehs. The U-shaped device surrounding the boteh's base appears as a further stylisation of a similar device which can be seen in Plate 198. The origin of this design derives possibly from opposing, joined botehs. The shawl was woven in two separate pieces as can be seen by the faint line running across the central medallion, and the way in which the boteh patterns face each other at this junction.

Plate 198. 'Moon' shawl. Sikh, c.1825. 174cm x 188cm.
Plate 199 (overleaf top). 'Moon' shawl. Sikh, c.1825. 168cm x 173cm.
Plate 200 (overleaf bottom). 'Moon' shawl (fragment). Sikh, c.1825. 16cm x 48cm.

The salient characteristic of this chandar group is, of course, the dense mosaic-like foliate nature that composes the medallions. In all three we find a sawtooth style in the field's design elements. Plate 200 shows an interesting trellis pattern which covers the field of leaning 'bent-tip' botehs. In the hashia of Plate 198 we see a novel variation of the fool's cap which bifurcates a repeating medallion-like device.

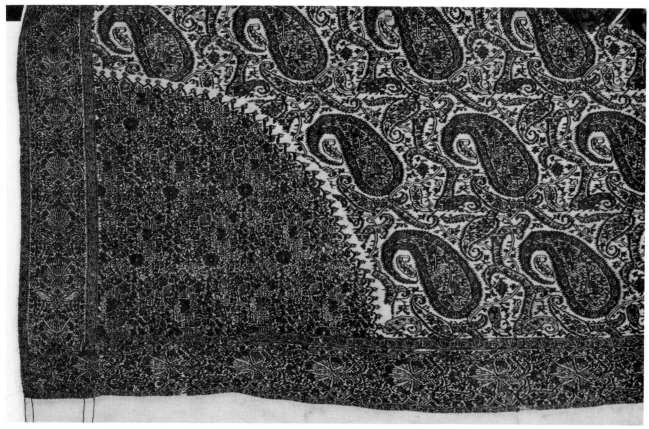

Plate 199. See previous page for caption.

Plate 200. See previous page for caption.

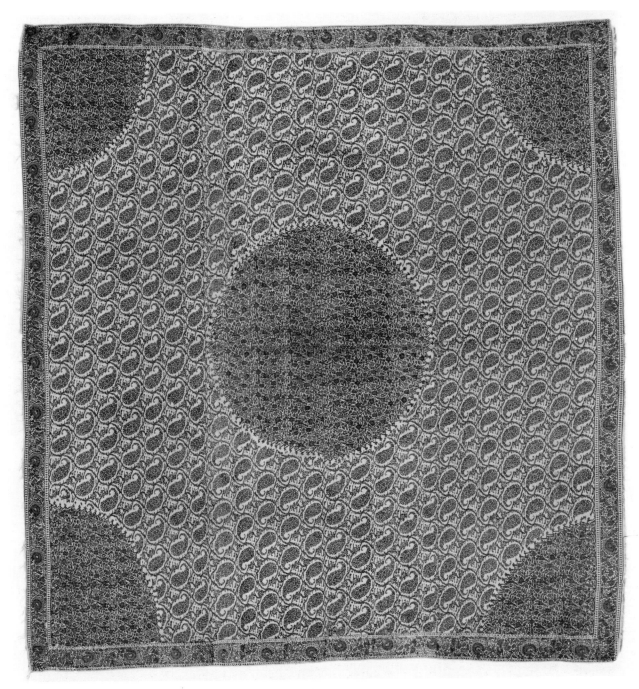

Plate 201. 'Moon' shawl. Sikh, c.1825. 162cm x 162cm.

Usually found as decoration of the long shawl's dhor, the small leaning butis here provide the overall field pattern. The central medallion and corners retain the popular theme of dense foliage that characterise nearly 80% of all chandars of this period. Four separate panels join to make this moon shawl — a fact which probably led to the misalignment of the central medallion's circumference. The flattened roses of the matching hashias recall the late Afghan style, seen in the moon shawls of Plate 170 and Colour Plate 41, p.259.

Plate 202. 'Moon' shawl. Sikh, c.1830. 165cm x 166cm.

The idea of flora arranged around a straight-line axis developed during the late Afghan period and can be distinctly noticed in Plates 190 and 210. Here we find 'arrowhead' medallions 'strung-up' on a foliate ground that resembles somewhat the style of Colour Plate 41, p.259.

Plate 203. 'Moon' shawl. Sikh, c.1830. 160cm x 160cm.

One of the prettiest pieces among all the chandar styles is the one with the khatraaz field. Here again as in Colour Plate 41, p.259, we witness the aesthetic transparency of the medallions which is created by the polychrome warp threads.

Plate 204. Shoulder mantle. Sikh, c.1830. 101cm x 201cm.

By 1820, quick imitations of the kani shawl were made by embroidery as opposed to the time consuming loom-woven patterns. This led to the appearance of a host of human and animal figures. Being simpler and less eye-exhausting, embroidered shawls did not require the strict surveillance which reigned within the crowded Kharkandars, or weaving ateliers. Instead they developed a folk style all of their own as they slowly began to bear the personal household stamp of the Kashmir families that designed them. On this particular shawl only the matan's corners are embroidered, showing two courting couples with the women admiring a flower offered as a gift and peacocks (the peacock is northern India's national emblem but here it is more likely a symbol of romance). The embroidered botehs echo the palla's boteh style of concentric and snake-like decoration.

Plate 205. Shoulder mantle (embroidered). Sikh, c.1820. 130cm x 310cm.

'Amli' or embroidered shawls frequently imitated the kani ones by abstracting their essential design features. The reverse effect was no less of a phenomenon. This example contains a well thought out pattern in fine style and opposing contrasts. The hooked vine's meander sweeps in and out of the cone. Upon re-entering it splits in two and suspends a fool's cap within the boteh's lance-like tip and centre. The remaining ground decoration is gracefully enhanced by leafy fronds.

Plate 206. Shoulder mantle. Sikh, c.1830. 277cm x 121cm.

Botehs outlined by deep sky-blue angular flowers and hollowed by a white inner cone render this bright cochineal shawl a very eye catching piece. The botehs are separated into compartments by the vertical line of 'stringed' forms which may be compared with the rows of 'arrowhead' shapes in Plate 202.

Colour Plate 49. Shoulder mantle. Sikh, c.1825. 140cm. x 305cm.

Stylistically this example bears a fair resemblance to the types of sample boteh drawings sent to England by Moorcroft in 1823. The fern-like foliage at the boteh's base is absent. Nevertheless the treatment of the branches and flattened roses relates closely to Plate 38a of Moorcroft.

Apart from the matan which is sewn in, the shawl is woven in eight sections as follows: the two vertical hashias, the two pallas including their top and bottom lateral hashias, and the four dhors of leaning botehs which surround the black matan.

Plate 207 (above). Shoulder mantle (fragment). Sikh, c.1830. 46cm x 50cm.
Plate 208 (opposite). Shoulder mantle. Sikh, c.1830. 135cm x 315cm.

The above and following two pieces belong to the same design family; the sharply serrated boteh, the arching U-shaped form and the moon crescents being the main unifying features. However, the pervading style consists of the angularity with which the flower petals are drawn and systematically arranged in a linear fashion. As a result these distinct symbolic elements combine to provide a sweeping sinuous movement. Plate 207 is an exceptional piece. The fool's cap hashia lends a feeling of fantasy to an already wild palla design. A tiny lantern-like object appears balanced at each end of the arching U-shaped element, while the base of each boteh and mound is joined by a thick sinuous vine. The dhor pattern cleverly imitates the palla; notice how the cypress tree is looped about itself, thereby maintaining volume and symmetry. In Plate 208 the sharp bristled aspect of the concentric cones is nicely softened by the hashia's winding hooked vine. These three pieces may be compared to their antecedents in Plates 198, 199 and 200.

Plate 208

Plate 209. 'Moon' shawl. Sikh, c.1830. 175cm x 180cm.
The same theme continues here as in Plates 207 and 208, lending itself well to the smaller repeat of leaning, hooked-tip botehs. The pattern is novel, innovative and rather lively.

Plate 210. Shoulder mantle (fragment). Sikh, c.1820. 53cm x 74cm.

This bizarre piece is of a type only very occasionally found in Western markets. However, similar pieces are quite commonly seen in Northern India and more especially in Lahore, Pakistan, which had once been the Sikh capital of the Punjab. For this reason we may label them 'Lahore' or 'Lahore-type' shawls. Besides their coarse yarn, which may be a mixture of sheep's or ordinary goat's wool, their generally sombre dyes were not very fast. Colour Plates 50 and 51, p.313, are of the same type.

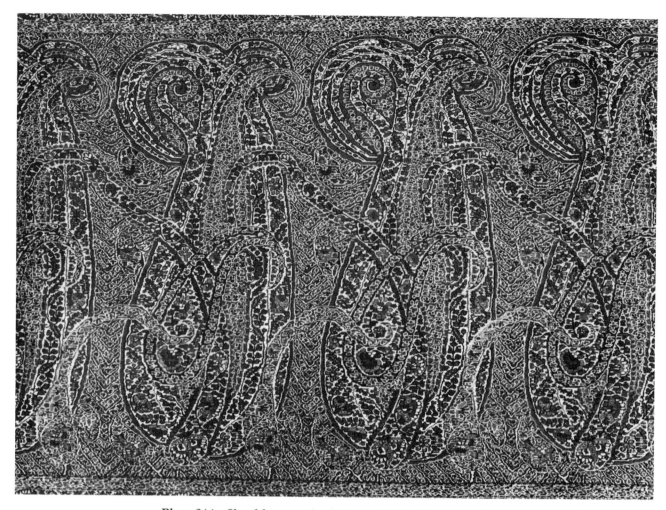

Plate 211. Shoulder mantle. Sikh, c.1820. 145cm x 305cm.

No shawl has captured so well, in visual form and pattern, the riotous undercurrents of an Islamic culture in full revolution. A tumultuous inner-cone movement appears to challenge the confining traditions of the boteh's classic curves. Within this frenzy of contorted shapes a new dynamic, if not radical, form of artistic expression finds its full growth potential. Each of the sweeping design elements interacts in such a way as to disintegrate the staunch notion of Kashmir's ubiquitous emblem, the boteh.

Plate 212 (above). Shoulder mantle. Sikh, c.1830. 139cm x 340cm.
Plate 213 (overleaf). Shoulder mantle. Sikh, c.1830. 295cm x 146cm.

These two tapestry shawls are monuments of design composition. Because of the festive floral nature of their fancy patterns they are called 'celebration shawls'. In both pieces, the sweeping botehs invade the lateral hashias — an idea which influenced, to a large degree, the Jacquard shawls. The swaying fan-like flowers in Plate 212 are descendents of the flattened rose.

The outlined sweeping botehs of Plate 213 in pink, yellow, blue and white alternating on various ground colours of green, vermillion and black, might be a burst of fireworks illuminating the sky.

Plate 213. See previous page for caption.

Plate 214. Shoulder mantle. Sikh, c.1825. 142cm x 333cm.

This incredible pattern appears to be a stylistic study in design research. The bold intertwining curves, arches, niches, large eight-pointed stars, all combine to camouflage the large hooked-cone botehs. The hashia's meander consists of oval emblems joined by a heavy vine. The emblems are further separated by leaning cone botehs. The weaving is very fine and the colours are most attractive: mustard yellow, sky blue, blue grey, navy blue, pink, cream, forest green, light green, cochineal and black. An embroidered inscription on the shawl reads 'Ordered by the royal [one] a novel and unique shawl — a thing of heavenly beauty studded with variegated, floral pattern, a delight to the eye was made'.

This shawl relates remarkably well to Chavant's shawl patterns (see, for example, Plate 76, p.164) which were published in Paris in 1837.

Plate 215. Shoulder mantle. Sikh, c.1830. 144cm x 327cm.

Here we see in a stylised form, the Sacred Mountain, which can be seen in less abstracted form in Colour Plate 54, p.315. Apart from the three laurel wreaths the design similarities, except for the dhor and hashia patterns, are noticeable upon brief inspection. The long hashias in this plate are not of the same design as the inner ones, and therefore they would have been replaced. Once again, as in Colour Plate 54, we have an almost superfluous role played by the botehs. Compare also with Colour Plate 55, p.315.

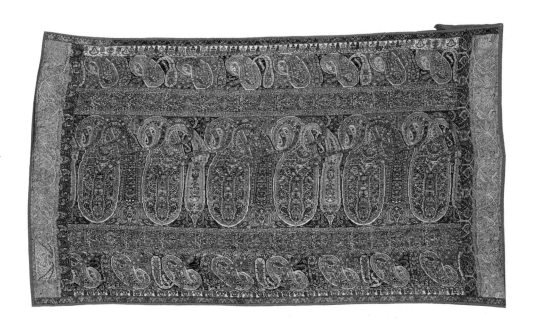

Colour Plate 50 (above). Shoulder mantle (fragment). Sikh, c.1820. 46cm x 132cm.
Colour Plate 51 (below). Shoulder mantle (fragment). Sikh, c.1820. 46 cm x 122cm.

These pieces are 'Lahore' or 'Lahore-type' shawls similar to Plate 210. The colours have been extensively 'pricked in'. The botehs appear hooked on the chimerical vines as they alternate in contrasting colours. Flowers are almost completely absent and the design theme is dominated by a juxtaposition of almost pure symbolic forms. Plates 207 and 211 share a similar design style.

Colour Plate 52 (left). Shoulder mantle. Sikh, c.1830. 137cm x 300cm.
Colour Plate 53 (right). Shoulder mantle. Sikh, c.1830. 146cm x 320cm.

An identical chromatic range of rich rainbow-like colours and similar design features pair these two rare Sikh pieces. The repeat which patterns Colour Plate 52 is composed of a large spearhead placed upon a sturdy block-like pedestal the face of which contains a vase of flowers framed by a mihrab. Hanging from each side of the pedestal are two pendants in the form of long cones. The spearhead's base splits in two and each end curls upward, terminating in a cornucopia shape from which spills a small boteh. Flanking the spearhead's point, which is surmounted by a crescent moon pierced by the thin stem of a fan-like object, are two minarets.

Superimposed across all of the above, by its outlined form only, is a tall bent-tip boteh. Adjacent to the boteh and rising vertically above a mound to an equal height is a spray of fern-like leaves the central stem of which is constructed of stacked, multicoloured chevrons. On the saffron coloured matan is a kani woven repeat of floral bedecked pavilions separated by fern-like plants. The lateral hashias are particularly interesting for their architypal meander. The vertical hashias, although contemporary, are not original to the shawl.

The palla of Colour Plate 53 contains three pairs of opposing, bent-tip botehs, each pair intersected by a large cone throwing off on either side a spray of fern-like leaves. The cone's centre is decorated by a kind of totem pole of various shapes typical of the Sikh period. Above the top lateral hashia's fine prototypal pattern is a continuation of the same design as the palla. As in Colour Plate 52 the vertical hashias here are probably not original to the piece.

**Colour Plate 54. Shoulder mantle.
Sikh, c.1825. 144cm x 314cm.**

The unique pattern of this shawl arouses one's curiosity. The trilobed scalloped spandrel, the ends of which terminate in cornucopias, illuminates a 'sacred mountain' of pointed cypress trees all reaching up towards a large central spear, a phallic symbol. Indeed, the subjects have a symbolic and mystical ring to them.

**Colour Plate 55. Shoulder mantle.
Sikh, c.1830. 138cm x 308cm.**

This piece is similar in style to both Colour Plate 54 and Plate 215. Again the Sacred Mountain features among the design elements. A similar idea is very often seen on early Chinese robes in the form of stylized mountains which loom up from a churning ocean, and are topped by crashing waves.

Colour Plate 56

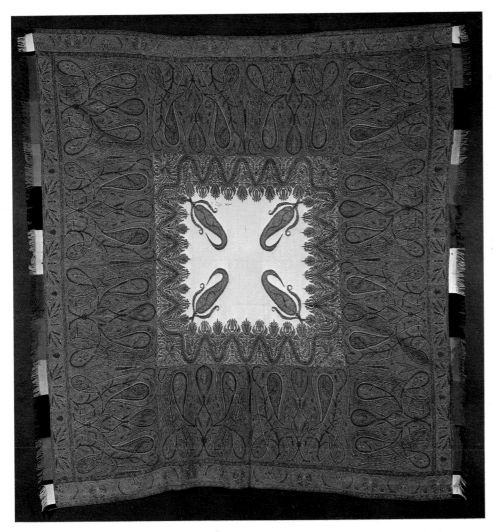

Colour Plate 56 (opposite). Shoulder mantle. Sikh, c.1840. 142cm x 312cm.
Colour Plate 57 (above). 'Rumal' shoulder mantle. Sikh, c.1840. 165cm x 165cm.

As in Colour Plates 52 and 53 here we find yet another design using stacked floral arrays. The theme is set by the stalks of pineapple-type leaves found in both shawls. In the rumal we see the curiously pointed arrow heads protruding from the bent-tip botehs. This idea appears to have been expanded in Colour Plate 56 in the form of tall arrays of pointed, fish-hook type plants. The latter overlaps four sinuous stems which terminate elegantly in botehs and spearheads in the dhor. The pattern is completed by serrated outlines of two large opposing botehs which fuse into the whole through a play of various shades of colour tones. The subtle, chromatic harmony imparts a graceful force despite the entanglements of interlacing foliage. In the rumal, Plate 57, the repeat consists of a pair of sweeping outlined botehs the tips of which terminate in the form of a protruded lancehead, curled upwards. The botehs are separated by a foliate spray similar to Colour Plate 56. A rising hooked vine invades the hollow outline of each boteh while the spray appears contained within a vase formed by the additional curving loop of a vine. The feathered edge of the sinusoidal vine in the centre field, although contemporary in style, does not reflect the same design as the shawl's borders. Nonetheless the draftsmanship in Plate 57 is extremely well done and the small realistic palm trees in each corner are an exotic addition. Similar trees can be seen in Couder's shawls.

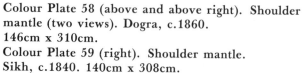

Colour Plate 58 (above and above right). Shoulder mantle (two views). Dogra, c.1860.
146cm x 310cm.
Colour Plate 59 (right). Shoulder mantle.
Sikh, c.1840. 140cm x 308cm.

The repeat motifs of these two pieces are created through arches or mihrabs and columns. They contain comparatively large fields of open colour (compare with Plate 216). Colour Plate 58 is particularly unusual not only because it is completely void of the ubiquitous boteh motif, but because the lateral hashias have been traded off for the mihrab repeat. Colour Plate 59 shows a dominant influence derived from Mughal architecture. Again we find the pineapple-type leaves in the mihrab decoration, a decoration which mirrors that seen on many Indian palaces.

Plate 216. Shoulder mantle. Dogra, c.1850. 132cm x 306cm.

This piece shares a distinct artistic style with Colour Plates 58 and 59, with comparatively large fields of open colour.

Plate 217 (above). Shoulder mantle. Sikh, c.1840. 135cm x 310cm.
Plate 218 (opposite). Shoulder mantle. Sikh, c.1840. 139cm x 328cm.

Exemplified by these two shawls is the incredible and inexhaustible virtuosity of the Kashmiri artist in his use of the hooked vine motif. In Plate 217 each tall boteh is overlaid by two vertically rising, interlaced hooked vines and a snaking floral meander. They cross the top hashia to end in a swirling riot of leaning botehs and pineapple cone leaves located in the field.

Plate 218

Colour Plate 60. Shoulder mantle. Sikh, c.1840. 140cm x 300cm.

The leafy frond vines join with the central field to run clear across the whole shawl. The matan's palm trees, as in those of Colour Plate 57, p.317, form the finishing touches to the palla's rising hooked vine. No doubt, both palm-tree motifs were inspired by Couder's great shawl, the 'Nou-Rouz', exhibited in 1839 (Colour Plate 18, p.154).

Colour Plate 61. 'Rumal', shoulder mantle. Dogra, c.1870. 180cm x 180cm.

From a standpoint of colour range and weaving execution, this shawl was found to be a particulary fine example of a late rumal. The number of 'patchwork' pieces has been kept to a strict minimum and the inserted black and white strips which form the large fleur-de-lis and scalloped lobed pattern have been scrupulously joined.

Colour Plate 62. Rumal, shoulder mantle. Dogra, c.1870. 175cm x 175cm.

This curious rococo and dense cursive leaf design is of a type of shawl which falls into a standard pattern. Many of these 'vase' shawls have been found in private collections of Iranian exiles after the fall of the late Shah Phalavi.

**Colour Plate 63. Shoulder mantle (two views).
Dogra, dated 1875. 144cm x 344cm.**

One of the most strikingly graphic patterns seen on a tapestry shawl. Indeed a living proof of the artistic heights to which creative weaving was raised just before the collapse of the kani weaving industry. Clearly visible in the detail are the tiny people, animals, birds and even pavilions used to decorate the palla. The overall trellis, fashioned by the hooked vine rising in an ogive pattern, provides an added Islamic touch. The shawl's magnificent saffron-centre (matan) recalls the chinoiserie style found in Chavant's album (see Plate 80).

**Colour Plate 64. Shoulder mantle (two views).
Dogra, c.1875. 140cm x 320cm.**

An exceptionally fine sinuous pattern is created by the sweeping
botehs interlaced within each of the palla's three mihrabs. This
pattern recalls that of the Turkish 'saph' rugs in which multiple
niches repeat across the rug's field.

**Colour Plate 65. Shoulder mantle (two views).
Dogra, c.1875. 152cm x 327cm.**
The detail illustrates the meticulous care which was invested
in this fine kani weave. The swirling mauve flames
sharpened by a burning yellow outline recalls the Chinese
clouds seen in early Mughal art. The embroidered fringe on
this shawl is one of the largest and most elaborate ever
found.

**Colour Plate 66. Shoulder mantle (two views).
Dogra, c.1875. 140cm x 320cm.**

Exemplified in this chef d'oeuvre of kani weaving is the beautiful synthesis of Hindu-Islamic styles. The serpent, symbol of procreative male force, is given particular attention by the Kashmiri artist. The large flame-tipped, serrated-edge botehs, the heads of which brush up against the mihrab spandrels, are held by truncated, stubby branches. The criss-crossing of long serpents across the whole palla renders a marvellous zoomorphic aspect to this picture of jungle morphology. A perfect contrast of changing ground colours is achieved through the use of conservative ground embellishment to enhance the shawl pattern's turbulent and almost nightmarish impact.

Appendix I
A brief review of French painting: the Empire Style

The fact that the sheer number of French paintings illustrating the Kashmir shawl during the Empire Period exceeds that of any other country is, in a way, indicative of the unique status that the French nobility had bestowed on it as an object of fashion. Style shows that the 'dernier cri' was undoubtedly the diaphanous long shawl, the extreme ends of which were patterned with stately botehs on a plain ground; buti patterns were also found though to a lesser extent. Certain characteristics of style, the details of which will be discussed below, indicate that the artists of Kashmir were well aware of the ornaments that characterized the Napoleonic period.

Apart from the boteh of the Kashmir shawl, popular floral motifs characterising the First Empire include: Greek palmette, laurel crown, garland, rectilinear leaf branch, cornucopia and split-leaf rosette. Animal figures included the winged sphinx and lion, and the swan; musical instruments the lyre, flute and cymbal. Classical divinities, vases and urns were also used in decoration.

The Empire boteh usually contained compact flowers and followed a curvilinear and bulbous shape in which a vase and dish appeared. The apex, when it did not have a large flattened rose, was terminated by a sinuous play of racemes; the botehs barely touched each other, the ground was free of ornament except near the top where a small detached branch of flowers, known as a 'coif', arched over the boteh's back, and at the bottom we find a buti or small cross of flowers.

One of the earliest paintings with a distinctive shawl pattern is a portrait of Madame de Sorcy-Thélussen, by Jacques-Louis David, painted in 1790. We observe a long saffron shawl with butis drafted in the Mughal manner, i.e. a small bouquet of three blossoms held by V-shaped racemes which in turn are secured by a possible Chinese character root; a hashia of similar flowers complements the palla. In the portrait of the coquette Madame de Recamier (1805), Gerard reserves a dominating portion of the canvas for a long flowing saffron shawl. It too reflects a late Mughal style and the delicate hashia with a tri-lobed flower in the meander is very typical of this period. In Jean Mosnier's portrait of Madame Chakhovskaa, the shawl appears to clash with the date, 1806. The boteh is full blown, rather bulbous, and it sits on a large dish. The large rose at the apex is crowned by a tiny serrated leaf or stamen; the ground is free of ornaments. Because the shawl appears to have been cut down from another one to form a square, indicated by the white palla and red matan, the palla itself may be older by several decades.

From the Empress Josephine (1805) by Prud'hon we discover a number of

Figure 32. Hashia tracing, showing an arrow-leaf meander, from the 'Comtesse Daru' by Jacques-Louis David, 1810.

revealing details: an all round 'dhor' pattern of large butis with serrated fronds and split-leaf flowers; an unusually large patka-type border flanked by large diamond-shaped dots in the guard borders; a sinuous vine device upon which the boteh's are slightly raised. In David's 'Comtesse Daru' (1810) we again see this diamond guard border in the hashia but here is something new: a sinuous chain-like floral meander in the hashia.

A similar shawl to the latter is seen in Ingres' 'Comtesse de Tournon' (1812). The hashia shows a new meander composed of large split-leaf floral rosettes (similar to the ones on the Josephine shawl) spaced within the interstices of a rectilinear vine.

Figure 33. Split-leaf rosette hashia, from the 'Comtesse de Tournon' by Jean-Auguste-Dominique Ingres, 1812.

A running 'dhor' of tiny niches reminds us of Couder's later harlequin shawl painting, 1823, which is on display at the Conservatoire National des Arts et Métiers, Paris.

In two other paintings, notably 'Mme de Verinac' (1799), and also the 'Sermont des Horaces' (1785), both by David, we find a plain European shawl except for the extreme borders. The borders contain a narrow sinuous line pattern which alternates with greek palmettes. It is felt that this may have engendered the earliest 'dhor' patterns, first seen in Prud'hon's 'Josephine'.

Finally, no review of European painting is complete without Baron Gros' 'the Empress Josephine' (1809) (Plate 29, page 69), a remarkable study in Kashmir opulence and revelation of character; Ingres' 'Madame Riviere' (1805) (Plate 28, page 69), sinuously swathed in meticulous Kashmir; and Girodet's 'Revolt of Cairo' (1810), teeming with Oriental drama. See page 70.

The Empire style, as further research will undoubtedly confirm, demonstrates the links between courtly taste in Kashmir and France.

Appendix II
A note on some Oriental Carpets

The development of Kashmir's curvalinear boteh during the eighteenth century appears to have been a phenomenon reserved only for the shawl and practically unrelated to carpet patterns. During the early Mughal period, however, both weaving mediums shared natural and freely spaced flowers. In the latter part of the eighteenth century, the boteh, as discussed in Chapter Four, underwent a radical transformation from a unique floral to an unmistakably curvilinear form; it was a fundamental part of the aesthetic evolution of the shawl. Yet a careful survey provides no evidence that the cone boteh was employed even as a minor design element in Oriental carpets and other weaving prior to 1800.

On the other hand, the nineteenth century saw a tremendous profusion of carpets, embroideries, etc., which utilized 'boteh' repeats and other Kashmiri patterns so often found in the kani shawl. Prior to this period Kashmir shawl designs may have influenced carpet weaving in the group of carpets popularly known as 'millefleurs'.[1] The origin of this distinctive group of carpets has been the subject of controversy, but it is now felt they were actually woven in India and that Kashmir itself is the most likely source of their manufacture. Their general design format is quite bold, consisting of a large central panel, the middle of which is shaped in the

Plate 219. Millefleurs prayer rug. Kashmir c.1800. Senneh knot, 188cm x 120cm.

---

1 cf. Millefleurs carpet (17th century): Museum of Decorative Arts, Vienna, T1539.

Plate 220. Shirvan prayer rug, Caucasian, c.1800. 114cm x 89cm.

form of a prayer niche. The field is generally cluttered with flower blossoms and branches, hence the appellation 'millefleurs'. The field's symmetry is balanced and harmonized by the use of a large vase and dish elevated by a mound situated at the bottom of the niche. Important pieces of this group are found in the well-known McMullan and Biltmore collections in the U.S. (see Plate 219), while the millefleurs shawl (the earliest of this type known, see Plate 161b) conserved by the Musée Historique du Tissu, Lyon, provides possibly the main link between this group and contemporary shawl patterns. The treatment and disposition of branches of flower blossoms (racemes), the graphic rendering of the top rose (radial flower) and of course the use of the vase, dish and mound, combine in late millefleurs carpets to suggest a close relationship between the 'millefleurs' carpets and Afghan-period shawls (1753-1819). Other examples of this carpet group can be seen in plates 30 and 32 of McMullan's *Islamic Carpets,* 1965. In the former we again find the apex flower drawn in the radial technique. In comparing plate 161a the apex rose shows the use of what the French called during the nineteenth century the 'caillouté' technique. Similarly, the dish's slanted or zigzag lines and the flower petals drawn on the vase itself, independently of the rest of the rug's flora, bears a strong resemblance to what might be found on a shawl woven towards the end of the eighteenth century.

Among the earliest carpets known at present which employ the Kashmiri cone boteh are those found in the region of Caucasus, in the village of Marasali.[2] These common prayer carpets display rows of boteh inside a mihrab (see Plate 220). Their

---

2 For examples of these carpets see *The Oriental Rug Collection of Mary Jane and Jerome Straka*, NY, 1978 pp.105-106 pl. 102-103. Also Schürmann, p.220, pl.78.

Plate 221. Mughal rug, India. Attributed to Shah Jehan period (1628-1658). 137cm x 294cm. Weave 34 x 37 or 1,258 knots to sq. in.

unique main borders are flanked by two insignificant minor borders, characterized by a meandering vine pattern composed of 'bent-tip' strawberries (or abstracted roses) laid end to end and arranged within a sinuous geometric vine which runs over and under them in an alternating fashion. Horizontal lines placed in a staggered manner fill this special border, an obvious carry over from the Chinese cloud-band trails. Such meandering motifs were the main theme of the seventeenth and eighteenth century patka hashia borders.

The last carpet I would like to mention is a fabulous Mughal fragment, a masterpiece of Imperial court weaving, hanging in the Metropolitan Museum of Art (see Plate 221). It is worth comparing the cog-wheel type flower in the rug's field to that of the shawl in Plate 102. The mounds too, located in the rug's border, with their leafy protrusions, also appear to stem from the same school of design as Plate 102. The elegantly drawn floral meanders in the rug's guard borders relate stylistically to those hashias found in Plates 88 and 90. These comparisons are not necessarily to prove that Plate 102 is of the same period as the rug but rather to demonstrate the transgression of one art medium to another.

Appendix III
The Reversible Shawl

(1) French espouliné

The reversible shawl was often made by the espouliné method. Legentil, a reporter of the 1844 exhibition, described how reversible shawls had been made in Russia for a long time, but in France only since 1827 and, until the time of his report, without success.[1] He does not mention reversible shawls originating from Kashmir, which he certainly would have done, had any been known at the time.

He describes in detail two reversible shawls displayed at the exhibition, exceptional for their quality and execution. They were shown by Heuzey and Marcel in collaboration with Deneirouse whose espouliné methods were used in making them.

The first was a long, richly designed shawl with a white centre, woven entirely of pure Kashmir wool; the second was an 'écharpe', or scarf, woven of very fine wool coming from a flock of sheep in Mauchamps, France. Both of these unusual products were part of a special commission and were to be exported to the Orient. Legentil wrote of the long white shawl:

> 'There is a very curious shawl at the booth of MM. Heuzey junior and Marcel, following Deneirouse, and Lagorce. This shawl, in pure Kashmir and completely white, is brocaded [in this case he means espouliné] *without a reverse side* ['sans envers'] in natural flowers, with stems, leaves and scalloped edges. It is fine, soft and light, delicate and beautiful, of excellent colours and artistically designed. In 1817 something of this nature was tried: very pretty borders were made with reverse side unapparent; but the 'brocade' was finely cut off or clipped. While on the contrary, the former is full, solid, with stitches which have some relation to the work of beautiful tapestry. Two things characterize this endeavour: first, the work does not give a reverse side, the warp finding itself enveloped in such a way that a relief is obtained which gives a vivacity simulating perfectly a velvetiness when woven with a twilled ground; second, the nature of the design breaks off entirely with all these 'crochets' [probably the hooked vine], floral designs ['ramages'], and eternal palms of Indian design, and reproduces here beautiful flower bouquets such as nature spreads before our eyes. *The appearance of this shawl is an event. It encompasses, maybe, a whole revolution.*'[2]

The 'impartial' observations of exhibition reporters should however be treated with some caution. The shawl manufacturers of Paris represented a closely knit group and secrets of the trade were tightly guarded. Often a maker was part of the review committee or jury to the commission reporting on the exhibits. Fortunately, the National exhibitions were reviewed by various writers and one may hope to form an unprejudiced opinion by reading several different reports.

(2) Russian espouliné

During the early organization of the shawl industry in Paris, competition from England and Germany was already recognized.[3] Ternaux drew his inspiration from the beautiful printed shawls form Vienna, while the Russians were beginning their shawl weaving industry, much like the French in 1800, by carefully dissecting the unique Kashmiri weave.

The Russian reversible shawl is described in an anonymous document found at

---

1 Expo. 1844, vol. I, p.205.
2 Expo. 1844, Musée Challamel, p.40.
3 National Archives, carton F12-2412, letter dated 20 Feb., 1808.

the Musée de Textile, Lyon.[4] It describes how the French ambassador to Russia, General Louis, Marquis de Caulaincourt and Duc du Vicence, recorded an account of Russian shawl weaving in 1808. During his second sojourn in Russia, he visited a famous weaving atelier in a small village called Skorodoumovka, near St. Petersburg. At the establishment of a Madame Merlaine he saw shawls and scarves which he considered more beautiful than those made either in France or in the Orient and he decided to purchase the most beautiful piece as a gift for the Empress Marie Louise. To the diplomat's great suprise, however, despite being offered the enormous sum of 10,000 roubles, Madame Merlaine refused to sell saying that as a devoted patriot, she was unwilling to let one of her most beautiful pieces of 'tapestry' out of her country.

Madame Merlaine had begun her atelier that year as a direct offshoot of the Kashmir shawl's popularity. Her success, due in part to the bondage of young serf women, was attributed to her patient and meticulous efforts. Her shawls were made with the Indian technique. Each weft was attached to the warp by a 'noeud special' and often separately woven bands were sewn together. This process demanded extreme, skilful attention so that the patterns and colours of the assembled pieces when joined would give the impression of having been made in one piece.

The distinction of the Russian shawls is that they have no 'wrong' side — each side is absolutely identical. Four times more work was required to make a reversible shawl than to make an ordinary one. The weft was not allowed to traverse the whole width of the shawl but only each specific area of colour, after which the thread had to be returned — a very tedious chore. The weaving progressed at the rate of 6 to 7mm a day.

Madame Merlaine was not alone in her efforts. Prince Nicolas Youssoupov from Koupavinsk, Prince Enikeev of Penza, the State Cousellor Kolokolzov from Saratov and Madame Elisseev of Voronége, who began her atelier in 1813, all made shawls. Only Merlaine and Elisseev manufactured them in any quantity; the former employed fifty weavers, all serfs, with an output of forty-six shawls and five scarves per year, the latter, depending on the season, employed from thirty-five to fifty people.

The technique varied little from one atelier to another and it is impossible to attribute with certainty any one shawl to a particular maker, with the exception perhaps of those of Madame Merlaine, who wove the initials H.M. into her shawls. At the time of the Public Exhibition of Russian Products in St. Petersburg in 1829 her shawls were the object of great admiration. The Czar, Nicolas I, acquired a splendid piece for 12,000 roubles. With her achievements crowned by the reception of a gold medal, Madame Merlaine incorporated in her designs the Imperial Russian Eagle, woven in above her initials. This emblem measured 15mm in diameter. The eagle was emblazoned with the Moscow coat of arms, an equestrian figure of St. George, the city's patron saint. The making of this woven emblem was considered a *tour-de-force* unequalled in the history of tapestry.

It was difficult, if not impossible, for Russian weavers to procure the wool of the Tibetan mountain goat. As a result, Elisseev was obliged to finance expeditions to the steppes of Western Siberia in order to assure her own personal supply of the wool. After appropriate sorting, the wool was soft, silky and very light. In 1802 a special scraper was devised to remove impurities from the goat's fleece, but, although this gave a fine lustre and softness to the yarn, not all impurities were completely eliminated. It was then necessary to remove the remaining impurities with a tweezer once the shawl had been woven.

---

4 'Châles tissés par les serfs Russes', Lyon. By 1841, Moscow recorded 13 shawl makers, with a total of 284 looms (*Dictionnaire Universel du Commerce etc.*, vol. 2, p.384).

Plate 222. Reversible square shawl. European, c.1860.

In France, Ternaux also had problems obtaining this rare fleece, and as a result undertook an expedition to Western Kazakhstan in 1818.[5] Earlier his purchasing agents in Russia had smuggled the coveted fleece into France where its scarcity was due in part to foreign shawl manufacturers who went to expensive extremes to satisfy a lucrative market.

Towards 1820 Russia gained direct access to the Kashmir shawl trade and at the same time allowed France to establish a consulate in Tiflis. This city, located midway between the Black and Caspian Seas, represented an important trading centre for Kashmir and Oriental shawl goods converging from the East, and then heading towards the major cities of Russia and the rest of Europe.

Evidently, the Russians experienced the same initial difficulties as the French in processing the goat fleece. Not until 1813 did Hindenlang in France develop a spinning method whereby, for the first time, pure Kashmir wool could replace silk or 'organsin' as warp threads.[6] In Russia, by 1823, hanks of warp measuring

---

5 See Irwin for a detailed discussion of attempts to naturalize the Oriental goat used for shawls in Europe.
6 Although 1813 is the date given for the discovery of a method proper for spinning Kashmir wool in France for shawl weaving, it appears that several large companies and especially Ternaux had conquered this difficulty at least three years previously (see *Bulletin de la Société d'Encouragement pour l'Industrie National,* Nov. 1810, Vol. 9, p.278).

4,500 metres and weighing not more than 13grams, were spun with remarkable skill.

For someone who has never come in contact with any of these reversible shawls, it is difficult to imagine the intricacy of their design. They are so fine that even when compared with similar weavings such as those of Huari, Peru or the Chinese 'K'ossu' their complexity still confounds the imagination. The sensation of touch, due to their softness and lightness is similar to handling a fine piece of silk satin. Only a country with slavery was capable of producing such articles. The work required was inhuman. However, in the case of Elisseev, who enjoyed universal respect for her kindness, the female workers were completely freed after ten years of work in her ateliers. Nevertheless most of them were by then almost blind; it is clear that the working conditions in Russia were no different from those in Kashmir or even France. Elisseev founded a hospice for blind weavers, unique of its type, regarded as an act of outstanding charity at the time.

In France, neither Bauson nor Girard, who operated weaving ateliers, discussed these hardships but nevertheless they were very real. Even a Jacquard weaver, working from 5am to 9pm in the summer or from 7am to sundown during the winter, was lucky if he still retained his eyesight at the age of 45 — so difficult was the chore of following the disposition of the yarns and as a result, many were forced to abandon their profession.[7]

(3) Jacquard Loom

The reversible loomed shawl, characterized by its traditional square format, small repeat pattern and few colours, is familiar to collectors of European shawls. It was often made of pure silk, or at least the warp was silk. Reversible shawls other than those made by the espouliné method were known to exist before the 1844 exhibition.

In 1827 Deneirouse and Gaussen senior exhibited a reversible shawl and a model of the draw loom on which it had been woven.[8] Another reversible shawl known as 'châle sans envers' was made popular by Ternaux.[9] The English also acknowledged the novelty of this type of shawl durng the 1820s, calling it a 'double shawl', but as yet it is impossible to be certain when the first one was woven on the Jacquard loom.

The technique was based on the use of two sets of warp threads that served to weave two shawls simultaneously back-to-back. Simplicity of design and sparsety of colour were a prerequisite in order for harmony to be achieved. The normally large number of floating wefts was reduced in such a way as to make the shawl as thin, and thus as light, as possible, and to allow the wefts to form the design. Since each weft shot served to pattern both sides of the fabric at the same time, it followed that the ground on one side would correspond to the figured work on the other.

It is not clear whether the reversible shawl originated in an attempt to weave two shawls simultaneously which would then be cut apart, but certainly a 'new' technique was presented at the 1844 exhibition in which two competing exhibitors each presented a method for manufacturing two shawls at the same time. The concept was similar to, yet different from the above technique; the aim here was to slice the 'double' shawl in half, and thus provide the commercial market with two saleable products. The same procedure is being used today in Pakistan to create two carpets at once, achieved by slicing the pile side of two parallel semi-mechanically produced carpets.

7 One is recorded as having become a vegetable merchant. *Ouvriers de Deux Mondes,* vol. 1, p.38.
8 Expo. 1844, vol. 2, pp.213-4.
9 Expo. 1827, 'Rapport du Jury etc.,' vol. 2, p.67.

Glossary

amli: embroidered; an embroidered shawl from Kashmir.

banian: banker, money lender.

battant brocheur espoulineur: an obscure loom which was capable of imitating the **kani** weave.

bedris: a tightly packed bale of woven goods for transport by caravan.

bent-tip strawberry: expression for a popular rose-type flower often seen in the **hashias** of the 17th and 18th century and sometimes in the **botehs** of the 17th century. It usually formed a repeat with the pin-wheel flower.

broché: brocaded. A weave whereby the weft does not travel the full width of the cloth but forms the pattern only when its colour is required.

buta: flower in Indian. See **boteh.**

buti: small flower.

caillouté: early French word meaning 'pebbly'. It denotes a particular floral style of the late Afghan shawls; compact flowers resembling a mosaic.

celebration shawls: refers to those exuberant and rare patterns mainly of the Sikh period whose effusively woven flora often appear like exploding fireworks.

chandar: the moon shawl. A square shawl containing a central medallion and quarter medallions at each corner of the field.

coif boteh: a boteh whose arching apex is highlighted by a detached **raceme.**

cone: see **boteh.**

counterfeit shawl: European kani shawl which was often passed off as a genuine Kashmir shawl.

dagshawl: a severe system of excise tax imposed during the Afghan period.

dhoor: a running motif which borders the matan.

diapered field: allover pattern of diamond-shaped figures.

dochalla: one of two long shawls woven exactly alike. Literally a 'double' shawl.

doruka: literally 'two-sided'. Reversible kani shawl from Kashmir.

dorunga: a 'doruka' whose ground colour on one side differs from that of the other, due to a very intricate couching stitch.

drawloom: loom whose warps are attached to vertical cords called simples, which in turn are raised by a drawboy.

espouliné: French term for **kani** woven.

espoulins: see **tojis.**

exact imitation shawl: see **counterfeit shawl.**

foldover shawl: square shawl which when diagonally folded in half displays its full design.

fool's cap: a floral device of the Sikh period which looks like a hat.

fringe gates: the different coloured bands of wool which, often embroidered with **mihrabs,** composed the fringe of the **kani** shawl. Fringe gates began about mid-19th century.

garden shawl: a shawl whose design imitates running water in the Mughal fashion by a chevron pattern.

grenadine: a yarn composed of two silk strands slightly twisted but given a high torsion when combined together.

harlequin shawl: type of long shawl popular around the 1820s; each **boteh** of the **palla** is highlighted by a different ground colour. Thus a compartmentalized effect is achieved.

hashia: the narrow lateral borders which run the length of the shawl, the pattern of which is usually composed of a floral meander.

ideogram root: expression coined for a 17th century Mughal style in which the **boteh's** roots were secured with a device resembling a Chinese ideogram.

ikat: a resist dye process in which designs are dyed on yarns by tightly wrapping bundles of yarn to prevent dye penetration.

Jacquard loom: a loom whose **warps** are raised by a system of hooks controlled by a series of punched cards.

jamawar: gown piece. Usually a long decorative shawl.

kani: woven. The Kashmir weave: twill tapestry weave with interlocked wefts.

karkhana: the building in which the shawls were woven.

karkhandar: proprietor of a weaving factory.

khatraaz: striped shawl pattern.

lancé: weaving method whereby the **weft** crosses the full width of the cloth and appears on the surface only where the design calls for its colour; otherwise the weft remains flotting on the reverse side or is trimmed off once the cloth leaves the loom

lena: goat's fleece from Ladakh.

matan: the unworked central field of the shawl.

mihrab: prayer niche in a mosque oriented toward Mecca, the holy city of Islam. This architectural form is found often in Islamic decorative arts.

millefleurs: 'thousands of flowers'. Often used for a type of prayer rug whose mihrab is completely filled with flowers.

mise-en-carte: the setting up of a given weaving pattern on special grid paper.

moon shawl: see **chandar.**

mugim: shawl appraiser.

naqqash: pattern maker.

paisley: see **boteh.** Also a town near Glascow, Scotland, where large numbers of cheap 'Kashmir' shawls were woven.

palla: the patterned borders at each end of the shawl.

palme: early French equivalent for **boteh.**

papier briqueté: grid paper whose pattern resembles that of a brick wall, on which the shawl pattern was drawn.

pashm: goat fleece.

pashmina: woven goat fleece.

patchwork shawl: shawls of the late 19th century composed of many separately woven pieces then joined together by the **rafugar.**

patka: waistband. A very long and narrow Kashmir shawl wrapped several times around the waist. It could also be used as a turban.

perfoliate leaves: botanical. Leaves that completely clasp the stem and are apparently pierced by it.

pin-wheel flower: expression for a particular yellow flower whose pointed petals appear arranged radially around a central axis. See also **bent-tip strawberry.**

pricked-in colours: a process by which faded colours are enhanced by painting in new or fresh colours directly by brush on the wool.

putto: crudely woven Ladakhi sheep-wool.

Qajar boteh: a coined term for bulbous, 18th century style of semi-curvilinear **boteh** the apex of which is composed of arching **racemes.**

raceme: botanical. Stalked flowers arranged singly along a common main axis.

radial flowers: flowers whose petals or buds are arranged in a precise circular fashion around a central axis, a style developed in the third quarter of the 18th century under the Afghans.

rafle: machine spun wool derived from merino sheep.

rafugar: shawl tailor or seamster.

raised boteh: a style popular about 1815 where the **boteh** was often shown raised on a mound or other type of ornament.

rank shawl: an early Mughal shawl which may have indicated military rank because of the symmetrically arranged rows of leaves.

renaissance shawls: shawl patterns popular in Europe during the 1830s in which neo-gothic architecture was in vogue.

reversible shawl: European square shawl whose pattern is composed of small repeats.

ring shawl: a **shah tus** shawl whose extreme fineness may be demonstrated by slipping it through a finger ring.

rumal: square shawl.

sash: see **patka.**

shah tus: literally king's wool. The fleece comes from the ibex, a wild Himalayan mountain goat of the genus capra, which grazes at very high altitudes. The rarest and most expensive fleece in the world.

shikarga: a shawl pattern depicting a hunting scene with animals.

shuttle: wooden bobbin with pointed ends which is slid back and forth across the loom to insert the weft.

talim: cards coded in the Kashmiri language on which the shawl pattern, according to **warp** number and its associated colour is indicated.

tangir: the horizontal border which lies above and below the **palla.** Normally it is identical to the **hashia,** which is why in the text the word **hashia** is often used to denote both.

tarah guru: colour caller.

technique of characterization: a coined term for an early Mughal style of mimicking nature in which case the **boteh's** flora, cartoon-like in quality, display a certain novel caricature effect.

tojis: needle-like wooden sticks used in the **kani** weave and around which the various dyed yarns are wrapped.

toshakhana: imperial wardrobe.

tree boteh: a boteh style popular around 1815 whose tall, thick central branch is drawn like a tree trunk.

tus or tooch: literally wool, but generally refers to shah tus.

twill weave: a cloth texture of oblique ribs formed by the **warp** and **weft.**

umbrella-handle stem: a type of stem that terminates in a slight hook and usually found in the **buti.**

ustad: master weaver.

vase shawl: square **kani** shawl the design of which is composed of vases in the form of leafy scrolls which approach the centre from each corner. The ground is usually heavily overfilled with other nondescript flora.

warp: the yarns which are stretched on the loom to form the underlying structure of the cloth.

weft: thread which crosses the cloth at right angles to that in which it was woven; the thread which forms the pattern.

winged-leaf buti: a type of small **buti,** the stem of which support a lateral projection of a serrated leaf or flower or both. It is usually seen on late 18th century shawls patterned with a trellis, chevron, or checkerboard design.

Bibliography

General

Anonymous
  Ouvriers de Deux Mondes. La Société d'Economie Sociale, vol. 1, Paris, 1857.
  Kashmeer and its Shawls, London, 1875.
  The History of the Sikhs, Calcutta, 1846.
Aijazuddin, F.S.
  Sikh Portraits by European Artists, London, 1979.
Alcan, Michel
  Essai sur l'Industrie des Matières Textile, Paris, 1847.
  Traité du Travail des Laines, Paris, 1866.
  Les Inventions et Les Perfectionnements Aportés à la Fabrications des Châles par M. Eck, Paris, 1848.
Ames, Frank
  'The Fashion of the Kashmir Shawl in France', *Hali,* London, Vol.5, No.1, 1982.
  'Le Châle Cachemire en France au 19ème Siècle', *Hali,* Vol.6, No.2, 1984.
  'Lost Horizons: The Stylistic Development of the Kashmir Shawl', *Hali,* Vol.6, No.4, 1984.
Baden-Powell, B.H.
  Handbook of the Manufacturers and Arts of the Punjab, vol.2, Lahore, 1872.
Bamzai, Prithivi Nath Kaul
  A History of Kashmir, New Delhi, 1973.
Barret, Douglas, and Gray, Basil
  Indian Painting, New York, 1963.
Bell, T.F.
  Jacquard Weaving and Designing, London, 1895.
Bernier, François
  Travels in the Mogul Empire, 1656-1668, 2 vols., London, 1891.
Biétry, Laurent
  Réponse à une Brochure d'un Fabricant de Châles, Le Châle Cachemire Français, le Châle des Indes et la Marque de Fabrique, Paris, 1849.
  Lettre Adressée à Messieurs les Membres du Jury de la 20ème Classe à l'Exposition Universelle de 1855, Paris.
Birdwood, George C.M.
  The Industrial Arts of India, London, 1880.
Blair, Mathew
  The Paisley Shawl, Glasgow, 1904.
Blanqui, Jérôme-Adolphe
  Conservatoire des Arts et Métiers, Cour d'Economie Industrielle, Paris, 1837-38.
  Histoire de l'Exposition des Produits de l'Industrie Française en 1827, Paris.
Bogle, G.
  Voyages au Thibet par Bogle, Turner at Pourungir, Paris, 1806.
Burnes, Alexander
  Travels into Bokhara, 2 vols., London, 1834.
Chandra, Moti
  'Kashmir Shawls', *Bulletin of the Prince of Wales Museum,* No.3, pp.1-24, Bombay, 1954.
Chassagne, Serge
  Oberkampf, Paris, 1980.
Chattopadhaya, K.
  Carpets of India and Floor Coverings D.B. Taraporevala Sons and Co., private edition, 1969.

Coffinet, Julien, *Arachiné ou l'Art de La Tapisserie,* Paris, 1971.
Cunningham, Alexander
  Ladak, Physical, Statistical, and Historical, London, 1854.
Cuvillier-Fleury, A.A.
  Notes Historiques sur le Général Allard et sur le Royaume de Lahore, Paris, 1836.
  Voyages et Voyageurs, Paris, 1854.
Couder, Amédée
  Analyse du Dessin des Cachemires et Moyens de vendre les Schalls Français Supérieurs à Ceux des Indes, Paris, 1834.
  Description des dessins Exposés en 1849, Paris.
  Quelques Idées sur l'Exposition Universelle en France, Paris, 1854.
Daclin, C.
  Table Générale Analytique et Raisonné etc., Paris, 1838.
Deloche, Jean, *Voyage en Inde du Comte de Modave 1773-1776,* Paris, 1971.
Deneirouse, Eugène, *Traité sur la Fabrication de Châles des Indes,* Paris, 1851.
  Notes sur la Situation de la Fabrique de Châles etc., Corbeil, 1849
  Notice sur la Nécessité de Remplacer par un Tissage Mécanique les Brochés à la Main, Paris, 1863.
Deslandres, Y.
  'Joséphine and the Arts', *Apollo,* July, 1977.
Dow, George Francis
  'The Paisley Shawl with Some Account of the Shawl Made in Kashmir', *Old-Time England,* vol.2, pp.113-121, Boston, 1921.
Duprès, Adrien
  Voyage en Perse fait dans les années 1807, 1808, 1809, 2 vol., Paris, 1819.
Elphinstone, Baron Mountstuart
  An Account of the Kingdom of Caubul, London, 1815.
Eymard, Paul
  Historique du Métier Jacquard, Lyon, 1863.
Falcot, P.
  Traité de la Fabrication des Tissus, 2 vols., Paris, 1852.
Falk, S.J.
  Qajar Painting, London, 1972.
Fichel, P.
  Un Mot sur le Cachemire des Indes et le Cachemire et le Cachemire Français, Paris, 1834.
Flachat, Jean Claude
  Observation sur le Commerce et sur les Arts etc., 2 vols., Paris, 1766.
Forster, George
  Journey From Bengal to England, London, 1798.
Fraser, James B.
  Narrative of Journey into Khorasan in the Years 1821 and 1822 etc., London, 1825.
  Journey of a Tour Through Part of the Snowy Range of the Himalayan Mountains etc., London, 1820.
  Travels and Adventures in the Persian Provinces etc., 1821-1822, London, 1826.
French, C.J.
  Journal of a Tour in Upper Hindustan etc., 1838-1839, Simla, 1872.
Ganju, M.
  Textile Industries in Kashmir, Delhi, 1945.

Geijer, Agnus
A History of Textile Art, England, 1979.

Grandsard, A.
Jacquard, Sa Vie, Paris, n.d.

Grose, J.H.
Voyage to the East-Indies, London, 1757.

Hanway, Jonas
An Historical Account of the British Trade over the Caspian Sea, 4 vols., London, 1753.

Honigberger, J.
35 Years in the East, London, 1852.

Hunter, J
'The Paisley Textile Industry 1695-1830', *Costume,* No.10, pp.1-15, 1976.

Ireland, John B
Wall-Street to Cashmere, New York, 1859.

Jacquard, Joseph Marie
Biographie Universelle, Paris, 1834.

Jacquemont, Victor
Voyage Dans l'Inde Pendant les Années 1828 à 1832, 4 vols., Paris, 1841.

Jehangir
The Tuzuk-i-Jehangiri; or the memoirs of Jehangir, Trans. Alexander Rogers, Delhi, 1968.

Jaubert, P. Amédée
Voyage en Arménie et en Perse Fait dans les Années 1805 et 1806, Paris, 1821.

Kahlenberg, Mary Hunt
'A Study of the Development and Use of the Mughal Patka (Sash) etc.' *Aspect of Indian Art,* Brill Pub., 1971, pp.153-166.

Kaul, S.N.
Kashmir Economics, Srinagar, 1954.

King, Margaret R.
'Cashmere Shawls', *Cincinatti Museum Review,* No.5, Oct. 1892.

Klaproth, Henrich Julius von
Voyage Dans les Steppes d'Astrakhan et de Caucase par le Comt Jean Potocki, 2 vols., Paris, 1829.
Tableau Historique, Geographique. . .entre La Russie et La Perse, Paris, 1827.

Koul, Anand
'The Kashmir Shawl Trade', *The East and West,* Srinagar, vol.XIV, Jan., 1915, No.159, pp.28-42.

Leavitt, Thomas W.
'Fashion, Commerce and Technology in the 19th Century: The Shawl Trade', *Textile History,* Dec. 1972, vol.3, pp.51-64.

Legoux de Flaix
Essai Historique, Geographique et Politique sur L'Hindustan, 2 vols., Paris, 1807.

Leitner, G.W.
An Account of Shawl Weaving. . .from Linguistic Fragments Discovered in 1870, 1872 and 1879, Lahore, 1882.

Lomüller, Louis M.
Guillaume Ternaux 1763-1833, Paris, 1979.

Martin, Henri
Historie de France, 9 vols., Paris, 1875.

Niclausse, Juliette
Tapisserie et Tapis de la Ville de Paris, 1948.

Olivier, Guillaume, Antoine
Voyage dans l'Empire Ottoman, l'Egypté et la Perse etc., 4 vols., Paris, 1804.

Pearse, Major Hugh
Memoirs of Alexander Gardner, Soldier and Traveller, Colonel of Artillery in the Service of Maharaja Runjit Singh, 1898.

Perleberg, H.C.
Persian Textiles, Newark Museum Association, 1919.

Picard, Charles, *Saint-Quentin, de son Commerce et de ses Industries,* 2 vols., Paris, 1867.

Posselt, E.A.
The Jacquard Machine Analysed and Explained, Philadelphia, 1893.

Prat, D. de
Traité de Tissage au Jacquard, Paris, 1921.

Reath, Nancy Andrews, and Sachs, Eleanor B.
Persian Textiles and their Technique from the 6th to the 18th Century, Yale University Press, 1937.

Rey, Jean
Etude pour Servir à l'Histoire des Châles, Paris, 1823.

Ruppert, Jacques, *Le Costume,* 5 vols., Paris, 1930.

Schürmann, Ulrich
Caucasian Rugs, London, 1974.

Sée, Henri
Esquisse de l'Evolution Industrielle de la France de 1815 à 1848, Paris, 1923.

Shah, Hajji Mukhtar
A Treatise on the Art of Shawl Weaving, Koh-i-Nor Press, Lahore, 1887. Translated from the Persian by Prof. Bashir Ahmad Dar, Srinagar, 1981.

Simpson, W.
India Ancient and Modern, London, 1867.

Singh, Ganda
Early European Accounts of the Sikhs, Calcutta, 1862.

Skelton, Robert
A Decorative Motif in Mughal Art, Aspects of Indian Art, Brill pub., 1971.

Soltykoff, Prince Alexis
Voyage dans l'Inde et en Perse, Paris, 1853.

Sonnerat
Voyage aux Indes Orientales et à la Chine depuis 1774 jusqu'au 1781, 2 vols., Paris 1782.

Stewart, A.M.
The History and Romance of the Paisley Shawl, Paisley, 1922.

Sufi, Dr. G.M. (AL-Hajj)
Kashir, A history of Kashmir, 2 vols., New Delhi, 1974.

Tavernier, Jean Baptiste
Les Six Voyages en Turquie et en Perse, 2 vols., Paris, 1981.

Tessier, M.
Mémoire sur l'Importation en France des Chèvres à Duvet de Cachemire, Paris, 1819.

Torrens, Lieut.-Col.
Travels in Ladak, Tartary and Kashmir, London, 1862.

Turner, Samuel M.
Ambassade au Thibet et au Boutan, Trans. into French by J. Castéra, Paris, 1800.

Vigne, G.T.
Travels in Kashmir, 2 vols., London, 1842.

Waheeduddin, Fakir Syed
The Real Runjit Singh, New Delhi, 1976.

Watson, J. Forbes
The Textile Manufacturers and the Costumes of the People of India, London, 1866.
Textile Fabrics of India, 18 vols., London, 1977.

Watt, Sir George
Indian Art at Delhi, London, 1904.
The Commercial Products of India, London, 1908.
Whiteley, J.
Ingres, London, 1977.
Whyte, Dorothy
'Edinburgh Shawls and their makers', *Costume,* No.10, London, 1976.
Whyte, Dorothy, and Swain, M.H.
'Edinburgh Shawls', *Old Edinburgh Club,* vol.31, 1962.
Wilson, H.H.
Travels in the Himalayan Provinces by Moorcroft and G. Trebeck, 1819 to 1825, 2 vols., London, 1841.

Museum Publications and Exhibition Catalogues

Archer, W.G.
Painting of the Sikhs, Victoria and Albert Museum, London, 1966.
Irwin, John
Shawls, Victoria and Albert Museum, London, 1955.
The Kashmir Shawl, Victoria and Albert Museum, London, 1973.
Lévis-Strauss, Monique
Le Tissage des Châles au Cachemire et en France, exhibition catalogue: 'La mode du châle cachemire en France', Paris, 1982.
Les Châles Tissés en Inde et en France, exhibition catalogue: 'Le Châle Cachemire en France au XIX siècle', Lyon, 1983.
Rothstein, Natalie
Introduction of the Jacquard loom into England, Studies in Textile History, Royal Ontario Museum.
Singh, Chandrmani and Ahivasi, Devaki
Woollen Textiles and Costumes from Bharat Kala Bhavan. Benares Hindu University, 1981.
Vial, Gabriel
La Technique du Châle, catalogue of the exhibition: 'Le Châle Cachemire en France au XIX siècle', Lyon, 1983.
Yale University Art Gallery
The Kashmir Shawl, Connecticut, 1975.
West Surrey College of Art and Design
The Art of the Shawl, England, 1977.
Conservatoire National des Arts and Métiers
Catalogue de Musée Section I (Industries Textiles, Teintures et Apprêts), Paris, 1942.
The Oriental Rug Collection of Mary Jane and Jerome Straka, New York, 1978.

French National and Universal Exhibitions
(chronologically arranged)

1798   Première Exposition des Produits de l'Industrie Française (*abbr:* E.P.I.F.)
1801   Seconde E.P.I.F.
       Procès Verbal, E.P.I.F.
1802   Troisième E.P.I.F.
       Procès Verbal, E.P.I.F.
1806   Catalogue des Produits de l'E.P.I.F.
       Rapport du Jury presenté par M. De Champagny of l'E.P.I.F.

1819   Rapport du Jury Central sur les E.P.I.F. présenté par Decazes et L. Costaz.
       Rapport du Jury d'Admission sur l'Exposition des Produits des Manufactures du Dept. de la Seine.
1823   Rapport du Jury d'Admission, Louvre, presenté par L. Héricart de Thury.
       Rapport sur les E.P.I.F., au Nom du Jury Central, rédigé par M. le Vicomte Héricart de Thury et par M. Migneron.
1827   Rapport sur les E.P.I.F., par Héricart et Migneron.
       Rapport du Jury Départemental de la Seine sur les Produits de l'Industrie Admis au Concours de l'Exposition Public par M. Payen, vols. 1 et 2, 1829 et 1832.
       Compte Rendu des E.P.I.F.
       Histoire de l'E.P.I.F. par Jean Adolphe Blanqui.
1834   Musée Industriel.
       Notice des E.P.I.F.
       Rapport du Jury Central sur des E.P.I.F., par Baron Charles Dupin, 3 vols.
       l'Industrie par Stephane Flachat, Paris.
1839   E.P.I.F., 3 vols., 1839.
1844   Musée Challamel par Jules Burat.
       Rapport du Jury Central, Vol.3.
       Vol.I, reporteurs: Deneirouse et Legentil.
       Vol.II, reporteur: Théodore Olivier.
       Catalogue Official des Produits de l'Industrie.
1849   Exposition Française à Londres, Description des Dessins Exposés par Amédée Couder.
1851   Travaux de la Commission Française, 13 vols. sur l'Industrie des Nations. Vol. 4: Industrie des Châles etc., rapport de Maxime Gaussen.
1855   Rapport du Jury Mixte International, Vol.1, et 3.
       Visite à l'Exposition Universelle de Paris, Tresca.
       Paris Universal Exhibition 1855, Committee reports Part I., Great Britain: Huddersfield Chamber of Commerce.
       Catalogue Spécial des Envois d'Autriche.
       Catalogue de l'Exposition de 1855.
1862   Rapport du Jury International published sous direction de Michel Chevalier.
       Catalogue Officiel.
1867   Rapports des Délégations Ouvrières, 3 vols.
       Rapports du Jury International, 13 vols. 'Châles' par David Gerson.
       Catalogue General publié par le Commission Impériale.
       Exposition Universelle de 1867, illustré par Prosper Poitevin.
1878   Exposition Universelle International de 1878, rapport sur les châles par M. Gaussen, Paris.

Dictionaries and Encyclopaedias

Nouveau Larousse Illustré, 7 vols., Paris, 1900.
Dictionnaire Technologique ou Nouveau Dictionnaire Universel des Arts et Métiers, 22 vols., Paris, 1823.
Dictionnaire Universel du Commerce de La Banque et de Manufactures, Pillet Imprimeur-Libraire, 2 vols., Paris, 1838, 1841.
Dictionnaire Universel de Commerce, Banque, Manufacture, Duane, etc., 2 vols., Paris, 1805.

Kashmir Design Albums

Musée des Arts Décoratifs, Paris:

Oberkampf

Dessins Copiés sur d'ancienne châles et écharpes de Cachemire, frontispiece reads: 'La plupart ont été copiés sur les premiers châles et écharpes qui furent introduits en France au commencement de ce siècle d'Egypte, Fabrique de Jouy.'

Recueil des premières empreintes de dessins pour le fabrique d'étoffes imprimnée, Jouy, 1804-1811.

Dessins copiés d'après des anciennes toiles peintes de la Perse et de l'Inde Jouy, 1760-1790.

Empreintes et dessins pour toiles imprimées, mouchoires et fichus, Manufacture d'Indiennes à Nantes, vols. I et II, 1770-1822.

Petitpierre

Manufacture d'Indiennes à Nantes, mouchoirs et fichus, 1770-1822.

Fay and Brulé

Dessins pour dentelle, 1809-1902. (It is felt that these designs were not reserved for lace only but were employed for embroidery and weavings also.)

Gonelle Frères

Dessins pour cachemire. (Inside label reads 'Dessaigne, successeur de Chavant 1854-1862'.)

Berrus

Dessins de châles fonds pleins. 5 albums. (Album I dated 1848-50, album II dated 1849-50.)

Pochades Longues, 6 vols., 1858-60.

Dessins de châles longs, 7 albums.

Pochades Carrée, 3 albums, 1865-66.

Dessins de châles carrés, 22 albums. (Album I dated 1851-53.)

Bibliothèque Nationale, Paris (departement des estampes):

Chavant F.

Souvenir de l'Exposition des Produits de l'Industrie Française de 1839. 'Reproduction exacte des principales étoffes façonnées et imprimées, 350 dessins réunis en 50 feuilles.'

Album du Cachemirien. 'Reproduction exact de tous les beaux châles des Indes et de la Perse Fabriqué à Lahore, Ispahan, Téhéran, Caboul, Kashmir, et Candahar qui arrivent en Europe calqués fidèlement et dessinés aux traits simple dans leurs grandeurs naturelles. Ouvrage précieux pour servir de matériaux aux dessinateurs de manufactures.' Paris et Kashmir, 1837.

Journal du Fabricant d'Etoffes Façonnées, 1837.

Guide du Dessinateur de l'Industrie, 1837.

Le dessinateur de Cachemire. 'Recueil de motifs et matériaux pour les dessinateurs de manufactures, composés sur pierres par des artists spéciaux.' Paris, 1837.

Delaye, V.

Indo-Parisien (1850-69).

Costumes féminins (albums from 1792-1803, 1804-13, 1814-21).

Dessins de Cachemire, 2 vols. (mid-19th century).

Costumes of Turkey, printed for William Miller, London, 1804.

Archives

National Archives, Paris:

Carton

F12-2199, Métier Jacquard.

F12-2414, Châles.

F12-2175, Vingtième extrait de divers avis sur le commerce fasicule, Fev. 1822.

F12-254, Recettes et dépense faites par les Sieux Fourcade à l'établissement des Indiens à Thieux, 1785.

F12-1004, F12-1005A (contain documents relating to patents delivered to Ternaux).

F12-600-603 (contain important documents on the raising of fleece goats and Ternaux's expedition to Russia to bring back the Kashmir goat).

Chambre de Commerce, Paris:

Registre de Correspondence, T4, 'Rapport de Ternaux et de Ballenger sur l'industrie parisienne de châles et de gazes.' Séance du 17 Juillet, 1822.

Indian Office Library, London:

Strachey, R.

'Memoire on the Revenue and trade of Cabul, etc., with other points of information relative to that Kingdom. (Contains interesting report on 'shawl manufactory'.) Unpublished, 1812.

Index

Note: The index covers the first seven chapters of the book only.
Page numbers given in italics refer to picture captions.

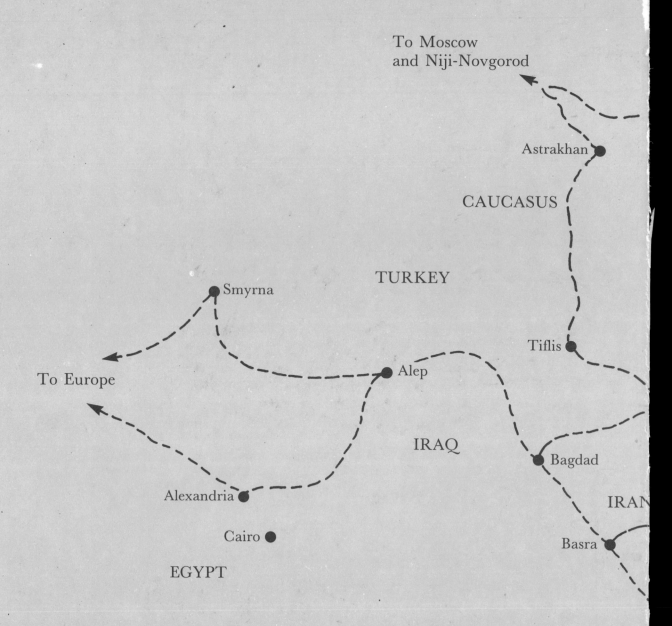

To Moscow
and Niji-Novgorod

Astrakhan

CAUCASUS

TURKEY

Smyrna

To Europe

Alep

Tiflis

IRAQ

Bagdad

Alexandria

IRAN

Cairo

Basra

EGYPT

ARAB

Shawl Routes of the Orient